HOW I LEARN BEST FOR HISTO

- highlight textbook according
- annotate with classnotes to h
- flashcards + summary sheets ..., ᴜ ᴜ ------ -, ʋ t8 etc.
- mindmaps grouping different factors within topics / events
- bulletpoint essay plans on what to mention + judgement point.
- explain events to others who don't study that eg. Mo to see where your knowledge thins out. → review this in detail
- mindmaps only in pictures (acts) → flashcards + detail

History

for the IB Diploma

PAPER 3

Civil Rights and Social Movements in the Americas Post-1945

SECOND EDITION

Mark Stacey,
Michael Scott-Baumann

Series editor: Allan Todd

CAMBRIDGE
UNIVERSITY PRESS

University Printing House, Cambridge CB2 8BS, United Kingdom

One Liberty Plaza, 20th Floor, New York, NY 10006, USA

477 Williamstown Road, Port Melbourne, VIC 3207, Australia

4843/24, 2nd Floor, Ansari Road, Daryaganj, Delhi – 110002, India

79 Anson Road, #06–04/06, Singapore 079906

Cambridge University Press is part of the University of Cambridge.

It furthers the University's mission by disseminating knowledge in the pursuit of education, learning and research at the highest international levels of excellence.

www.cambridge.org
Information on this title: www.cambridge.org/9781316605967

First published 2012
Second edition 2016
20 19 18 17 16 15 14 13 12 11 10 9 8 7 6 5 4 3 2 1

Printed in the United Kingdom by Latimer Trend

A catalogue record for this publication is available from the British Library

ISBN 978-1-316-60596-7 Paperback

Contents

1 | Introduction

This book is designed to prepare students for *Civil Rights and Social Movements in the Americas Post-1945*. This is Topic 17 in HL Option 2, History of the Americas for Paper 3 of the IB History examination.

It will focus mainly on the US, and will examine the history of the struggle for African American civil rights from the Civil War to the late 1960s, with the emphasis on the peak of the movement in the 1950s and 1960s. It will also examine the campaign for Native American and Hispanic American rights and assess the achievements of the women's and youth protest movements of the 1960s and 1970s. The extent to which these movements succeeded and the role of governments will be regularly assessed. Small case studies of the impact of similar movements in other parts of the Americas are also included.

ACTIVITY

Research the lives of Native Americans (traditionally called American Indians) before and after the arrival of Europeans. Who were the main tribes and how did they make their livings? What impact did the Europeans have on the lives of the Native Americans?

Figure 1.1: A modern map of the US (excluding Alaska and Hawaii).

Themes

To help you prepare for your IB History exams, this book will cover the main themes and aspects relating to *Civil Rights and Social Movements in the Americas* as set out in the IB History Guide. In particular, it will examine civil rights and social movements in the Americas after 1945 in terms of the major areas shown below:

- the goals, methods and achievements of the Native American movements for civil rights
- the origins, tactics and organisation of the early US African American civil rights movement in its campaign to challenge white supremacy in the South
- the role of the Supreme Court and legal challenges to segregated education in the 1950s; the emergence of Martin Luther King
- the civil rights campaigns and the ending of segregation in the South from 1960 to 1965
- the role of the federal government in achieving civil rights for African Americans
- the growth of African American radicalism from 1965 to 1968, including Malcolm X, the Black Muslims, Black Power and the Black Panthers
- youth cultures of the 1960s and 1970s, including the growth of a counter-culture and the impact of the Vietnam War protests
- feminist movements in the Americas; their origins, goals and achievements.
- the Hispanic American movement in the United States, the issue of immigration and the role of César Chávez.

ACTIVITY

Research the demographics of the US over the last 70 years. How have the different groups referred to in the course changed and grown. For Hispanic Americans, African Americans and Native Americans look at overall numbers and the main areas in which they live. For women and young people, you might look at jobs, higher education or even voting patterns. What do your findings suggest about change and continuity for these groups?

Key Concepts

Each chapter will help you focus on the main issues, and to compare and contrast the main developments that took place during the various periods for the different groups concerned. In addition, at various points in the chapters, there will be questions and activities which will help you focus on the six key concepts – these are:

- change
- continuity
- causation
- consequence
- significance
- perspectives.

Theory of Knowledge

In addition to the broad key themes, the chapters contain Theory of Knowledge links, to get you thinking about aspects that relate to history, which is a Group 3 subject in the IB Diploma. The *Civil Rights and Social Movements in the Americas* topic has several clear links to ideas about knowledge and history, notably in the language that we use, the perspectives that we trust and even the thorny issue of indigenous knowledge systems. Many of the matters covered, such as race relations and abortion still divide opinion today and historians cannot help but be influenced by contemporary opinion. This presents a huge challenge to the historian, and is an issue that has clear links to the IB Theory of Knowledge course.

Historians have to decide which evidence to select and use in order to make their case, and which evidence to leave out. But to what extent do the historians' personal, political and social views influence their decisions when they select what they consider to be the most important or relevant sources, and when they make judgements about the value and limitations of specific sources or sets of sources? Is there such a thing as objective 'historical truth'? Or is there just a range of subjective historical opinions and interpretations about the past, which vary according to the political leanings and social values of individual historians?

Much of this book is concerned with the sensitive issue of race. Our current values make it intensely difficult to understand the deeply entrenched attitudes and beliefs of white supremacists in the American South in the 1950s and early 1960s. Yet, without an empathetic understanding of those racist views, it is impossible to understand fully why the campaign for African American civil rights met such bitter resistance. We need to be both sensitive and dispassionate, both understanding and impartial to understand why the issue of otherness has led some to call for integration and assimilation while others cleave to segregation and elimination.

You are strongly advised to read a range of books on the subject – historical novels as well as historians' accounts. The novels *To Kill a Mocking Bird* by Harper Lee and *The Help* by Kathryn Stockett give a historically well-founded portrayal of racial prejudice and inequality in the 1930s and early 1960s respectively.

IB History and Paper 3 questions

In IB History, Paper 3 is taken only by Higher Level students. For this paper, IB History specifies that three sections of an Option should be selected for in-depth study. The examination paper will set two questions on each of the 18 sections – and you have to answer three questions in total.

Unlike Paper 2, where there are sometimes regional restrictions, in Paper 3 you will be able to answer *both* questions from one section, with a third chosen from one of the other sections. These questions are essentially in-depth analytical essays. It is therefore important to study all the bullet points set out in the IB History Guide, in order to give yourself the widest possible choice of questions.

Exam skills

Throughout the main chapters of this book, there are activities and questions to help you develop the understanding and the exam skills necessary for success in Paper 3. Your exam answers should demonstrate:

- factual knowledge and understanding
- awareness and understanding of historical interpretations
- structured, analytical and *balanced* argument.

Before attempting the specific exam practice questions that come at the end of each main chapter, you might find it useful to refer *first* to Chapter 11, the final exam practice chapter. This suggestion is based on the idea that if you know where you are supposed to be going (in this instance, gaining a good mark and grade), and how to get there, you stand a better chance of reaching your destination!

Questions and mark schemes

To ensure that you develop the necessary skills and understanding, each chapter contains comprehension questions and examination tips. For success in Paper 3, you need to produce essays that combine a number of features. In many ways, these require the same skills as the essays in Paper 2.

However, for the Higher Level Paper 3, examiners will be looking for greater evidence of *sustained* analysis and argument, linked closely to the demands of the question. They will also be seeking more depth and precision with regard to supporting knowledge. Finally, they will be expecting a clear and well-organised answer, so it is vital to do a rough plan *before* you start to answer a question. Not only will this show you early on whether you know enough about the topic to answer the question, it will also help maintain a good structure for your answer.

So, it is particularly important to start by focusing *closely* on the wording of the question, so that you can identify its demands. If you simply take the view that a question is *'generally about this period or person'*, you will probably produce an answer that is essentially a narrative, with only vague links to the question. Even if your knowledge is detailed and accurate, it will only be broadly relevant – if you do this, you will get half-marks at the most.

The next important aspect of your answer is that you present a *well-structured* and *analytical argument that is clearly linked to all the demands of the question.* Each aspect of your argument, analysis or explanation then needs to be supported by carefully selected, precise and relevant own knowledge.

In addition, in order to access the highest bands and marks, you need, where appropriate, to show awareness and understanding of relevant historical debates and interpretations. This does not mean simply paraphrasing what different historians have said. Instead, try to *critically evaluate* particular interpretations: for example, are there any weaknesses in some arguments put forward by some historians? What strengths does a particular interpretation have?

Examiner's tips

To help you develop these skills, most chapters contain sample questions, with examiner tips about what – and what *not* – to do in order to achieve high marks. These chapters will focus on a specific skill, as follows:

- Skill 1 (Chapter 2) – understanding the wording of a question
- Skill 2 (Chapter 3) – planning an essay
- Skill 3 (Chapter 4) – writing an introductory paragraph
- Skill 4 (Chapter 5) – avoiding irrelevance
- Skill 5 (Chapter 6) – avoiding a narrative-based answer
- Skill 6 (Chapters 7 and 9) – using your own knowledge analytically and combining it with awareness of historical debate
- Skill 7 (Chapter 8) – writing a conclusion to your essay.

Some of these tips will contain parts of a student's answer to a particular question, with examiner comments, to help you to understand what examiners are looking for.

This guidance is developed further in the exam practice chapter, where examiners' tips and comments will help you focus on the important aspects of questions and their answers. These will also help you to avoid the kind of simple mistakes and oversights which, every year, result in some otherwise good students failing to gain the highest marks.

For additional help, a simplified Paper 3 mark scheme is provided in the exam practice chapter. This should make it easier to understand what examiners are looking for in examination answers. The actual Paper 3 IB History mark scheme can be found on the IB website.

The content covered by this book will provide you with the historical knowledge and understanding to help you answer all the specific content bullet points set out in the *IB History Guide*. Also, by the time you have worked through the various exercises, you should have the skills necessary to construct relevant, clear, well-argued and well-supported essays.

Background to the period

When the United States was created in 1783, it was made up of 13 states, from New Hampshire in the north to Georgia in the south (see the map in Figure 1.1). These states had been 13 colonies of the British Empire. Most of the colonists were of British origin, together with a small number from other European countries. In their Declaration of Independence of 1776, the American colonists stated:

'We hold these truths to be self-evident, that all men are created equal… with certain inalienable Rights, that among these are Life, Liberty and the pursuit of Happiness.'

Yet three large minorities of Americans were not entitled to these rights: they were neither equal nor free in the newly independent United States of America.

These minorities were the Native Americans, the Hispanic people of the south-west and the black slaves. Seven of the chapters in this book examine the 20th-century campaigns by the descendants of these groups and those that joined them in the US to gain equal rights.

The first of these groups, Native Americans, were the country's original inhabitants. As the European colonists arrived and settled the land, the Native Americans were forced back. When the colonists moved further west, the Native Americans were often deprived of their lands. In the late 18th and the 19th centuries, the citizens of the newly independent US pushed their way into the heart of the continent, often forcing the nomadic Native Americans to live on reservations – lands that were allocated to them by the government.

Figure 1.2: A Navajo, Tom Torlino, before and after his assimilation at the Carlisle Indian Industrial School in Carlisle, Pennsylvania, circa 1882.

The second large minority were black slaves, mostly living in the South. Slavery was nothing new in the 18th century. It had existed since ancient times. The Greeks and Romans practised it in Europe, and the Arabs did so in Asia and Africa over many centuries. Then, from the 16th century, Europeans started to capture black Africans and to transport them, virtually as livestock, to their colonies in America. African Americans today are nearly all descended from slaves whom the British, in particular, shipped to America. They were regarded as property, and large numbers were employed in the southern colonies of the British Empire in America, in what today are the southern states of the US (see the map in Figure 1.1). Huge numbers were employed in hot, back-breaking work on white-owned plantations growing sugar, rice, tobacco and, above all, cotton.

After the creation of the United States of America in 1783, the vast majority of these African Americans remained as slaves. A small minority were able to buy their freedom, some escaped, and some were employed in the northern states of the US where slavery was not so widely practised. However, over 90% of African Americans were 'employed', as slaves, in the South.

The final group were Hispanic Americans. When the US was created in 1783, Spain still laid claim to around half of the territory of what we think of as the United States. In the following 60 years, through treaties, diplomatic manoeuvring, the purchase of land and, in 1846–48 the Mexican War, the south-west was gradually absorbed from Mexico into the US. Though the Treaty of Guadalupe-Hidalgo promised to respect the rights of Mexican Americans in the newly acquired territories the reality of their experience was very different.

In this book, the terms 'African American' and 'black' are used interchangeably. Until the 1960s, the term 'Negro' was widely used, both by blacks and whites, and it was acceptable. It was later replaced by 'black' or 'African American'.

DISCUSSION POINT

The issue of language is always a pertinent one where the rights of groups are concerned. Consider four of the groups covered in this book, Native Americans, Hispanic Americans, African Americans and women and see if you can answer these questions.

- Which is more acceptable, 'Native American' or 'Indigenous American'? Consider why 'Red Indian' is no longer acceptable.
- How do Spanish-speaking Americans feel about being lumped together under the term 'Hispanic Americans' when Havana to Mexico City is only slightly closer than Amsterdam to Moscow?
- How have we arrived at a situation where African Americans can refer to themselves using a word that is unacceptable for others to use?
- How many pejorative terms for a woman are there compared with the terms for a man?

Terminology and definitions

Civil rights

Civil rights are the rights of an individual to political and social freedom and equality by virtue of citizenship. In the US, they are enshrined in the Constitution. They include:

- the right to vote in elections
- the right to equal treatment under the law
- the right to a fair trial
- the right to free speech, religion and movement.

Most of the civil rights and protest movements examined in this book aimed to secure these rights through changes in the law or through changes in the way the laws were interpreted. That meant winning the support of the government in Washington, DC, the capital of the US.

The US system of government

The rules and regulations for the government of the United States were set out in the Constitution of 1787. One of the primary aims of the Founding Fathers who drew up the Constitution was to establish a balance between the powers of the individual states and of the central government. The 13 states that made up the United States had come together to fight for their freedom from Britain, but did not want to replace one strong central government – that of the British monarch – with another in Washington, DC. They were keen to retain their autonomy.

The solution was to create a federal system of government. This provided for a federal (national) government in the capital and for separate governments in each of the states. The head of the federal government would be the president. He would be elected by all the citizens, which meant white men. He could propose laws but these would have to be passed by an elected law-making body, the Congress. The Congress was to consist of two houses – the Senate and the House of Representatives. The Senate would consist of two elected representatives, or senators, from each state. In this way, the smaller states could not be dominated by a few bigger states.

This system of government would be copied in the individual states, each of which would have an elected governor and legislature (law-making body). The states would be responsible for law and order, education and many other matters. States are protective of the areas they have control over and resent Federal government interference, this is why issues such as sales taxes, the use of the death penalty, the use of marijuana, gun ownership and the teaching of creationism in schools can differ from state to state.

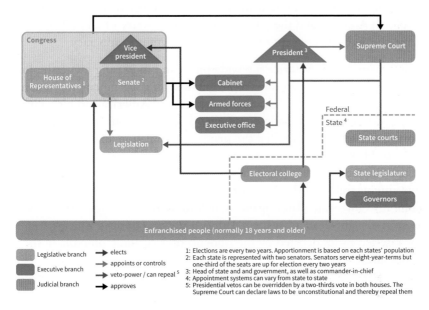

Figure 1.3: The US system of government.

There was much scope for dispute between the federal government and the states over their respective powers. It was the job of the Supreme Court to act as arbitrator in such disputes. As the highest court in the land, its job was to protect the Constitution and decide, when asked, if laws passed by the federal or state governments were constitutional or not. Changes could be made to the Constitution but they had to be passed by a majority of two-thirds in both houses of Congress and ratified (agreed) by the states, which was rare. These changes were added as Amendments to the Constitution.

The campaigns in the United States run by Native Americans, Hispanic Americans, African Americans and the women's movement all involved demands for changes in federal law, and appeals to the Supreme Court for favourable interpretations or changes in the interpretations of existing laws.

Elsewhere in the Americas

In his 2011 book *Civilization: The West and the Rest*, historian Niall Ferguson argues that the fundamental difference between the success of North America and the relative failure and poverty of Latin America came through the concept of the property-owning democracy.

Whereas in North America the widespread and increasing ownership of property brought demands for representation in government, the system introduced by the Spanish in South and Central America was virtually feudal, ensuring that a landowning élite descended from Spanish and Portuguese settlers controlled the majority population and kept them in poverty. Here in Latin America the issues of rights began with the stuff of subsistence, land, food and safety. (The Canadian experience of social movements followed the American pattern but in a less confrontational fashion.) Only much later, against much more draconian governments, were civil rights leaders in Latin America able to consider aspiring to the rarefied issues debated by the students of Yale and Columbia in the 1960s and 1970s.

Summary

By the time you have worked through this book, you should be able to:

- understand and explain how the Native Americans had improved their civil rights by the 1980s
- understand and explain the role of the civil rights movement in challenging and outlawing racial segregation in the US
- evaluate the role of Martin Luther King and of the federal government in achieving civil rights for African Americans
- assess the significance of Malcolm X and Black Power

- understand how the aims and the techniques of the African American civil rights movements were adapted by other groups
- understand the nature and assess the impact of youth protest in the 1960s and 1970s
- assess the success of the feminist movement in the Americas
- draw parallels between the rights movements in the US and those in other parts of the Americas.

2 | Native American movements in the Americas

Introduction

This chapter deals with the development of Native American movements in the Americas, and focuses in particular on the United States. It will examine the situation of Native American peoples at the end of the Second World War, in the context of colonial rule and the development of the modern states. The chapter will then seek to address why the Native American movements emerged in the 1960s and what their aims and grievances were, before considering how successful the movements were in achieving those aims. Finally, it will look at how far the civil rights of Native Americans changed in the post-war period. The chapter also includes case studies of indigenous peoples in other countries of the Americas.

TIMELINE

1944 National Congress of American Indians (NCAI) formed

1956 Indian Vocational Training Act (1956) passed

1958 Battle of Hayes Pond between Ku Klux Klan (KKK) and Lumbee Indians

1961 National Indian Council (NIC) formed in Canada; National Indian Youth Council (NIYC) formed

1968 American Indian Movement (AIM) formed; Civil Rights Act contains Indian 'Bill of Rights'

1969 **Nov:** Occupation of Alcatraz by Navajo Indians

1970 Publication of *Bury My Heart at Wounded Knee* by Dee Brown

1972 AIM leads Trail of Broken Treaties to Washington, DC

1973 Armed confrontation between AIM members and government officials at Wounded Knee

1975 Indian Self-Determination Act passed

1978 American Indian Religious Freedom Act passed

1992 Rigoberta Menchú wins Nobel Peace Prize for work on behalf of Guatemalan Indians

KEY QUESTIONS

- What was the situation of Native American populations in 1945?
- Why did Native American movements emerge in the immediate post-war period?
- What were the goals of the reformers in the Native American movements?
- How did Native Americans seek to affirm their identities during the 1960s?
- To what extent did the civil rights of Native Americans change from the 1960s to the 1980s?

Overview

- US federal policy towards Native Americans was paternalistic through most of the 20th century. There was an expectation that tribes would die out eventually but this gradually faded as the population recovered.
- Native Americans are comprised of discrete tribes who were often unwilling to work together, this made coordination more difficult than in the African American and women's rights movement
- The formation of the National Congress of American Indians (NCAI) in 1944 gave Native Americans a national voice to address the issue of rights for the first time.
- Native Americans faced considerable disadvantages in terms of unemployment, healthcare and education.
- The slow progress of change led to the creation of the National Indian Youth Council (NIYC) in 1961, which was inspired by the black civil rights movement.
- The American Indian Movement (AIM), founded in 1968, used increasingly radical and media-friendly stunts to put pressure on the federal government, such as the occupation of Alcatraz and the Trail of Broken Treaties.

- By the 1980s, advances had been made in terms of legislation and addressing social problems, but Native Americans were still the most disadvantaged group in US society.
- In other parts of the Americas, indigenous people were similarly disadvantaged. They were more frequently disenfranchised (deprived of the right to vote) than in the US.

2.1 What was the situation of Native American populations in 1945?

Colonisation and modernisation

The indigenous peoples of North and South America suffered heavily at the hands of the European colonists who began arriving after Hernán Cortés's victory over the Aztec Empire in 1519. In the following two centuries over ¾ million Spanish people arrived in Latin America.

The Spanish in the South and British and French in the North brought disease and sought to 'civilise' native people, while native lands were taken for derisory sums, most notably the island of Manhattan for $24 worth of glass beads and cloth. Traditions were disrespected and suppressed, but worse still was the impact of alcohol, which was introduced to the Native Americans by the white settlers. On both continents, indigenous peoples were treated as subhuman.

As the colonial period developed into the agricultural and industrial revolutions, more and more land was needed to house and feed the expanding population. The subsequent impact of these forces of modernisation on indigenous people was even more damaging than the arrival of the Europeans.

Skirmishes between settlers and natives were frequent and were later immortalised in (fictional) cowboy films. Over 50 'wars' were fought in the lands west of the Mississippi in the period from 1823 to 1900. At their conclusion treaties with the natives were signed which purported to recognise certain native rights to lands and fishing areas as well as promises of investment in the needs of the tribes.

Civil Rights and Social Movements in the Americas Post–45

In practice these treaties, though legally binding, were rarely honoured, owing to the superiority of settler numbers and forces and the racial and religious prejudices against native people that persisted. These prejudices were reinforced by the concept of Social Darwinism. The idea that certain races (here meaning white Europeans) were superior to others was being hotly debated at the time. Social Darwinism provided a pseudo-scientific justification for anything from ignoring native customs to genocide.

Theory of Knowledge

History and language:

The term 'genocide', meaning the deliberate killing of a large group, especially those connected by nationality, ethnicity or religion, is fraught with difficult connotations. The Second World War genocide of the Jews is widely recognised but other large-scale deaths such as the Armenian 'genocide' of 1915 are disputed. As you work through this chapter consider whether the US government can be seen as having perpetrated a genocide against Native Americans and why the term is problematic.

The ideas of the free market also contributed to the colonisation of Native American lands. The opening and exploitation of new territories was seen as part of a natural progression of capitalism, and more progressive Europeans expected indigenous people to either assimilate or die out.

Railroads and settlements brought displacement, starvation and, in some cases – such as the Trail of Tears following the Indian Removal Act of 1830 – genocide. These genocides were achieved using forced relocation to reservations, 'treaties' that were little more than diktats, and outright warfare and extermination campaigns carried out in both North and South America.

ACTIVITY

Find out more about the Indian Removal Act of 1830 and the Trail of Tears. Why does the term 'genocide' apply to events such as the Trail of Tears?

Figure 2.1: A 1911 advertisement promoting the sale of former Native American land which had been taken by the government.

US paternalism and the 1887 Dawes Act

As the European colonists moved west and settled the land the Native Americans were forced off and into government-allocated reservations. Native Americans had no desire to become assimilated into the mainstream of American society. However, the government's attitude towards the Native Americans was guided by paternalism. A paternalistic government is one that interferes with people's lives, against their will, 'for their own good'. In 1887, the US Congress passed the General Allotment Act (also known as the Dawes Act). The aim of the act was to break up native reservation lands in order to 'free' Native Americans to assimilate into the mainstream.

The idea was that the reservations would be divided up among families to give them land of their own. Historian Niall Ferguson calls this idea of the property-owning democracy one of the 'killer apps' (jargon for an exceptional computer application) of Western economic success, but the concept of 'owning' anything was alien to the Native Americans and unworkable in the often desolate reservation territory. Historian Howard Zinn claims that, in fact, much of this land was taken by white speculators who suspected there might be commercial value in it or under it, and reservations – now reduced in size – remained.

Over time it became clear that the Dawes Act was a disaster. Many Native American families were forced to abandon their barren smallholdings and head to the cities. Their situation was exacerbated during the Great Depression of the 1930s, because their lack of land meant they did not qualify for federal aid as larger-scale farmers did.

The failure of the policies of assimilation and termination (see section 2.2) had a twin outcome. It made Native Americans more determined to retain their traditional culture and way of life as opposed to assimilating to the American norm. It also made them more determined to claim their rights as American citizens. In particular, Native American leaders came to be most concerned with their right to their tribal lands.

Native Americans differed from the other groups discussed in this book in their relative lack of unity. Where other groups could be defined by colour, gender or language, Native Americans resisted homogenous definition and wanted self-determination by tribe rather than as a wider group. To Americans raised on cowboy legends, Native Americans were simply 'Red Indians', but huge differences existed between Crow in the north, Choctaw in the south-east and Navajo in the west. This meant that it would always be difficult for a grassroots group to emerge that could claim to represent them all.

Theory of Knowledge

History and generalisation:

The term 'Red Indians', which grouped the tribes into one homogeneous entity, is a generalisation that is no longer in use. The French novelist Alexandre Dumas famously claimed *'all generalisations are dangerous, even this one'*. Can you think of any dangerous generalisations that are common in the modern world?

Developments in the early 20th century

Some progress in challenging the idea of the helpless native was made by individual Native Americans such as the actor Will Rogers and the ballerina Elizabeth Marie Tall Chief, but even limited progress for others brought its own problems, with few opportunities for work on the reservations. School-educated Native Americans often had to choose between the tribe and the mainstream. This dilemma, along with the associated problems of alcoholism, is addressed in the 1969 novel *House Made of Dawn* by **N. Scott Momaday.**

N. Scott Momaday (b. 1934):

A Kiowa-Cherokee poet and writer, Momaday grew up both in small south-western communities and on reservations. This, along with his Native American father and European American mother, helped him to understand the problems facing young Native Americans. His 1969 Pulitzer Prize-winning novel *House Made of Dawn* describes the complex and challenging experiences of young Native Americans in the period following the Second World War and relocation. He continues to write, and was awarded the National Medal of Arts in 2007 by President George W. Bush.

The first pan-Indian group to attempt to address this dilemma was formed by 50 professional Native Americans in 1911. The Society of American Indians (SAI) campaigned for better education and health facilities and for civil rights, demands that were repeated nearly 60 years later at Alcatraz (see 2.4, The occupation of Alcatraz, 1969). However, the SAI lacked internal coherence and the financial strength required to mount successful legal challenges. It also suffered from the suspicion and lack of support of the tribes and collapsed within a decade.

Despite this fragmented Native American protest and the failure of the SAI, by 1941 the position of Native Americans had improved as a result of the policies of President Franklin D. Roosevelt and the head of the Bureau of Indian Affairs (BIA), **John Collier**. Some native lands were restored and the division of tribal lands was prohibited. Nevertheless, the options open to Native Americans were still limited and bleak. Those who sought to assimilate faced prejudice, and those who stayed on the reservations faced poverty.

> **John Collier (1884–1968):**
>
> Collier was a social reformer, bureaucrat and academic who became the commissioner for the Bureau of Indian Affairs from 1933 to 1945. He was the driving force behind the Indian Reorganization Act of 1934, which restored certain rights to Native Americans. Though sometimes seen as paternalistic by Native American leaders, he was a vocal supporter of Native self-determination and director of the National Indian Institute until his death in 1968.

The Second World War

Despite their uneasy relationship with the federal government some 25 000 Native Americans fought in the Second World War, of whom 500 died. The most famous of the Native soldiers were the Navajo code talkers, whose unique language skills proved vital in the war in the Pacific.

These marines created a secret, seemingly unbreakable, code based on the complex Navajo language. A total of 50 000 Native Americans also worked in the defence industries. Although the war did little to help Native Americans in concrete terms, as with African Americans the experience of fighting overseas led to an increased consciousness of rights and a willingness to question the paternalism of the government. It also gave white and black Americans who served with Native Americans an insight into indigenous people.

In 1945, Collier's term as head of the BIA ended. The bureau itself was moved from Washington to Chicago, and its budget was cut. However, the greater educational opportunities that Collier had worked for were beginning to show results, helped by Roosevelt's 1944 GI Bill, which provided college education for Second World War veterans.

There was also an increased number of Native Americans employed in the BIA. These factors combined to make Native Americans less reliant on non-natives to provide the skills needed to assert their rights.

Therefore, by 1945, there had clearly been progress. More Native Americans were educated and working in the professions; voting rights were being enforced; and the formation of the National Congress of

American Indians (NCAI) in 1944 gave indigenous people a national voice.

However, huge problems still existed. The issues of broken treaties had not been addressed, and so land rights were a major issue; young Native Americans struggled with the conflict between traditional and modern ways; and poverty and health problems were rife.

Figure 2.2: Navajo military code talkers using a portable radio set, Solomon Islands, 1943.

ACTIVITY

Draw a two-circle Venn diagram with one circle to represent Native American problems and the other to represent the problems of one of the other groups covered in this book. As you progress through the book, fill in the diagram to show which problems the groups had in common and which were distinct to Native Americans, blacks, young people or women.

2.2 Why did Native American movements emerge in the immediate post-war period?

The post-war years

By 1900 there had been a steep decline in population, which meant only 300 000 Native Americans were left in the US. It seemed as if the 'Indian problem' would soon solve itself. Yet, by 1960, the population had more than doubled to 800 000, with approximately half living in cities and half on reservations, meaning the issue of rights became increasingly pressing.

Following the war, there were hopes that the Truman administration would begin to instigate fairer policies. Rehabilitation programmes were developed, and there was an increasing recognition of and respect for Native American religious and social customs and their rights as American citizens. An example of this was the ending of the ban on alcohol, 20 years after prohibition (the national ban on alcohol) had been repealed for the rest of the country.

The ban was a classic case of laws being passed for 'their own good' rather than in consultation with the Native American community, although many reservations did opt to remain free of alcohol after 1953.

Termination

However, when John Collier left the BIA in 1945, one of the most vocal supporters of Native American self-determination was removed. Policy relapsed to assimilation in the form of 'termination', a policy developed by the federal government in the 1940s and eventually carried out from 1953 to 1964. The government felt that it would be better for the Native Americans if they were assimilated as individuals into mainstream US society. In the 109 terminations that occurred, beginning with that of the Menominee in 1954, the federal government brought an end to its recognition of the tribes as sovereign nations, its trusteeship of reservations, and the exclusion of Native Americans from state laws and federal taxes.

Termination was designed to move towards an ending of federal control by the BIA and to give the same rights and responsibilities to Native Americans as other minority groups. It therefore attempted to impose the American tradition of individualism on tribes for whom the importance of the collective was deep in their self-identity.

The desire to oppose termination re-energised Native protest and led to the formation of the National Congress of American Indians (NCAI). The denunciation of the policy at the 1954 NCAI convention, and the willingness of Native Americans to go to Washington to protest against it, stung the government.

Figure 2.3: Attendees at the NCAI Conference, in Browning, Montana, 1945.

In 1956, President Eisenhower announced that there would be no more terminations unless a tribe specifically requested it. By engaging with the government and organising themselves, Native Americans had begun to make progress in asserting their rights.

Voting rights

Establishment of voting rights was never a straightforward issue. The Indian Citizenship Act of 1924 had made Native Americans full citizens with voting rights, but loopholes in the act meant that some states excluded Native Americans from the franchise for over two decades. In 1948, Miguel Trujillo, a Laguna Indian and teacher in New Mexico, attempted to register to vote and was refused. In the subsequent court case, the state of New Mexico was found to have discriminated against him. Particular note was made of the fact that Trujillo, like other Indians, paid all state and federal taxes except for private property taxes on the reservations.

However, this precedent alone was insufficient as there were further legal problems because of the Native Americans' demand for sovereign (self-governing) status as separate nations while at the same time they were demanding their voting rights as Americans. Nevertheless, by 1953, the states of Maine, Arizona and New Mexico became the final three to incorporate the terms of the 1924 act into their state constitutions. In 1975, Barbara Jordan, a black member of the House of Representatives, successfully campaigned to extend the 1965 Voting Rights Act (see section 5.5) to address discrimination against 'language minority groups' with the provision of bilingual ballots in all states.

Education

There was some progress in education too – about 90% of native children attended school by 1965. However, their different cultural background and needs were largely ignored, and Native American children often dropped out of school before graduating. The growing, educated, middle class, upon which successful protest often depends, was conspicuous by its absence.

The Cold War and McCarthyism

In the immediate post-war period there was gradual, but not substantial, progress in Native American rights. Like the other civil rights movements, Native American campaigns did not take off in the years immediately following the Second World War. In this period, the influence of the Cold War and the paranoia of McCarthyism led to huge domestic pressure for conformity, and an almost religious fervour for the 'American way'.

Any questioning of government policy by minority groups could easily be linked with having communist tendencies. The resulting pressure on Native Americans to assimilate was difficult to resist without an established national movement.

The image of the 'tamed savage'

In addition, Native Americans were the victims of a powerful position in the American psyche which was emphasised by the growth of films and TV. As a new country with a short history, it was important for America to acquire its own heroes and legends. The battle between cowboys and Indians filled this gap. Books such as Owen Wister's novel *The Virginian, Horseman of the Plain* (1902) gave way to the later films of John Wayne (and Ronald Reagan!), which made it very clear that the Red Indian was the bad guy and the cowboy the good. Helen Hunt Jackson's 1881 book *A Century of Dishonor* had shocked readers with its graphic tales of the violence and deceit towards the tribes by the federal government, but the overwhelming image of the Native American in the rest of American culture was that of the tamed savage.

Theory of Knowledge

History and myth:

The myth of the West is a powerful part of the American psyche. Ideas of 'manifest destiny' and the importance of 'good' versus 'evil' have led many commentators, notably the political scientist Leo Strauss, to suggest that the US needs an enemy to fight against. First, there was the rejection of the old monarchies of Europe, then the conquest of the Native Americans, and later economic and then military rivalry with the Germans, the Soviets and now Islamic Fundamentalists. Do you think this need is real and, if so, is it unique to the US?

White prejudice was not as overt towards Native American people as it was towards black people. The Native American threat had been conquered in the push to the west and was reconquered nightly in TV dramas such as *Gunsmoke*.

This neo-colonial attitude meant that Native American problems were less connected to the social prejudices of whites. But the gradual drift of Native Americans into the cities brought tension, as with any ethnic minority group, especially as relocation was actively encouraged. After 1945, significant Native American populations developed in Chicago, San Francisco, Oakland and Oklahoma City, all near large reservations.

The government continued to try to address the 'Indian problem' in a paternalistic way. The Indian Vocational Training Act (1956) was designed to improve employment prospects for Native Americans in the cities. The new urban dwellers encountered the kinds of social problems that faced northern blacks, particularly poverty and unemployment. Around 25% of urban Native Americans were officially counted as 'poor', and almost 20% lived in substandard housing. Not surprisingly, Native American life expectancy was only two-thirds that of whites. Unemployment was more varied and was less of a problem in Chicago (4.3%) for example, than in Seattle (18%).

Lobbying

The NCAI, led by Joseph R. Garry, remained the main lobbying group for Native Americans, and was comprehensive in that it tried to recruit members from all tribes. Women were also well represented. The organisation aimed to achieve the setting up of a federal commission to hear and settle land ownership claims against the government, and improve administration from the BIA – which, it argued, should employ more Native Americans. It also wished to monitor congressional legislation affecting Native territory.

Because many of its demands were particular to the needs of the Native American community and did not impact on whites in the way that, for example, the Brown case (see 4.2, *Brown versus Board of Education of Topeka*, 1954) did, the NCAI never achieved the national recognition of organisations such as the NAACP (the National Association for the Advancement of Colored People), which campaigned for African American rights. Nonetheless, some comparisons could be made with black civil rights organisations: the concerns with voter registration and better health and educational services, for example.

However, successful lobbying and slow progress in the period from 1945 to 1960 did not make up for the prejudice suffered by the Native American people. In 1961, a more recognisable form of activism emerged from the American Indian Chicago Conference.

Divisions in the NCAI between Oklahoma and Plains tribes had made the organisation powerless, and contempt for the BIA was widespread. In addition, a new generation of younger, urbanised Native Americans was emerging, less tied to tribal customs and more willing to embrace Pan-Indian values. The conference produced a 'Declaration of Indian Purpose' and determined that Native Americans should be involved in the decision-making process for all programmes that would affect them.

But even this did not go far enough for some. In late 1961, Clyde Warrior, Melvin Thom and Herbert Blatchford formed the National Indian Youth Council (NIYC) and issued a 'Statement of Policy' that was scathing in its criticism of government policy:

SOURCE 2.1

Our viewpoint, based in a tribal perspective, realises, literally, that the Indian problem is the white man, and, further, realises that poverty, educational drop-out, unemployment etc. reflect only symptoms of a social contact situation that is directed at unilateral cultural extinction.

Witt, S. and Steiner, S. 1972. **The Way: An Anthology of American Indian Literature.** *New York, USA. Alfred A. Knopf. p.221.*

QUESTION

Why would the statement in Source 2.1 be highly controversial?

Inspired by the early successes of the more militant tactics employed by the black civil rights movement, the NIYC began to break away from the NCAI. The NCAI was accused of being largely dominated by more prosperous Native Americans and of not representing the views of the young.

The Student Nonviolent Coordinating Committee (SNCC) (see section 5.1) had been established the previous year, and as the SNCC

Civil Rights and Social Movements in the Americas Post–45

was the prelude to the Black Power movement (see 7.3), so the NIYC would inspire increased militancy with the development of the American Indian Movement (AIM) in 1968 (see 2.4). The Native American historian Waziyatawin argues, 'When people are educated to respect the knowledge, the scholarship, and the history and the background of everyone except themselves, then those people are miseducated.'

In the late 1960s this miseducation was addressed through the growing awareness of Native American history brought about by the writing of Vine Deloria Jr and Dee Brown. These factors resulted in a series of protests reflecting dissatisfaction with both the NCAI and the Native American policies of the federal government.

KEY CONCEPTS QUESTION

Causation and Consequence: Why did the Native American civil rights movement emerge at this particular time in US history? What were the most immediate results of its formation?

KEY CONCEPTS ACTIVITY

Significance: Read through this section and construct a table with the headings 'Social', 'Economic' and 'Political'. Try to classify the reasons given above as to why the Native American movement emerged in the 1960s into these three categories. Finally, add any other categories you think are needed to explain the emergence, and write a couple of sentences to explain which one(s) you consider to have been most important.

2.3 What were the goals of the reformers in the Native American movements?

SOURCE 2.2

In 1970 the median income for Native American men over the age of sixteen was barely more than $3500, compared to an average for European Americans of nearly $9000, and $5400 for Afro-Americans. Average annual earnings for Native American women in 1970 were $1700, compared to $6823 for European American women and $5258 for Afro-American women.

Olson, J. S. and Wilson, R. 1986. **Native Americans in the Twentieth Century.** *Chicago, USA. University of Illinois Press. p.187.*

QUESTION

What message does Source 2.2 portray?

Young Native Americans increasingly criticised those members of the NCAI who chose to work closely with the BIA, calling them 'apples' (because they were red on the outside but white on the inside) or 'Uncle Tomahawks' (in a nod to the 'Uncle Tom' insults sometimes levelled by militant blacks at figures such as Martin Luther King and Ralph Abernathy). Once more the legitimacy of a unifying Native American movement was under threat.

By the late 1960s Native Americans had begun to take ownership of their situation following the model of the black civil rights movement. Though there were still divisions at the tribal and generational level and Native Americans were still considerably disadvantaged there was considerably more promise for the future than at any time since the landing of the pilgrims.

Was poverty at the root of the problems faced by Native Americans in the post-war years? Read through this section about the goals of the reformers in the Native American movements, and see if any of these goals could be argued to be unrelated to the issue of poverty. Does this differ from the African American situation? Does it mean that Marx is right and that all history is a matter of economics?

Treaty rights

The NIYC began to attempt to achieve its goals by direct action, and the first goal it tried for was that of treaty rights. From 1787 to 1871, European settlers had signed over 650 treaties with Native American tribes that defined the tribes as sovereign nations.

These treaties covered such things as peace negotiations, borders of Indian territory and guarantees of Indian hunting and fishing rights. For example, the Treaty of Medicine Creek, signed in Washington State in 1854, stipulated that 'The right of taking fish, at all usual and accustomed grounds and stations, is further secured to said Indians in common with all citizens of the Territory.' However, the increasing marginalisation of Native Americans through the 19th century, along with the construction of dams, salmon canneries and further industrialisation of the Columbia River, made it difficult for Native Americans to uphold these rights.

In 1964, inspired by the 'sit-ins' in the African American civil rights movement, the NIYC organised a 'fish-in' in Washington State to test a congressional ruling from 1954 that Native Americans were exempt from state fishing and hunting regulations. The protest was attended by film star Marlon Brando who was arrested with others during a Puyallup tribe fish-in.

Further fish-ins in Oregon, Idaho and Montana followed. In 1966, the Department of Justice restored treaty rights to the protestors and the media picked up on the story, just at the time when there was a relative lull in the black civil rights movement.

Millions of ordinary Americans started to become aware of Native American demands. The issue of treaty rights would become more visible with the Trail of Broken Treaties in 1972 (see section 2.4).

Social issues

The second NIYC goal was to address poverty and its consequences: unemployment, health – both physical and mental – and housing. In 1970, unemployment levels were as high as 80% on some isolated reservations, and average life expectancy was 44 years compared to a national average of 64. Diseases continued to kill thousands and there were high suicide rates, particularly among 16 to 25 year olds.

Land rights

Finally, there was the question of land. The majority of Native Americans lived west of the River Mississippi in Oklahoma, Arizona and California. Life on the reservations was hard. Their size had been reduced following the 1887 Dawes Act, and what was left was often uneconomical to farm. In addition, the periodic discovery of mineral or oil wealth brought big business into the territories but Native Americans saw none of the benefits.

As a result, the Indian Land Rights Association was founded. This organisation aimed to restore tribal lands, and dismissed the idea that money was sufficient compensation.

Physical intimidation

One issue that Native Americans rarely had to deal with was physical intimidation. Unlike the black civil rights movement, Native Americans only occasionally faced physical threats and menace.

The Battle of Hayes Pond, in which 100 Ku Klux Klan members (see 3.1, 'Black Codes' and the Ku Klux Klan) attempted to intimidate a Lumbee reservation and were scattered by over 500 armed Lumbee, was a notable exception to this rule. Here, it could be argued, the Native Americans benefited from the popular perception of them in the US as a conquered people who were no longer a threat to white dominance.

2.4 How did Native Americans seek to affirm their identities during the 1960s?

Over the period from 1944 to 1980, large numbers of Native Americans left their reservations and moved to the cities. They were encouraged to relocate by government programmes that were based on the belief that if Native Americans could be integrated into white society, problems such as alcoholism and high mortality rates could be tackled more effectively.

By 1980, therefore, many of the million strong Native American population lived in urban areas – some in small towns, but many more in large cities such as San Francisco and Los Angeles. Congregating together in large numbers made many increasingly aware of their own economic and social inferiority compared to both whites and blacks. It also increased the possibility of the emergence of new and more effective protest movements.

Use of the judicial system

Learning from and paralleling the black experience, Native Americans initially sought to address the issue of their civil rights through the courts. The NCAI became the first organisation that claimed to represent a majority of Indians and used the judicial system in an attempt to get justice. Though they always lacked high-profile successes, such as the NAACP achieved in the Brown decisions, the same technique of using the courts was beginning to pay off.

The NCAI sued state and federal governments over discrimination in employment and education, and over the issue of treaty rights. For many Native Americans, this method of taking the white man on using his own laws was the best way to make progress.

However, the legal method was slow and frustrating, and some questioned the potential impact of entangling Native Americans more tightly into the federal system. Unlike most African Americans, it was never the intention of Native Americans to seek integration into American society, and the debate over whether voting undermined

Native American identity was now being played out on a larger scale. Some were concerned that invoking citizenship rights would damage tribal identity.

Given this lack of cohesion, the fact that the NCAI achieved any success is all the more impressive. When President John F. Kennedy pledged to develop the human and natural resources of the reservations to help Native Americans, as part of his New Frontier programme which aimed to erase poverty regardless of race, it seemed the federal government was genuinely addressing the demands of the NCAI. However, by then the organisation's central place in Native American protest was weakening.

The emergence of radical protest

During the 1960s and 1970s, the growing anger of the Native Americans was directed both against an unresponsive government and the slow-moving NCAI. By 1968, protest was growing stronger, particularly among younger Native Americans.

In 1969, Vine Deloria Jr published the book *Custer Died for Your Sins*. It was followed a year later by Dee Brown's bestselling *Bury My Heart at Wounded Knee: An Indian History of the American West*, which highlighted how deceitfully the government had behaved towards the Native Americans.

Recognition gave the more radical protesters momentum, and they drew inspiration from other protest movements, such as those demanding black civil rights or an end to the Vietnam War.

The occupation of Alcatraz, 1969

In November 1969, encouraged by the idea of protest and direct action, 14 Native American men and women occupied the disused island of Alcatraz. They offered to buy the island for $24 in glass beads and cloth – the same price paid by the white settlers for Manhattan. This was the second Native American attempt to use Alcatraz to grab media attention; the first, in 1964, was quickly driven off.

When their proposal to turn the island into a centre for Native American Studies for Ecology was rejected, 80 Native Americans, including notable figures such as Richard Oakes – the director of Indian Studies at San Francisco State College – returned and occupied the island. Hundreds of Native Americans flocked to join the protest and they were supported by students from UC Berkeley.

During the course of the protest, more than 10 000 Native Americans visited the island, which even had its own radio station 'Radio Free Alcatraz', named after the US anti-communist propaganda station 'Radio Free Europe'. Direct action at Alcatraz brought more national and international recognition than the BIA and NCAI had ever achieved.

Figure 2.4: Native Americans occupy Alcatraz; note the changes to the sign.

Eventually, after cutting off telephones, electricity and finally water to the island, federal forces landed on Alcatraz and physically removed the Native Americans who remained. Perhaps the most lasting legacy of the occupation was the proclamation made by the first group on to Alcatraz, entitled 'We Hold the Rock'. It mockingly addressed the problems of reservation life and implicitly demanded redress.

SOURCE 2.3

We feel that this so-called Alcatraz Island is more than suitable for an Indian reservation, as determined by the white man's own standards. By this we mean that this place resembles most Indian reservations in that:

- It is isolated from modern facilities, and without adequate means of transportation
- It has no fresh running water
- It has inadequate sanitation facilities
- There are no oil or mineral rights
- There is no industry and so unemployment is very great
- There are no health care facilities
- The soil is rocky and non-productive; and the land does not support game
- There are no educational facilities
- The population has always exceeded the land base
- The population has always been held as prisoners and dependent upon others.

Extract from the 'We Hold the Rock' proclamation, November 1969. Source: www.jstor.org

QUESTION

With reference to its origin, purpose and content, analyse the value and limitations of Source 2.3 for a historian studying the Native American rights movement.

The Alcatraz incident showed what could be achieved by direct action, and encouraged many Native Americans to call for and believe in 'Red Power'. This was a more militant approach to achieving separation from whites, which was inspired by the Black Power movement and the Nation of Islam's demands for a separate black state within a state (see Chapter 7).

After Alcatraz, Native Americans occupied federal lands and disobeyed state and federal fishing regulations with increasing regularity. In Maine, members of the Passamaquoddy tribe even collected tolls on busy highways crossing their land.

The American Indian Movement (AIM)

Militancy and media savvy clearly brought results. The most militant Native American group was the American Indian Movement (AIM), which was founded in Minneapolis–St Paul in 1968 by **Dennis Banks** and Clyde Bellecourt. In response to police harassment, young Native Americans, dressed in a striking uniform of red berets and jackets, patrolled the streets monitoring the police in the same way that groups of Black Panthers did in Oakland, California (see Figure 7.4). As a result, there was a decline in the arrest of Native Americans, and their numbers in local jails fell by 60%.

AIM also sought to improve the housing, education and employment of Native Americans in the cities, and to project a more positive image. Between 1969 and 1970, they set up 18 branches and held their first National Convention in 1971.

> **Dennis Banks (b. 1937):**
>
> An Anishinaabe Indian, Banks co-founded AIM in 1968. He participated in the Alcatraz occupation and helped to organise the 1972 Trail of Broken Treaties. Banks continued to be involved in direct action and was arrested along with 300 others for the occupation of Wounded Knee in 1973. Banks controversially re-emerged in a small armed AIM group that disbanded after the unsolved murder of Native American rights activist Anna Mae Pictou Aquash. Banks was offered sanctuary in California and went on to teach at Stanford University. He also founded the Sacred Run movement and appeared in a series of Hollywood films.

The Trail of Broken Treaties, 1972

In 1972, together with other organisations, AIM took part in the Trail of Broken Treaties to the BIA in Washington, DC. The Trail took its name from the Trail of Tears, the forced removal of Cherokees from the south-eastern United States under President Andrew Jackson following the Indian Removal Act of 1830.

After travelling all the way from the west coast, picking up participants from the major Native American states on the way, the protesters arrived in Washington in November, the week before the presidential election, paralleling the venue and timing of the 1963 March on Washington (see section 5.3). Here, AIM members took over the BIA's offices, going through files and calculating that each Native American family in the country could receive a further $4000 per year if the bureaucracy of the BIA was removed.

The list of 20 demands that followed was ignored by the Nixon government, perfectly encapsulating the frustration of the protesters. In the preamble to the demands they had written:

SOURCE 2.4

The government of the United States knows the reasons for our going to its capital city. Unfortunately, they don't know how to greet us. We go because America has been only too ready to express shame, and suffer none from the expression – while remaining wholly unwilling to change to allow life for Indian people.

Extract from **Preamble to the Trail of Broken Treaties** *20-point position paper, October 1972. From www.aimovement.org.*

The Trail highlighted the problem of broken treaties and the hypocrisy of a government that said it regretted the mistreatment of Native Americans, but was unwilling to put its hand in its pocket to remedy them, particularly following a costly war. An escalation in militancy was almost inevitable, and Native American protest came full circle in 1973 at Wounded Knee in South Dakota.

Confrontation at Wounded Knee, 1973

In 1973, militant members of AIM brought about an armed confrontation with government officials at Wounded Knee in South Dakota, where 83 years previously US cavalry had massacred the Sioux. Wounded Knee was chosen carefully for its historical significance, and its contemporary resonance following Dee Brown's book. The incident was widely reported despite the limited number of AIM participants (only about 300 members supported the confrontation), largely because it gave journalists the chance to joke that Richard Nixon was about to become the first US president for a century to fight a war against the Native Americans.

Other than contributing to the growing media awareness of Native grievances, the confrontation achieved very little. Vine Deloria later commented in 1993 that the era 'will probably always be dominated by the images and slogans of the AIM people. The real accomplishment in land restoration, however, were made by quiet determined tribal leaders.'

The desire by Native American people to affirm their identities after the Second World War arose for a number of reasons. Fear of the loss of tribal heritage and Native American identity was heightened by the rapid spread of a homogeneous 'American' culture aided by the growth of the mass media. The inspiration of the legal methods of the black civil rights movement gave middle-class Native Americans the idea of asserting their treaty rights through the courts, and this was helped by the founding of organisations such as the NCAI and the evolution of groups such as AIM.

These groups were willing to copy and adapt the more militant tactics of black people, women and anti-Vietnam protesters in a bid to assert native rights and address issues of education, poverty and unemployment. Meanwhile, the mass media machine brought attention to the Native American plight through celebrity endorsement, and the rediscovery of native writing and history slowly infiltrated the intellectual mainstream. Progress was slow but tangible.

ACTIVITY

Research a treaty between the early American government and a native tribe. Examine the terms and the extent to which they were kept in subsequent years. If you were a member of the American Indian Movement what would be the most appropriate (in keeping with tribal tradition but exciting media attention) way of protesting against your 'broken' treaty?

2.5 To what extent did the civil rights of Native Americans change from the 1960s to the 1980s?

Legal recognition

Native Americans in the US certainly made some progress from the 1960s to the 1980s, much of it under the Nixon administration. Opinion polls suggested that white Americans had considerably more sympathy for Native American demands than those of African Americans. The increased assertiveness of the Native Americans also led to changes in government attitudes, although their lesser numbers reduced the impact of their activism. They had greater equality both *de facto* (in reality) and *de jure* (in legal terms), and the legal system had provided precedents for supporting their rights.

Native American culture was legally recognised and preserved in the American Indian Religious Freedom Act (1978). This act granted the right to 'believe, express and exercise traditional religions including access to sites, use and possession of sacred objects and freedom to worship through ceremonials and traditional rites'. Land was restored to a number of tribes, such as the 48 000 acres of sacred mountain land restored to the Taos Pueblos Indians in 1970.

Where restoration was unmanageable, compensation was paid. In fact, between 1946 and 1968 the Indian Claims Commission gave around $400 million to compensate for land loss.

There were also advances in self-government, including the Indian Self-Determination Act (1975), which attempted to give Native Americans more control of their reservations.

Continuing social problems

Native Americans were among the greatest beneficiaries of President Lyndon B. Johnson's attack on poverty, but it was an uphill struggle to address the underlying problems of welfare dependency and job creation. Reservations were unattractive to employers owing to their limited pool of poorly educated workers. In 1966, Johnson appointed Robert L. Bennett as the first Native American to head the BIA, although he achieved far less than Collier before him.

In 1969, the Nixon administration appointed a Mohawk–Sioux, Louis R. Bruce, as Commissioner for Indian Affairs. In 1970, Bruce assured the tribes that they would be given greater autonomy 'without being cut off from federal concern or support'. The intention was to free Native Americans from federal supervision and to transfer the cost of their support to the states, but this policy was filled with problems and soon failed. Historian Paula Marks noted: 'All of this governmental activity to address Indian problems and concerns actually fed activism rather than defused it.'

Indeed, many problems and difficulties remained. Progress had undoubtedly been made by Native Americans in the US, but much of this was in the form of legal recognition. As with the African Americans, the real problems of poverty had yet to be addressed in any coherent way.

By 1980, the average annual per capita income for Native Americans on reservations was less than $1000 per year. Poverty in turn brought the attendant problems of poor housing and sanitation, malnutrition and health issues. Native Americans in 1980 were six times more likely to contract tuberculosis than the national average, and 70 times more likely to get dysentery. Suicide rates were six times higher than the national average and deaths from liver disease, as a result of alcoholism, were five times the national average. These combined health problems made the life expectancy of Native Americans in the US seven years under the average (64 compared with 71, though this had increased considerably in the past two decades), and they remained indisputably the poorest people in the US.

Discrimination also remained a problem. This ranged from the mild form found in history textbooks that referred to 'Red Indians' and TV shows such as *Bonanza* (a western soap opera that ran from 1959 to 1973) to more concrete statistics, such as those for imprisonment which, in towns close to reservations, ran 30 times higher than non-Native Americans. And when the economy suffered, Native Americans were, together with blacks, usually first to lose their jobs.

Decline of the movement

Many Native Americans disliked the approach of militant groups such as AIM. They felt it was not in keeping with traditional ways. As a result, the Native American protest movement dissipated in the 1980s as Reagan's assertively traditional Republican presidency refocused national attention on the Cold War.

SOURCE 2.5

The presence of 1,878,285 American Indians living in hundreds of rural and urban communities in the United States in 1990 was evidence that Native Americans had not disappeared from the American scene as so many observers, officials and researchers had predicted over the years. It is not only the case that Indians have not disappeared as distinct individual ethnic identities in the United States; it is also the case that Indian communities as distinctive ethnic enclaves remain very much a part of the American ethnic mosaic. We take for granted the presence of these many Native American societies scattered across the United States. From what we know of American history, however, it is quite remarkable that any Indian communities managed to weather the many assaults on their viability mounted during the past half-millennium.

Nagel, J. 1997. **American Indian Ethnic Renewal: Red Power and the Resurgence of Identity and Culture**. *Oxford, UK. Oxford University Press. p.187.*

DISCUSSION POINT

Where Nagel (Source 2.5) sees the resilience of Native Americans in the post-war years as part of a long tradition of patient opposition to outside agents of change, Rooney (Source 2.6) sees a way of life that is an anachronism. Which of these opinions do you find most convincing in the light of what you have studied? Is there a fundamental difference between the Native American campaign for civil rights and those of African Americans or women? How viable or desirable is it for societies to maintain and support those who choose to live in a traditional way?

SOURCE 2.6

It's interesting that for all the problems they've had with white Americans, American Indians were never subjected to the same kind of racial bias that blacks were. They were never forced to sit in the back of the bus. In spite of the fact that they surrounded the wagon trains and shot flaming arrows into the stagecoach carrying the new schoolmarm, Indians were always considered to be brave, strong, stoic, resourceful, true to their word and unconquerable. Anyone with a touch of Indian blood in their ancestry is proud of it. There have been many efforts to assimilate the Indians into our society but, for the most part, Indians don't want any part of it. While American Indians have a grand past, the impact of their culture on the world has been slight. The two million American Indians alive today are reluctant to concede that it's no longer practical to maintain a lifestyle that is an anachronism. The time for the way Indians lived is gone and it's doubly sad because they refuse to accept it. They hang onto remnants of their religion and superstitions that may have been useful to savages 500 years ago but which are meaningless in 1992.

Commentator and journalist Andy Rooney in an interview with the newspaper **Sacramento Union**, *1992.*

QUESTION

Compare and contrast what Sources 2.5 and 2.6 reveal about attitudes to Native Americans in the 1990s.

DISCUSSION POINT

Since 1980, tribes have successfully sought to augment their income by allowing gambling on their land. This practice was codified by the Indian Gaming Regulatory Act of 1988. By 2011 this was a highly lucrative practice bringing in $27 billion to the 240 tribes operating casinos (the Hard Rock Cafe franchise is, for example, owned by the Seminole tribe). Discuss the ethical implications of this method of preserving tribal history.

International legislation

In 1957, the International Labour Organization (ILO), part of the United Nations, produced a document entitled *The Indigenous and Tribal Populations Convention*, which was designed to recognise and protect the rights of indigenous peoples in cultural, religious, civil and social areas, and to provide a framework for addressing their economic issues. The convention was widely ratified but also widely ignored in the Americas. Argentina, Brazil, Columbia and Paraguay were among the countries who signed up to the convention in the 1960s, but the US and Canada did not.

In 1989, the Indigenous and Tribal Peoples Convention replaced the 1957 convention. The ILO itself admits that the 1957 convention was formulated in the belief that indigenous and tribal populations (ITPs) were 'temporary societies' that would disappear as a result of 'modernisation'. The 1989 convention redresses this by recognising that indigenous peoples have the right to preserve their culture and traditions.

Case study: Canada

Canadian Indians suffered similar problems to American Indians in the US and responded in similar ways, with a new phase of activism among native peoples in the 1960s. The National Indian Council (NIC) was set up in 1961 to strengthen unity among native peoples and build understanding between native and non-native Canadians. However, the NIC lacked sufficient focus and funding, and the organisation dissolved in 1968.

Two new groups were formed to replace it, the Canadian Métis Society (later renamed the Native Council of Canada) and the National Indian Brotherhood. The identification of the wealth of raw materials in Canadian forests and prairies meant that there was a desire to move Native American groups, but the developments in the US made many Native Canadians more willing to campaign for action. The Canadian government failed to learn from the mistakes made by the US, and a White Paper on federal Indian policy in 1969 caused considerable controversy when it recommended assimilation, having been drawn up without consulting Native Canadians.

2

Case studies: Latin America

The prevalence of dictatorship and civil war in Central and Latin America in the latter half of the 20th century made it extremely difficult for native groups to assert their rights. It was only with the weakening of dictatorships and the uneasy peace agreements in the final two decades of the century that native populations began to see change. Nevertheless, there are a number of success stories that would be worthy of further research to contrast with the experience of Native Americans in the US.

Guatemala

The key figure in Guatemalan Indian native rights in the latter part of the 20th century and the early 21st century has been Rigoberta Menchú, who was awarded the Nobel Peace Prize in 1992.

Menchú is a K'iche' Guatemalan whose father Vicente was a member of the Guerrilla Army of the Poor. This was a communist movement inspired by Che Guevara that fought against the US-backed military dictatorship that had crushed political opposition and civil rights since coming to power in 1954. Her book *My Name is Rigoberta Menchú and this is how my Conscience was Born* gave her an international profile, and enabled her to campaign more forcefully for justice for her fellow indigenous Guatemalans who suffered during the 30-year civil war.

Figure 2.5: Rigoberta Menchú in 1998.

In 2007, Menchú formed an indigenous political party but lost in the first round of the presidential election after suffering a campaign of intimidation. She was aiming to become Latin America's fourth indigenous president after Mexico's Benito Juárez, Peru's Alejandro Toledo and Bolivia's Evo Morales.

Mexico

Mexico has an indigenous population of around 10%, mainly living in the south of the country. It differs from other Latin American countries in the way in which indigenous culture has been co-opted by the government. The Mexican Revolution of 1910 to 1920 produced a national feeling that indigenous peoples were the foundation of Mexican society. This 'Indigenous Sentiment' can be seen in the work and writing of artists such as Frida Kahlo and Diego Rivera. Successive governments have provided bilingual education in indigenous communities and published free bilingual textbooks, and some states, such as Chiapas, sought to reinforce their identity by adopting indigenous culture.

Nevertheless, as elsewhere in the continent, economic underdevelopment of the communities has been noticeable, and indigenous people have suffered most badly in the economic crises of the 1980s and 1990s. The answer for many indigenous Mexicans has been escape to the US or to the major cities. Elsewhere, some of the Maya peoples of Chiapas have rebelled against local government, demanding better social and economic opportunities.

The Mexican central government has responded to legal challenges, promoting the development of indigenous communities and the preservation and promotion of their languages. The most notable of these was the amending of the second article of the Constitution, in order to grant indigenous people the right of self-determination, and require state governments to promote and ensure the economic development of indigenous communities, as well as the preservation of their languages and traditions.

Summary

Native Americans in the US had made huge progress by the 1990s recovering both their numbers and their dignity as the paternalist attitude of the federal government in the 19th century gave way to a greater appreciation of the unique problems facing their indigenous population. The techniques of the black civil rights movement were vital in this turnaround but elsewhere in the Americas the issue of indigenous peoples' rights lagged behind the US and was intertwined with wider problems within the political system.

Paper 3 exam practice

Question

Compare and contrast how native peoples in the Americas sought to affirm their identities in the period after the Second World War.
[15 marks]

Skill

Understanding the wording of a question

Examiner's tips

Though it seems almost too obvious to need stating, the first step in producing a high-scoring essay is to look closely at the wording of the question. Every year, students throw away marks by not paying sufficient attention to the demands of the question.

It is therefore important to start by identifying the **key or 'command' words** in the question. With this one, the key words are as follows:

- compare and contrast
- the Americas
- affirm their identities
- after the Second World War.

These key words are intended to give you clear instructions about what you need to cover in your essay – hence they are sometimes called 'command' words. If you ignore them, you will not score high marks, no matter how precise and accurate your knowledge of the period.

For this question, you will need to cover the following aspects of the issue of native people's rights:

- **compare and contrast:** the question is focused on the similarities and differences in the reasons behind the efforts to affirm native identities
- **the Americas:** the question requires discussion of issues in a number of different countries in the region; it can focus on one (probably the US) but must cover others

- **affirm their identities:** this is a rather vague term but is referring to all the issues that were protested; your answer should therefore cover economic, cultural and political protests
- **after the Second World War:** the whole of the post-1945 period is included, so your points can cover the events in the 1980s and 1990s where Latin American protest becomes more important.

Common mistakes

Under exam pressure, two types of mistake are particularly common.

One is to begin by giving some pre-war context, but then to continue giving a detailed account of the different kinds of protest. It is true that a brief reference to the situation before the war will be relevant for putting your answer into context. However, the period before the war must not be a significant part of your answer. Such an answer will only score the very lowest marks, no matter how detailed and accurate your knowledge of native people's grievances in the 19th century may be.

The other – more common – mistake is to focus entirely on the situation of native people in the US. This is almost certainly likely to end in the production of a narrative account of what happened during this period. Such a narrative-based account will not score highly, as it will not explicitly address the issue of comparison and 'the Americas' parts of the question.

Both of these mistakes can be avoided if you focus carefully on the wording of the question.

For more on how to avoid irrelevant and narrative answers, look at the exam practice sections of Chapters 5 and 6 respectively.

Activity

In this chapter, the focus is on understanding the question and producing a brief essay plan. So, look again at the question, the tips and the simplified mark scheme in Chapter 11. Now, using the information from this chapter, and any other sources of information available to you, draw up an essay plan – perhaps a spider diagram – that has all the necessary headings for a well-focused and clearly structured response to the question.

Paper 3 practice questions

1 Evaluate the effects of the Second World War on indigenous people in any two countries in the Americas in the decade after 1945.

2 To what extent did native people successfully affirm their rights in the second half of the 20th century?

3 Discuss the reasons why indigenous people began protest movements in one country of the region in the 1960s.

4 With reference to two countries of the region, to what extent did the civil rights of indigenous people change from the 1960s to 2000?

5 Evaluate the successes and failures of native peoples' protest movements in one country of the region since 1945.

3

The African American experience: from slavery to the Great Depression

Introduction

This chapter examines what life was like for African Americans during the period of Reconstruction, after the Civil War, when key civil rights for black Americans were enshrined in the Constitution. The chapter also examines how, when and why the notion of white supremacy was re-established in the South at the end of the 19th century, and the impact this had. It then considers the roles of Booker T. Washington and W. E. B. Du Bois in the origins of the civil rights movement. Finally, the chapter examines the impact of the First World War and the Depression of the 1930s.

TIMELINE

1863 Lincoln's Emancipation Proclamation promises to end slavery in Confederate states

1865 13th Amendment abolishes slavery

1868 14th Amendment provides 'equal protection of the laws' to all citizens

1870 15th Amendment grants black male suffrage

1890 State of Mississippi introduces laws to prevent blacks from voting

1895 Booker T. Washington's 'Atlanta Compromise' speech

1896 *Plessy versus Ferguson* ruling declares that 'separate but equal' facilities are not unconstitutional

1909 National Association for the Advancement of Colored People (NAACP) formed

1915 Supreme Court ruling outlaws 'grandfather' clause

1919 Race riots in Chicago and other cities

1925 A. Philip Randolph becomes leader of the Brotherhood of Sleeping Car Porters

KEY QUESTIONS

- What was life like for African Americans during the period of Reconstruction?
- What were the effects of 'Jim Crow' laws and white supremacy in the South?
- What were the origins of the early civil rights movement?
- How did the First World War affect African Americans?

Overview

- African Americans were granted political and legal rights, but not land, during Reconstruction.
- After 1890, when northern forces had withdrawn from the South, 'Jim Crow' laws allowed southern states to re-establish white supremacy. Blacks were systematically and 'legally' disenfranchised.
- Booker T. Washington, W. E. B. Du Bois and the National Association for the Advancement of Colored People (NAACP) were significant in the origins of the civil rights movement.
- Black migration to the North, during the First World War, led to increasing racial discrimination and segregation. This, in turn, produced varying forms of black resistance.
- African Americans experienced mixed fortunes during the Depression and the New Deal (1929 to 1938).

3.1 What was life like for African Americans during the period of Reconstruction?

In 1865, 90% of all black people lived in the South of the US, especially in the fertile belt of land that stretched from southern Virginia to eastern Texas; three states – Louisiana, Mississippi and South Carolina – had black majorities.

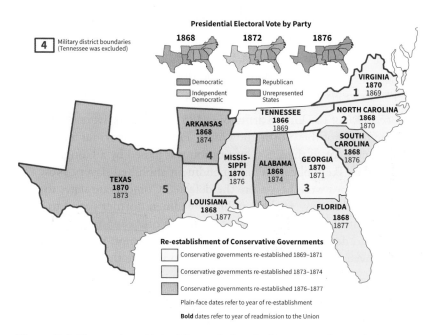

Figure 3.1: The southern United States during the Reconstruction period, 1865 to 1890.

As white Americans moved west in the 19th century, settling on land in the Midwest and beyond, there was increasing friction between the North and the South about whether new states admitted into the Union (the USA) should be free or slave states. Most northerners wanted them to be free states so that there would be no slave labour to undercut free men working their own land. The Republican Party, which emerged in the 1850s, represented these people. Many northerners also feared that the South might come to dominate the federal government in Washington and national politics. Disagreement over this matter, of whether newly admitted states should be free or slave states, formed the background to the Civil War.

The fighting broke out in 1861, soon after the Republican Abraham Lincoln was elected president. Eleven slave-owning southern states seceded (broke away) to form the Confederacy: they were South Carolina, Mississippi, Florida, Alabama, Georgia, Louisiana, Texas, Virginia, Arkansas, North Carolina and Tennessee. This was a loose alliance of states that resented what they saw as increasing domination by the federal government and sought more autonomy.

Civil War and the abolition of slavery

3/5
white
person

Despite the North's larger population, stronger industry and superior weapons, the war was prolonged. Lincoln had promised in 1863 to end slavery in the Confederate states hoping this would encourage slaves to disrupt the Confederates' war effort and fight alongside Union forces.

By 1865, 10% of the Union army, over 185 000 soldiers, were black. In 1865 the forces of the North, the Union, emerged victorious and the 13th Amendment to the US Constitution was passed by a Congress dominated by Republicans. This Amendment abolished slavery. Now the big questions were how were the defeated Confederate states to be treated, and how were the 4 million freedmen (former slaves) to be integrated into society? This was the challenge of Reconstruction, the term used to describe the federal government's attempts to rebuild the South between 1865 and 1877, which was to include the readmission of the defeated states into the Union and the provision of help to former slaves.

Executive
Order for
emancipation
1863
→ didn't
apply
everywhere .

Reconstruction in the South

The freedmen had no money, no land and no property, but many were under the impression that they had been promised land by the Union army to fight for them. Many left the plantations on which they had been employed and looked for family and friends they had been separated from. After that, they wanted land, education and the vote, in that order. Lincoln spoke of granting the vote to educated freedmen and 'those who serve our cause as soldiers'. This was going too far for many people, even for some northerners, including a Confederate sympathiser called John Wilkes Booth. On hearing Lincoln's promise he declared

'That means nigger citizenship. Now, by God, I'll put him through. That is the last speech he will ever give.' Three days later, on 14 April 1865, Booth assassinated Lincoln.

Lincoln was succeeded by his vice-president, Andrew Johnson, who was keen to readmit the Confederate states as quickly as possible to the Union, and leave it to them to decide whether to grant the vote to former slaves. Johnson felt that, as long as the states swore allegiance to the Union and accepted the end of slavery, they should be free to run their own affairs in line with the principles of states' rights.

Meanwhile, the freedmen themselves set up schools and their own independent churches. They were helped by northern charities and, above all, by Congress's newly established Freedmen's Bureau, which provided food and clothing to millions and established hospitals and schools. But the Union promise of '40 acres and a mule' for every freedman never materialised. → economically: little education.

Most ended up sharecropping, a system of agriculture in which a landowner allows a tenant to use their land in return for a share of the crops produced. This meant they worked for planters, often former slave owners, who granted the freedmen land and basic housing and, in return, the freedmen shared their crop with the landowner.

Whole families could work together, free from close supervision, and decide what hours they worked. In practice, they were now enslaved by debt rather than law as they had to borrow money to buy seed and implements from the landowners or merchants. Freedmen could set up businesses but very few could actually afford to do so and most remained as poor sharecropping labourers.

'Black Codes' and the Ku Klux Klan

Most white southerners wanted to keep things that way. They wanted blacks to remain subservient to and dependent on whites, and to preserve white supremacy (the belief that whites are superior to non-whites). To make sure of this, several southern states enacted laws, called 'Black Codes', which allowed whites to whip blacks for indiscipline, to send them back to their previous owners if they were deemed to be 'vagrants', to prevent them being witnesses in court, and to limit the areas – especially in the towns – where they could live. If these strategies did not work, intimidation and terror usually did, most notably through the first Ku Klux Klan (KKK).

Civil Rights and Social Movements in the Americas Post–45

The Ku Klux Klan was a secret terrorist society formed by former Confederate soldiers in 1866. The Klan's aim was to maintain white supremacy at all costs. Its members, wearing hoods and long robes of different colours, terrorised and lynched many blacks for daring to rent or buy land, go to school or get a better job. White supporters of the Republican Party were also victims of the KKK, and the historian Eric Foner has suggested the Klan was effectively the military wing of the Democratic Party in the South.

Figure 3.2: A *Harper's Weekly* cartoon from 1874 showing a black family subjugated by the KKK and the White League, two of the many anti-reconstruction groups operating at the time.

Ku Klux Klan members, dressed in robes and hoods, intimidated and murdered those who dared to push for the changes stipulated in the 13th, 14th and 15th Amendments.

'Equal protection of the laws'

For most Republicans, whose party had a huge majority in Congress after the elections in 1866, this situation was intolerable. It was an insult to those who had fought for freedom, whether black or white, and it was an insult to the martyred Lincoln. Congress overrode Johnson's opposition and passed a Civil Rights Act in 1866 to protect the freedmen's basic civil rights. They also passed the 14th Amendment, in 1868, which guaranteed 'equal protection of the laws' for all citizens. This reinforced the Civil Rights Act so that it could never be overturned by a bare majority of 51% in Congress. (For an Amendment to be passed or revoked, it had to pass Congress with a two-thirds majority.)

gave power to intervene but not followed + increased KKK.

The Amendment struck down the Black Codes and declared that the federal government could intervene if any states tried to deny the rights, including the right to vote, of any citizen. Ten of the eleven southern states refused to ratify the Amendment. Violence increased and many blacks who were active in politics were murdered. In one county in South Carolina where whites lost the elections, 150 freedmen and their families were driven from their homes. Thirteen people were killed, including a white judge who had been elected with black votes.

Congress then went further and enacted laws to establish military rule in the South and make sure southern states drew up constitutions that guaranteed black civil rights: this was a condition for readmission to the Union. These laws had the effect of hardening white supremacist feeling in the South even further and increasing support for the Klan. Most southerners resented northern domination and interference as much as they resented blacks exercising their civil rights.

The impact of black male suffrage

The third and most dramatic Amendment, the 15th, was passed in 1870 and granted black male suffrage. This was controversial, and not just in the South. White women who were campaigning for the vote for women were split by this measure. Some resented the fact that black men were being granted the vote before them. After all, many white women had contributed to the war effort.

DISCUSSION POINT

One white suffragist, Elizabeth Stanton, said that black male suffrage would 'culminate in fearful outrages on womanhood in the Southern states'. Many black women put racial pride before any feminist feeling and supported black male suffrage. However, one black woman, Sojourner Truth, who had helped many slaves escape to freedom before the Civil War, said: 'If coloured men get their rights, and not coloured women theirs, you see the coloured men will be masters over the women, and it will be just as bad as it was before.' How do you explain these two contrasting views?

Black advancement during Reconstruction

During Reconstruction, certainly up until the mid 1870s, a number of black men gained political power. With the vote, they were able to elect senators and congressmen, magistrates and sheriffs, especially in black majority areas in states such as Mississippi and South Carolina. Sixteen black men were elected to Congress and hundreds to state legislatures, including P. B. S. Pinchback who became Governor of Louisiana in 1872. But this progress proved to be short-lived.

The North grew weary of its involvement in the South and withdrew its troops. It wanted the southern states to be reconciled, not alienated. Besides, most believed liberty was more about freedom from government interference than use of government power to stand up for minorities, an idea summed up by the concept of States' rights.

By 1877, all the southern states had rejoined the Union and slavery was ended. This was enough for most northern whites who were keen to put the war behind them. Many northern politicians were now far more concerned about managing America's rapid industrial growth.

Although many of its achievements were to be reversed, Reconstruction gave black people great self-confidence and set a series of precedents. Blacks held political office, voted and established churches, universities, schools and businesses, including black-owned newspapers.

Long after the end of Reconstruction and the loss of political power, black people cherished their own institutions. They continued to seek an education when they could afford it, and a black middle class of teachers, church ministers, small businessmen, and a small number of lawyers and doctors, emerged. The black colleges of higher education institutions, especially universities such as Howard and Fisk, produced many of the black leaders who would carry on the struggle for civil rights into the 20th century.

KEY CONCEPTS QUESTION

Perspectives: Why was it so difficult to achieve the goals of reconstruction?

KEY CONCEPTS ACTIVITY

Perspectives: Imagine you are a journalist in 1877. Write a newspaper article on what has been achieved under Reconstruction. You can choose to write either in a favourable light, for a northern newspaper or, in a less favourable light, for a southern newspaper. A third alternative is to write for a northern newspaper, explaining why you think Reconstruction should now be left to the southern states.

3.2 What were the effects of 'Jim Crow' laws and white supremacy in the South?

The period of Reconstruction ended in 1877. With the removal of troops, and the loss of interest from the North, a wide range of 'Jim Crow' laws were passed by southern states. Jim Crow was a figure of mockery, a fictional character that had appeared in travelling minstrel shows in the South since the days of slavery. He was originally a crippled black stable boy, unsteady on his feet, slow and stupid. He was played by a white man with his face blacked up and came to represent a black stereotype.

These 'legal' means re-established segregation by keeping the races apart in schools and hospitals, hotels and restaurants, cemeteries and parks while also being symbolic of states' rights. A further everyday aggravation for black people was segregation on public transport: blacks were forced to sit at the back on tram cars and to sit in separate carriages, usually older and dirtier, on railways.

In order to avoid opposing the 14th Amendment, which guaranteed equal rights to all citizens, southern politicians claimed that these Jim Crow laws did ensure that blacks had equal rights. It's just that they were separate. However, it was rarely the case that blacks were treated equally. This was most obviously the case in education, as was shown by the huge differences in spending on white schools and black schools. Older, unheated buildings, far fewer books, less well-qualified and poorly paid teachers were the norm in black schools.

Not surprisingly, rates of black illiteracy remained far higher than those for whites: by 1900 45% of blacks were illiterate compared with 6% of whites.

Disenfranchisement of blacks in the South

In order to get around the 15th Amendment, which forbade discrimination on grounds of race at the ballot box, southern states also developed 'legal' ways of preventing blacks from voting. The state of Mississippi introduced a poll tax in 1890 for those wishing to register to vote. Most poor blacks were unable to pay.

Literacy and citizenship tests were also used: a voter had to prove that he could read and answer questions about a state's constitution. Although the local registrar allowed many illiterate whites to pass this test, these laws did exclude a number of whites, so a 'grandfather test' was enacted which allowed a citizen to vote provided his grandfather was a free man before 1865.

In Mississippi, the number of black voters fell from 190 000 to 8000. Similar laws were passed by several southern states, and blacks were effectively disenfranchised. By 1900, only 3% of blacks were able to vote in much of the South and the advances of Reconstruction were reversed. Since the states largely controlled the conduct of elections, these laws mostly went unchallenged.

In these ways, a seemingly legal and democratic foundation for white supremacy was laid in the Jim Crow South. Southern whites justified the system biblically and by claiming that blacks were inferior and dangerous. In fact, many southern whites claimed that blacks had degenerated since the ending of slavery.

No longer so closely supervised by whites, they had – according to the prejudiced white view – become lazy, incompetent and even criminal. Above all, many whites believed that black men's lust for white women led to increased incidences of rape.

When a black newspaper editor in Wilmington, South Carolina, suggested that white women sometimes consented to have sexual relations with black men, whites went on the rampage: the newspaper offices were burnt down and 1400 blacks were forced to flee from the city, never to return.

Rape (or an allegation of it) came to be the most common justification for lynching, a brutal ritual form of execution in which the victim is killed (either by hanging or burning) by a mob. In fact, lynching more commonly arose out of a dispute between a black man and a white man over a business matter that led to violence. **Ida Wells**, the outspoken black journalist from Tennessee, said lynching was 'an excuse to get rid of Negroes who were acquiring wealth and property', a means of repressing the black community.

Worst of all, whites knew they would not be arrested or otherwise punished for these and other forms of violence against blacks, as the police, lawyers, judges and juries were all white. Few cases came to court, and, in any event, Jim Crow laws forbade black people from testifying in court against whites.

Ida Wells (1862–1931):

Ida Wells was born a slave during the Civil War. Both of her parents were of mixed race, the children of white fathers and female slaves. She went to school and later to Fisk University. She became a teacher but found her true calling as a journalist campaigning fearlessly against lynching and for women's suffrage, criticising both black and white leaders who opposed her.

Figure 3.3: Ida Wells, who one historian described as 'militant long before militancy found a national spokesman'.

Plessy versus Ferguson, 1896

Understandably afraid of white violence and 'legal' consequences, many black people did not overtly challenge the status quo. However, some resisted, as will be seen in the next section. One way was to challenge Jim Crow laws in the courts. The most famous case at this time was that of *Plessy versus Ferguson*, which reached the Supreme Court in 1896.

It originated when Homer Plessy, who was one-eighth black, sat in a whites-only part of a train in Louisiana. He refused to move and was arrested and jailed. The case was taken to the Supreme Court in

Washington, DC, on the grounds that it violated the 14th Amendment. However, the Court interpreted the Amendment as being concerned with political, not social, rights. It said that the states were free to follow their own customs and traditions in order to preserve social order and peace.

More significantly, it stated that segregation was not unconstitutional as long as separate facilities were equal. (It left it to judges in local federal courts to decide on this matter. Subject as these judges were to state pressure, it was unlikely that they would defy state authorities.)

It was to be 50 years before the Supreme Court changed its mind about the enforced separation of the races.

ACTIVITY

Make a list of the most significant effects of Jim Crow laws on black people in the South and categorise them into social, political and economic factors. Which do you think were most damaging?

The North's abandonment of black southerners

The Supreme Court decision appeared to epitomise the North's abandonment of southern blacks. The Republican federal government was effectively endorsing, or at least allowing, white supremacy in the South. Most northerners raised no objection to the South's solution to the 'Negro question'. With the blacks disenfranchised, Republican power in the South collapsed, leaving Democrats to dominate the South until Lyndon Johnson's Civil Rights Act of 1964.

Blacks in the North

Northern blacks usually voted freely and received fairer treatment in court. Although only some schools were integrated, there was not the huge difference in quality between white and black schools that there was in the South. However, northern whites kept their distance from blacks, not by law but by social pressure. There were no 'whites only' notices, but estate agents, builders and local politicians kept the black population out of the mainly white areas. This was *de facto* (in fact) segregation rather than the *de jure* (in law) segregation of the South.

Most urban northern blacks lived in ghettos, poorer, overcrowded inner city areas. Here they took the lowest-paid jobs as domestic servants, cleaners, porters and waiters, but faced competition from new immigrants from Italy and Eastern Europe.

In the factories, whites-only unions effectively excluded blacks or ensured that they only took the unskilled jobs. Unable to find work, many urban blacks took to gambling, prostitution or theft in order to survive. In this way, the racist southern stereotype of the lazy, criminal, inferior black person was reinforced in the minds of some northerners.

3.3 What were the origins of the early civil rights movement?

Booker T. Washington

The majority of blacks in the South learned to live with white domination. After all, the odds were stacked against them. Sitting in the wrong place on a tram or train or trying to register to vote could lead to the loss of a job or rented property. Worse still, it could lead to physical violence and even death. Most made no attempt to cross the 'colour line'. Some, however, attempted change.

Booker T. Washington was the principal of a college called the Tuskegee Institute. He had established the college with financial backing from northern philanthropists (people who give charitable donations). It was wholly staffed and run by black people, and became a symbol of what could be achieved by black Americans.

What made Washington even more well known, and controversial, were his beliefs and his influence. He believed that black schools and colleges such as Tuskegee should concentrate on teaching practical skills so that black people could become economically independent. He had no time for political agitators. Washington believed Reconstruction had been a mistake for black people. Freedom had led them to believe that they could start 'at the top instead of at the bottom', so that they focused on political equality rather than on hard work and earning a living, which Washington felt would bring the social and economic equality they needed. In this way, and through a strict Christian faith, blacks would prove that they were not inferior and deserved to be treated as equals. This policy became known as 'accommodationism'.

Booker T. Washington (1856–1915):

Washington was the son of a white man and a black female slave. At the time he was born, a person of mixed race was classed as a slave. He realised the importance of education, and struggled through poverty to gain a college education. He is credited with creating the 'Atlanta Compromise' as a result of a speech he made in Atlanta, Georgia, in 1895, in which he said: 'In all things that are purely social we can be as separate as the fingers, yet one as the hand in all things essential to human progress.' By the end of the 19th century, he was the most well-known black American.

Figure 3.4: Booker T. Washington addressing a crowd at Tuskegee in 1915.

The historian Adam Fairclough wrote: 'Washington never renounced the ultimate goal of equality. He advocated a tactical retreat in order to prepare the way for a strategic advance.' What do you think Fairclough meant?

Many whites approved of Washington because they thought he was accepting second-class status for blacks, encouraging them to focus on industry, not politics, learning vocational skills, not academic ones. Others saw him as encouraging blacks to become skilled, even set up their own businesses, and that this was dangerous as it would make them economically independent. However, the greatest horror for southern whites was caused by Washington being invited to dinner at the White House in 1901 when new President Theodore 'Teddy' Roosevelt sought his advice on appointing black people to office in the South.

For most blacks, this was a source of pride. The Tuskegee Institute had become the most successful black college in America. Washington attracted huge donations from white northern businessmen and liberals and was able to set up hundreds more schools. With a basic education and vocational skills, poor blacks could become farmers, carpenters, mechanics and set up their own businesses. By 1900, a quarter of all black farmers had become owners of the land they farmed, despite the lack of land allocated to them after the Civil War and all the additional obstacles of discrimination.

However, Washington had his black critics, who pointed out that his work and his influence did not bring equality any nearer. Blacks still came up against Jim Crow laws every day, and lynchings were reported regularly. Washington continued to be optimistic and claim that race relations were improving. He cited the city of Atlanta as an example, yet, in that same city, in 1906, tensions sparked race riots and whites turned on blacks in a frenzy; one of seven race riots over the next four years. Whites attacked black businesses and homes and pulled black people off trams and beat them up.

The white press later tried to explain the rioters' actions as an effort to punish criminals, but a black editor replied: 'There is evidence that the mob was not after the worst Negroes so much as they were after the best.' Washington probably felt most betrayed when President Roosevelt, speaking to Congress later in 1906, said that 'the greatest cause of lynching is the perpetration, especially by black men, of the hideous crime of rape'.

ACTIVITY

The historian Donald Spivey wrote that Booker T. Washington believed 'blacks should be taught to remain in their place, to stay out of politics, keep quiet about their rights, and work'. Adam Fairclough wrote that Washington's message 'was an inspiration to the emerging black middle class of teachers and small businessmen. To black farmers, it offered a road map out of tenancy and debt.'

What evidence is there to support each of these views? Conduct a class debate: one half of the class should defend Spivey's view, the other half Fairclough's view.

W. E. B. Du Bois and the NAACP

Washington's leadership did not go unchallenged. In 1905, a group of mostly northern blacks met at Niagara. They claimed that 'persistent, manly agitation is the way to liberty'. One of them, **W. E. B. Du Bois**, criticised Washington's policy of 'submission' and, unlike Washington, he praised Reconstruction and the work of the Freedmen's Bureau.

Du Bois went on to become a founder member, in 1909, of the National Association for the Advancement of Colored People (NAACP). This organisation had both black and white members and set out to publicise injustice, for instance by sending out white members to investigate lynchings (it was too dangerous for blacks to do this).

W. E. B. Du Bois (1868–1963):

Du Bois was born into a northern family that had been free for a hundred years. An urban intellectual, he was the first black man to gain a PhD from Harvard University. For 12 years, he was a professor at Atlanta University in the South. He campaigned tirelessly for civil rights throughout his long life. In 1951, during the Cold War, he was arrested on suspicion of being 'an agent of a foreign power'. Du Bois later joined the Communist Party and moved to Ghana, the first black African country to gain its freedom from colonial rule.

Figure 3.5: W. E. B. Du Bois, a highly educated black northerner who had travelled extensively in the South and experienced discrimination at first hand, called for 'open, frank agitation'.

Such atrocities were reported in *The Crisis*, the magazine that Du Bois edited for the NAACP. He was keen to reach a large number of black people and appeal to their hearts and minds through political cartoons and striking covers. *The Crisis* published articles about black history and literature to show what black Americans had achieved and to encourage voting. It was fearless in its reporting and even published photographs of lynching and advocated armed self-defence in the face of lynch mobs.

Du Bois called on black men to 'kill lecherous white invaders of their homes and then take their lynching like men. It's worth it!' By 1919, *The Crisis* had a circulation of over 100 000.

SOURCE 3.1

Atlanta must not force the South to see material prosperity as the be all and end all of success. This dangerous idea is already beginning to spread; replacing the better Southerner with the ostentatious wealth-seeker. The sweetness of Southern life is hidden beneath a veneer of pretension. Wealth has been held up as the answer to all southern problems: slave feudalism, disenfranchised black people, the incentive to keep people working, the end aim of politics, the basis of law and order; and even, instead of truth, beauty, and goodness, as the ideal of education.

Adapted from Du Bois, W. E. B. (ed) 1994. **The Souls of Black Folk**. *Dover Publications, Incorporated.*

ACTIVITY

What can you infer from Source 3.1 were the principle issues facing the South as far as W. E. B. Du Bois was concerned?

Figure 3.6: From 1920 the NAACP would draw attention to lynchings by hanging a banner outside its New York offices the day after a lynching had been reported.

The NAACP decided to act. It developed a legal tactic of employing the best black lawyers and took carefully chosen cases of discrimination to the Supreme Court in order to secure impartial enforcement of the Constitution, focusing on civil rights that were guaranteed by the 14th and 15th Amendments.

This policy had some success: in 1915, the Supreme Court knocked out Oklahoma's 'grandfather clause'. Even though white Oklahomans might find other ways of keeping blacks disenfranchised, this was the first time the Supreme Court struck down such a strategy.

In 1917, the Supreme Court ruled that a Kentucky law on residential zoning, keeping blacks and whites apart, was unconstitutional. Again, it might make little difference to daily life, as other ways of enforcing segregated housing would undoubtedly be found. But it showed that the NAACP could take the battle for civil rights to the centre of government, and that the Supreme Court could be an ally, setting a precedent that was to be followed up in the late 1940s and 1950s.

The Birth of a Nation

The NAACP suffered a setback in 1915 when it campaigned to ban the showing of a silent film called *The Birth of a Nation*, directed by D. W. Griffith. The film was based on a white supremacist novel, *The Clansman*, set at the time of Reconstruction. It showed blacks as rapists lusting after white women, and glorified the KKK as the saviours of civilisation. Considered purely as a piece of cinema, it was a visual masterpiece: vivid, spectacular, dramatic, and it held audiences spellbound at a time when films were becoming increasingly popular. *The Birth of a Nation* became the most successful silent film ever and prompted the revival of the KKK. The NAACP failed to get the film banned or censored except in a few places. However, their campaign created controversy, increased membership and led to a debate in Congress on lynching.

Theory of Knowledge

History and film:

President Woodrow Wilson was given a private screening of *The Birth of a Nation* in the White House. He allegedly said: *'It is like writing history with lightning. And my only regret is that it is all so terribly true.'* What do you think he meant? Which films have had a significant influence on how millions of people see the past? Is film a valid way of gaining historical knowledge?

3.4 How did the First World War affect African Americans?

At the start of the 20th century, 90% of black people in the US still lived in the South. The majority worked on the land, trapped by poverty, a lack of skills and all the obstacles created by Jim Crow laws. A small but steady number continued to move to the cities of the South, in order to find work and escape from the control of their rural, white landlords. Then, during the First World War, the 'Great Migration' began: between 1914 and 1918 more than 350 000 black Americans migrated to the North, to cities such as New York, Chicago and Philadelphia.

The Great Migration

Both pull and push factors accounted for this mass movement. The main pull factor was the offer of better, well-paid jobs in the fast-expanding industries of the big northern cities. Although America did not actually enter the fighting until 1917, US factories kept Britain and France supplied with weapons and other goods. Not only was more labour needed in the factories, but the flow of immigrants from Europe largely dried up during the war. The push factors, the reasons for leaving the South, were low pay, poor schools and the daily humiliations of Jim Crow laws, as well as the ever-present threat of lynching.

In addition, blacks flocked to join the army after 1917. They hoped that President Wilson's 'War for Democracy' might lead to the defeat of oppression at home as well as abroad. About 370 000 black Americans (13% of the total forces, higher than the 10% which was the percentage of blacks in the total US population) were called up. On a wave of patriotism and optimism, Du Bois called on blacks to 'forget our special grievances' and 'close ranks' behind the war effort.

However, many were to be embittered by their treatment in the army. Given menial jobs as cooks or labourers, or forced to fight in segregated regiments, many returning veterans were impatient, determined to resist white supremacy and assert their rights. Du Bois now changed his tune and claimed to speak for those returning veterans when he said that 'we return fighting.' In the South, there was little desire by whites to make states such as Alabama or Mississippi 'safe for democracy': blacks were still to be kept in their place. Returning African American soldiers met hostility. In fact, black men in uniform particularly angered some white racists, and there was a big increase in lynchings in 1919. In Texas, a white leader of the NAACP was beaten so badly that he died soon after. One of his assailants was a county judge.

ACTIVITY

Why would a black soldier in uniform anger whites? What does this say about attitudes to the ideals of the United States among white people in the South?

The situation in the North was not much better. After the war, factory production contracted, especially in the defence industries, and returning white soldiers wanted their jobs back. Competition for jobs and housing led to increased resentment and tension. In Chicago, in 1919, racial violence led to 38 deaths.

So serious were the disturbances that the city authorities decided to adopt a policy of residential segregation in order to keep the races apart and maintain peace. White owners were prohibited from reselling or renting their property to blacks through 'restricted covenants'.

The Supreme Court condemned such restrictions but they were still enforced privately, by estate agents and builders, and backed up by intimidation and violence. As housing became more segregated this had a knock-on effect on schools, and black children were increasingly taught in segregated classrooms.

As a result of wartime migration and Chicago city policy of housing racial groups together, 90 000 black people were confined to one square mile of overcrowded houses and schools in South Chicago. Similar patterns were reproduced in other northern cities.

SOURCE 3.2

The Great Migration may be the most momentous internal population movement of the twentieth century. In the decades before the 1950s 20 million southerners left the region. In doing so, they changed America. They transformed American religion, spreading Baptist and Pentecostal churches and reinvigorating evangelical Protestantism. They transformed American popular culture, especially music. The development of blues, jazz, gospel and R&B all depended on the southern migrants. The Southern Diaspora transformed American racial hierarchies, as black migrants in the great cities of the North and West developed institutions and political practices that enabled the modern civil rights movement.

Adapted from Gregory, J. (ed). 2005. **The Southern Diaspora**. *Washington, North Carolina, USA. University of North Carolina Press.*

Black resistance

Blacks did not accept ill treatment passively. Even the law-abiding NAACP sounded more defiant. In *The Crisis*, W. E. B. Du Bois wrote: 'When the mob moves, we prepare to meet it with bricks and clubs and guns.' The impact of the war and its aftermath led to a huge increase in support for the NAACP. By 1919 it had 90 000 members and over 300 branches, 130 of which were in the South. There had been only three in the region before the war.

The first genuinely mass movement emerged at this time, too. **Marcus Garvey**, a flamboyant Jamaican, arrived in the US in 1916. As founder and president of the Universal Negro Improvement Association (UNIA), he called on all Africans to unite and fight for freedom.

A powerful agitator, he told black Americans that they were blacks first, Americans second, and that they should be proud of their African past and strive for a heroic future. He instilled racial pride, particularly in poor urban blacks. He also set up his own Black Star shipping line to take black Americans back to Africa, but it was badly run and Garvey's American career came to an end after he was found guilty of fraud and jailed in 1923. Four years later, he was deported.

Marcus Garvey (1887–1940):

Born in Jamaica, Garvey later studied in England and was impressed by the black Africans he met who were campaigning for independence from Britain. In the US, he urged blacks to develop separately, without white support. He was the first black nationalist to create a mass movement in America. With his colourful costumes, flag, anthem and processions, he was mocked by other black American leaders. Du Bois, who no doubt felt overshadowed, referred to him as a 'little, fat black man' who was 'the most dangerous enemy of the Negro race in America and the world'.

Figure 3.7: Marcus Garvey caught the imagination of the masses and attracted widespread, enthusiastic support, most obviously seen in huge UNIA parades.

In the 1930s, a campaign against racial discrimination that had started in Chicago spread to other cities. Tens of thousands of black Americans implemented the slogan 'Don't buy where you can't work' and, in places, the boycotts led to blacks being employed in retail stores setting a precedent for the use of black economic power. Meanwhile a very different form of black activism emerged.

In 1925, **A. Philip Randolph** had become the chief organiser of the Brotherhood of Sleeping Car Porters. This was an all-black union and it represented the black porters on Pullman trains. While the Pullman company employed whites to build their railway carriages, they hired blacks to carry the luggage, serve the food and drinks, and shine the shoes of those who travelled and slept on the trains. After ten years of negotiation, Randolph finally persuaded the company to recognise the union and then to award better pay and allow shorter hours. This victory made the union a symbol of black solidarity, and it raised Randolph to national stature.

> ### A. Philip Randolph (1890–1979):
>
> Randolph was born in Florida. He moved to New York in 1914 and later edited a black radical magazine called *The Messenger*, criticising the élitism of the NAACP. Randolph organised the Brotherhood of Sleeping Car Porters from 1925. His threat of a March on Washington in 1941 led Franklin D. Roosevelt to ban discrimination in war industries. As the longest-serving civil rights leader, he organised the March on Washington in 1963 (see section 6.3), which helped to build support for the Civil Rights Act of 1964.

The Depression and the New Deal

Millions of people, white as well as black, suffered during the Great Depression of the 1930s. Worst of all for black Americans, the cotton plantations were decimated, first by the boll weevil infestation, then by a collapse in the market for cotton. As a result, huge numbers of black labourers lost their jobs.

From 1933 to 1938, the Democratic president, Franklin D. Roosevelt (often known by his initials, FDR) introduced a series of economic policies, the 'New Deal', to get the unemployed back to work. Many blacks benefi ted, even if racism often led to whites being employed fi rst by New Deal organisations. FDR took on many black advisers – his 'black cabinet' – and his wife, Eleanor Roosevelt, advocated 'fair play and equal opportunity for Negro citizens'.

For the fi rst time, large numbers of black Amer icans switched their support from the Republican Party, the party of Lincoln, to the Democrats. As the Democratic Party expanded its membership to include many immigrants and northern blacks, so the South lost its dominant infl uence in the party. These developments would have a signifi cant impact on the development of the civil rights campaign in the 1950s and 1960s.

The Great Depression, like the First World War, led to increased black migration to the North as mechanisation and drought eroded the jobs in agriculture in the South. Despite the discrimination that blacks suff ered in northern cities, there were far more job opportunities and there was better pay than in the South. Blacks were free to vote and free to express their own views, even to protest.

Black culture, epitomised by jazz musicians such as Louis Armstrong and Duke Ellington, flourished in northern cities, while the 1938 victory of Joe Louis, the black boxer, over the German (Nazi) world heavyweight champion, Max Schmeling, was a source of racial pride for all African Americans.

In the South, it was far more difficult for African Americans to organise resistance and protest. On average 35 black men a year were lynched in the South in the first half of the century, creating a climate of fear that few were willing to challenge. White supremacy was at its strongest from 1900 to 1941 before US participation in the Second World War kick-started the civil rights movement.

Prior to this, sharecroppers could be evicted, employees fired and businessmen see their property burnt down if they defied segregation. And the fear of arrest, beating and murder was ever-present. Nevertheless, black teachers could instil racial pride and encourage self-improvement in their students, in the Booker T. Washington tradition.

The presidents of some black colleges allowed their students to set up branches of the NAACP. Mary McLeod Bethune organised the National Council of Negro Women, presided over President Roosevelt's 'black cabinet', and educated Eleanor Roosevelt about conditions for black Americans.

DISCUSSION POINT

'The Depression and New Deal had more impact on African Americans than the First World War.' To what extent do you agree with this statement?

Paper 3 exam practice

Question

Compare and contrast the effectiveness of Booker T. Washington and W. E. B. Du Bois in advancing the cause of African American rights. **[15 marks]**

Skill

Planning an essay

Examiner's tips

As discussed in Chapter 2, the first stage of planning an answer to a question is to think carefully about the wording of the question, so that you know what is required and what you need to focus on. Once you have done this, you can move on to the other important considerations:

- Decide your main argument/theme/approach before you start to write. For example, this question clearly invites you to compare the achievements of Washington and Du Bois. This will probably shape the structure of your essay.
- Plan the structure of your argument – the criteria against which to judge both men. Then plan the introduction, the main body of the essay (in which you present precise evidence to support your arguments against the criteria you have chosen), and your concluding paragraph about which leader did more to advance the African American cause.

For this question, whatever your view about which leader achieved more, you should try to put a balanced argument, covering the positive achievements and the limits of what each man achieved. These example sentences encapsulate a leader's achievement but qualify it with a note on the limit to what was achieved:

Washington's invitation to the White House was a source of pride for African Americans but the president later appeared to blame black men for the high incidence of rape – an insult and injustice to black Americans.

Du Bois encouraged blacks to show their patriotism (and hence their worth as Americans) and to 'close ranks' in the war effort from 1914 but, on realising what a poor deal many veterans had received in the army, was forced to backtrack and state, in The Crisis in 1918, 'We return fighting.'

Drawing up a table, spider diagram or mind map might help you with your essay planning. For this question, your table might look like this:

Criteria	Washington	Du Bois
Economic advancement		
Political and social advancement		
Advancement in pride, morale, self-confidence		
Conclusion about overall achievement of each		

When writing your essay, include linking phrases to ensure that each factor or paragraph is linked to the main issue (advancing the African American cause). For example:

'*However*, while Booker T. Washington was more effective in enabling African Americans to achieve economic independence, W. E. B. Du Bois did more to raise blacks' consciousness of their inferior political position and to pave the way for a black civil rights movement.'

'*Although* Washington inspired and enabled blacks to develop practical skills and qualifications, Du Bois enhanced black Americans' pride in their history and literature.'

Whatever the question, try to link the points you make in your paragraphs, so that there is a clear thread that follows through to your conclusion. This will help to ensure that your essay is not just a series of unconnected paragraphs.

There are many factors to consider, which will be difficult under time constraints. Producing a plan with brief details (for example, effectiveness plus evidence) under each heading will help you cover the main issues. It will also give you something to use if you run out of time and can only jot down the main points of your last paragraph(s). The examiner will be able to give you some credit for this.

Common mistakes

Once the exam time has started, one common mistake is for candidates to begin writing straight away, without being sure whether they know enough about the questions they have selected. Once they have written several paragraphs, they run out of things to say – and then panic because of the time they have wasted.

Producing a plan for each question you have to write in Paper 3 at the start of the exam, *before* you start to write your first essay, will help you see if you know enough to tackle the questions successfully. If you don't, you need to choose different questions!

Activity

In this chapter, the focus is on planning answers. So, using the information from this chapter and any other sources of information available to you, produce essay plans – using tables, spider diagrams or mind maps – with all the necessary headings (and brief details) for well-focused and clearly structured responses to at least two of the following Paper 3 practice questions.

For more on how to avoid irrelevant and narrative answers, see the exam practice sections of Chapters 5 and 6 respectively.

Paper 3 practice questions

1   Evaluate how far the position of African Americans in the US improved between 1877 and 1940?

2   'The First World War had more impact on the lives of African Americans in the US than the NAACP did.' To what extent do you agree with this statement?

3 Compare and contrast the position of African Americans in the North and African Americans in the South by 1940.

4 'Marcus Garvey and A. Philip Randolph did little to advance the cause of African American civil rights in the inter-war years.' To what extent do you agree with this statement?

5 Examine the reasons for, and effectiveness of, African American civil rights campaigns from Reconstruction to the Depression.

4

The emergence of the civil rights movement, 1940s–50s

Introduction

This chapter examines the impact of the Second World War on black Americans in the US, and the emergence of the civil rights movement during those years. It then focuses on two key events. The first was the Supreme Court's 1954 ruling on desegregation in schools. This was a significant breakthrough but aroused massive resistance in the South, as shown in Little Rock, Arkansas (see 4.2, Little Rock, Arkansas, 1957). The second was the Montgomery Bus Boycott of 1955 to 1956, which was hugely successful and also brought Martin Luther King to the forefront of the civil rights movement.

TIMELINE

1941 A. Philip Randolph plans March on Washington; Roosevelt establishes Fair Employment Practices Commission (FEPC) and bans segregation in defence industries

1944 Supreme Court outlaws all-white Democratic primary election in Texas

1947 Publication of report 'To Secure These Rights'

1948 Truman orders desegregation in armed forces

1954 **May:** *Brown versus Board* ruling declares 'separate but equal' schools unconstitutional

1955 **Aug:** Murder of Emmett Till

Dec: Start of Montgomery Bus Boycott

1956 **Mar:** Southern Manifesto denounces Brown ruling

Nov: Supreme Court rules segregation on Montgomery buses to be illegal, leading to end of boycott

1957 **Jan:** Southern Christian Leadership Conference (SCLC) formed

Sep: Eisenhower sends federal troops to Little Rock, Arkansas; Civil Rights Act passed

1960 **May:** Civil Rights Act passed

Overview

- The effects of the Second World War on the lives of African Americans contributed to the development of black activism.
- The growing strength of the NAACP and of a grassroots voter registration campaign signified the emergence of civil rights as a movement.
- The NAACP achieved successes in its legal challenges to the Jim Crow laws.
- The Supreme Court ruling against segregated schools eliminated the legal basis for segregation, but also triggered massive white resistance in the South.
- Events at Little Rock High School led to federal intervention, but also highlighted the tenacity with which the South defended segregation.
- The success of the Montgomery Bus Boycott has often been attributed to the heroism of Rosa Parks and Martin Luther King. Their roles were crucial but so were those of other individuals, and ultimate success was due to sustained, local, mass action.
- The boycott led to the formation of the Southern Christian Leadership Conference (SCLC).

4.1 How did the civil rights movement emerge during the Second World War?

The Second World War and its outcome would have a dramatic impact on the lives of all American people. Not only would 14 million Americans be called up to fight (and similar numbers migrate to the cities to work in war industries), but the US would emerge as a superpower claiming leadership of the 'Free World' whose only rival was the communist USSR.

Not surprisingly, the war had a huge impact on the lives of millions of black Americans as well as white. Nearly a million were called up to fight, still in segregated units, and a larger number would leave farms in the South to seek work in cities, both in the South and, more especially, in the North continuing the Great Migration. African Americans knew that the USA's entry into the war in 1941 meant that they were fighting to defeat an avowedly racist Nazi Germany. They were determined to exploit that.

Black Americans were eager to play their part in the war effort, but were determined not to go unrewarded as they had done after the First World War. As the NAACP magazine *The Crisis* argued: 'Now is the time not to be silent'. The black newspaper *The Pittsburgh Courier* launched a 'Double V' campaign for victory over racism both abroad and at home. President Roosevelt responded by appointing the first black general, Benjamin O. Davies, and calling for equal opportunities for all in the armed forces.

This was easier said than done. Many army leaders had a low opinion of black soldiers, and resisted pressure to enlist them in combat units, despite the heroism of men such as Private George Watson who was posthumously awarded the Medal of Honor for saving the lives of his shipmates. Many of the military training camps were situated in the South. As well as facing the racism within the camps, black soldiers from the North, unused to Jim Crow laws, were shocked by the treatment they received outside the camps. Insulted or refused service in shops and bars, they also came up against segregation on public transport.

Nowhere was this worse than on buses: there were numerous incidents where drivers ordered black soldiers not to sit in 'white' seats and, when they refused, were arrested and, in a few cases, shot.

Discrimination in the North

Discrimination in the North was not as extreme, but it was widespread. Over a million blacks left the South and found better-paid, more secure jobs than they had had on farms in the South. But, as in the First World War, race relations often became more tense, especially as competition for urban housing led to overcrowding and the deliberate exclusion of blacks from white neighbourhoods. Chicago's black population doubled in the 1940s and was increasingly squeezed into unsafe, insanitary housing, sometimes ten to a room. There were numerous outbreaks of violence in northern cities, the worst being in Detroit in 1943. During the war, 50 000 blacks arrived in the city, lured by job opportunities in arms production. Rumours of a white woman being raped by a black man triggered a race riot. Large mobs of whites swarmed the black ghetto and by the time order was restored by troops, 34 people had been killed, 25 black and 9 white, and hundreds injured.

The development of black activism

The black response to racial discrimination took many forms, while the NAACP persisted with legal cases. A. Philip Randolph took a more direct approach by organising thousands of blacks to march on Washington in 1941. The aim was to pressurise the federal government into banning all job discrimination in war industries; in other words, in all the shipyards, aircraft and weapons factories that were producing arms for the government's war effort. The mere threat of such a demonstration in Washington led Roosevelt to set up the Fair Employment Practices Commission (FEPC) by Executive Order (a form of power allowing the president to act with legal power but without Congressional approval) to ensure that blacks were employed in the war industries. This showed what the threat of mass protest could do, and it boosted confidence in the emerging civil rights movement by suggesting the president could act decisively if pushed. In reality, the FEPC had limited impact. There was widespread resistance in the South, where employers insisted that white workers would refuse to work alongside blacks. Even in the North, some unions organised 'hate strikes' where white workers walked out, refusing to work with blacks.

The growing impact of the NAACP

The campaigns run by the NAACP and many local black organisations were probably more significant, in the long term, in advancing the cause of black civil rights. Just as the First World War led to a huge rise in support for the NAACP, so did the Second. Membership leapt from 50 000 to 450 000 by the end of the war.

The organisation attracted far wider support in the South, especially in the growing urban population, and gave its backing to numerous small-scale, local campaigns. More and more blacks, freed from dependence on white landlords, had the confidence to attend NAACP classes where they learnt how to pass literacy classes and pay the poll tax so that they could register to vote. In addition, they had jobs and could fund the NAACP campaigns. The development of this sustained, grassroots activity marked a new phase in the campaign for black civil rights in the South.

This movement was complemented by the successes of the NAACP lawyers, who took an increasing number of legal cases to the Supreme Court. The court was now more receptive, thanks to the appointment, by President Roosevelt, of several more liberal judges. In 1944, the Supreme Court outlawed the all-white Democratic primary election in Texas.

A primary election is held in each state to decide who will be the candidate for that party in a general election, and white primaries (in which blacks were banned from voting) had been common in the South before this.

Now that blacks could not legally be excluded, many more of them tried to register to vote, including Rosa Parks who registered successfully, at the third attempt, in 1945. Although many still faced intimidation if they attempted to register, the percentage of blacks in the South on the electoral register rose from 3% in 1940 to 12% in 1950.

The NAACP's chief lawyer was Charles Houston, professor of law at Howard University, who was mentor to a whole generation of black lawyers trained to fight civil rights cases. His star student was Thurgood Marshall. Although Houston, Marshall and their legal team wanted to abolish segregated schooling completely, they first set about achieving equality within the segregated system. In other words, they wanted to ensure that facilities in black schools were equal even if they were separate. In this way they avoided direct confrontation and instead aimed to make the whole system of segregated schooling prohibitively expensive for the states.

A significant victory had already been achieved in 1939 when the Supreme Court ruled that it was unconstitutional for the state of Missouri to send a black student to a law school in another state (even with Missouri state funding) rather than to the University of Missouri's own – all-white – law school. Instead, the state of Missouri had to make sure he was treated equally to white law students and either allowed to go the all-white law school or to a new black law school in Missouri. Following this legal victory, Missouri financed and built a law school for black students. Other southern states followed suit or allowed black students entry to previously all-white schools.

Another carefully chosen legal campaign by the NAACP obliged the states of Virginia and Maryland to pay equal salaries to black and white school teachers. Victories in these border states of the Upper South in the early 1940s would not necessarily lead to immediate compliance by the most racist states of the South, but many did in fact fall into line in order to be able to maintain their separate schools. The salaries gap was virtually closed by the end of the war, and the legal basis for segregated schools was being gradually undermined by the NAACP's legal challenges.

QUESTION

What was the thinking of the NAACP that led them to target issues of Higher Education in border states first?

None of the gains made by the NAACP, whether at local level or in Washington, signified the end of white supremacy. The Jim Crow system of segregation was still entrenched in the South, supported by all-white courts, police and prisons. However, an increasingly educated and outspoken urban black population in the South, particularly in Atlanta, and growing awareness among blacks of the discrepancy between democratic values and white supremacy, were helping to win wider support for an activist approach.

With the emergence of more widespread, sustained and well-organised action, the foundations for the civil rights movement of the 1950s and 1960s were being laid. All the while the growth of mass media including newspapers, cinemas and the explosive growth of television (over 5 million sets were sold in each year of the 1950s) were bringing protests to the wider population.

DISCUSSION POINT

Adam Fairclough, in his book *Better Day Coming*, wrote: 'As World War II drew to an end, blacks were well aware that they had achieved no great breakthrough. The basic pattern of race relations remained intact.' By contrast, Robert Cook, in *Sweet Land of Liberty?* wrote: 'The Second World War did more than any other event to drag the South into the twentieth century.' Which of these two contrasting statements do you think better represents the impact of the war on the lives of black Americans in the South?

The aftermath of war

As the Second World War ended the economy was booming and did not contract as it had done after the First World War. Furthermore, Congress had passed a law that offered returning soldiers financial aid to attend college and gain qualifications, the 1944 GI Bill.

Many black army veterans benefited from this law, which led an educated black middle class to emerge with more confidence in the late 1950s and 60s. Having fought for freedom and democracy against fascism and racism, returning soldiers were determined to enjoy their rights. Yet, in the South, blacks were thrown off buses for sitting in the wrong place and could be shot for trying to vote. Black veterans, in uniform, were among those killed.

Truman and civil rights

These and other atrocities led Harry Truman, who had become president when Roosevelt died in 1944, to appoint a Committee on Civil Rights to investigate the causes of such violence.

Genuinely appalled though he was, both by the murders and the fact that 'nothing is done about it', there were also electoral reasons for Truman's action: the presidential election of 1948 was likely to be close, and he feared that blacks might vote Republican. Although only 12% of blacks were registered to vote (even if this was four times as many as in 1940), their votes could have a significant impact in northern cities.

Figure 4.1: Eleanor Roosevelt addressing the 38th annual conference of the NAACP in 1947, President Truman seated to the side of her. Truman was the first president to address the NAACP.

After the committee's report, 'To Secure These Rights', was published in 1947, Truman boldly proposed a Civil Rights Bill, the first since Reconstruction, that would ban segregation on public transport and make lynching a federal crime. In June 1948 he proclaimed 1 February National Freedom Day, to commemorate the outlawing of slavery. In July, he ordered the desegregation of the armed forces.

Truman was showing far more commitment to civil rights than any of his predecessors. Could he persuade Congress? He won a close presidential contest over his Republican rival in 1948, but a combination of Republicans and southern Democrats, known as Dixiecrats, killed his Civil Rights Bill in Congress. It would take another 20 years of sustained pressure from the civil rights movement to persuade Congress to pass such a comprehensive bill.

The impact of the Cold War

The immediate post-war period saw an increasing number of black people registering to vote: the number rose from 250 000 to over a million between 1940 and 1950. Nevertheless, the Cold War between the US and the Soviet Union had a stifling effect on the development of African American civil rights after 1945 as any protest against the government was seen as unpatriotic. This became particularly acute after 1949 when the Soviet Union became a nuclear power and China became communist.

Perceptions of civil rights weren't helped by the role of Randolph whose status as a union leader led to him being perceived as socialist and borderline communist in some quarters. It was in this climate that W. E. B. Du Bois, aged 82, was arrested in 1951 for being the 'agent of a foreign power'.

Many others, black and white, trade unionists as well as civil rights activists, were hounded and many ended up in prison. In the McCarthyist era it was widely believed that the Cold War with Soviet Russia could only be won by unity at home, and that any criticism of the US was unpatriotic.

When the anti-communist hysteria of McCarthyism died down in the mid 1950s, civil rights activists began to use the Cold War to their advantage – they pointed out that the US needed to be seen to uphold its ideals of liberty, equality and justice if it was to win friends and allies, especially in the newly independent former colonies of Asia and black Africa.

Soviet diplomats at the United Nations in New York wasted no opportunity to publicise every lynching and race riot to help win allies among the new non-white member states at the UN.

4.2 How far did the NAACP and Supreme Court achieve desegregation in education?

Brown versus Board of Education of Topeka, 1954

In 1950 the NAACP won two university education cases *McLaurin versus Oklahoma* and *Sweatt versus Painter* by proving that the facilities being provided at the University of Oklahoma and the University of Texas were inherently unequal and hence contradicted the ruling of *Plessy versus Ferguson*. This emboldened their lawyers (and brought in sufficient donations) for the organisation to begin an attack on segregation in schools.

In 1952 it brought five cases to the Supreme Court, the first of which was *Brown versus Board of Education of Topeka*. Linda Brown was an eight-year-old black girl who lived near an all-white school in Topeka, Kansas. Her father sued the Topeka Board of Education, claiming that his child should be able to attend her local, all-white, school rather than have to cross town to go to an all-black school. When the Court's newly appointed Chief Justice, **Earl Warren**, gave the Courts' unanimous ruling in May 1954, he stated that 'separate but equal' facilities were 'inherently unequal'.

He further said that, even if the schools were equally good in material terms, the psychological effect of segregated schooling was to breed feelings of 'inferiority' in the 'hearts and minds' of young blacks and thus infringed their rights to 'equal protection of the laws'. He called for the desegregation of schools in order to comply with the 14th Amendment to the Constitution.

Earl Warren (1891–1974):

Warren was a former governor of California who Eisenhower appointed as the 14th Chief Justice of the United States, where he served for 16 years. The Warren Court transformed civil rights and increased the power of the Supreme Court but created controversy by repeatedly undermining the rights of individual states to rule on issues such as education and voting.

This was a seismic result and gave great hope to the NAACP and its supporters, both black and white. It finally eliminated the legal basis for segregation in education and by implication the whole concept of 'separate but equal' on which Jim Crow laws were built and prompted Thurgood Marshall to declare that all segregation would be eliminated by 1963, the 100th anniversary of Abraham Lincoln's Emancipation Proclamation.

Figure 4.2: Thurgood Marshall, centre, here standing outside the Supreme Court, led the legal team that challenged segregation in education.

Marshall's optimism was misplaced. The Supreme Court had not followed up its decision with a plan for implementation, preferring to stop before being accused of dictating to the States. Even when, in 1955, the Court's Brown II ruling called for desegregation 'with all deliberate speed', it did not set any timetable and it left it to lower federal courts to ensure schools were desegregated. These courts were vulnerable to pressure from the ruling élites in the white supremacist South.

President Eisenhower's response

Another reason for the delaying of desegregation was that the Republican President Eisenhower (elected in 1952) did not endorse, let alone express great support for, the Court's decision. Eisenhower didn't need black votes in the same way Truman had and was resigned to Dixiecrat domination of the South.

More damningly, Eisenhower described his appointment of Earl Warren as 'the biggest damn fool decision I ever made'. He believed that deeply entrenched racial feelings, traditions and customs could not – should not – be changed by law. Eisenhower instead adopted a gradualist approach seeking to maintain the comparative calm of mid 1950s America, and let rights develop incrementally. He also understood that the Supreme Court's decision threatened to disrupt the social order and lead to violence in the South.

Eisenhower's obvious lack of enthusiasm for the ruling did not suggest that federal support for desegregation would be forthcoming and emboldened segregationists to challenge the court's decision.

Opposition from whites

However, by far the most significant reason for the lack of immediate desegregation, at any rate in the South, was widespread opposition from whites. There was some desegregation of schools in border states such as Maryland, Missouri and Oklahoma, and in areas where black children formed only a small proportion of the school population.

Even in the Deep South, some white moderates in the churches, education and the press called for acceptance of the ruling, although the majority kept quiet. But there was virtually no desegregation of schools in the states of Georgia, Alabama, Mississippi, Louisiana and South Carolina. The Supreme Court decision was seen as an outright attack on the southern way of life, of long-standing customs and 'our Southern traditions'.

Above all, it was an attack on states' rights; in this case the right of states to organise their own education. Nearly all southern members of Congress went on to sign the 'Southern Manifesto'. This document, created in March 1956 and drafted by Strom Thurmond, a Democrat Senator from South Carolina, aimed to condemn the Brown decision and unite the South in resistance.

Most southerners believed in white supremacy or, at least, in white superiority. They opposed any kind of racial integration in public places, and above all miscegenation – interracial sex or marriage – which integrated schooling might lead to. The state governments and local school boards, who were in charge of education, put up obstacles to desegregation: token admission of a few blacks to white schools in order to show compliance with the Court's ruling; teaching according to 'ability groups', a euphemism for racial groups; over-complicated admissions procedures and paperwork for black people seeking to enrol their children in white schools.

White Citizens' Councils

The Ku Klux Klan (KKK), with its frightening ceremonies and its lynchings, revived in a third incarnation, though it lacked the wide membership of the 1920s. In addition, White Citizens' Councils, which claimed to be non-violent (wearing 'suits not sheets'), were also set up and attracted widespread support. Their members included doctors, lawyers, farmers, businessmen and politicians. They used economic threats such as threatening to sack black employees who took part in civil rights activities, as well as cruder methods, to deter integrationists: blacks who tried to admit their children to white schools were fired by their employers or evicted from their homes by their landlords.

Often these White Citizens' Councils received state funding, while state laws required the NAACP to reveal lists of their members and addresses, thus exposing them to intimidation and violence.

Fire-bombing the houses of black (and white) civil rights campaigners became common. Perpetrators were rarely arrested and, even when they were put on trial, the all-white juries nearly always acquitted the defendants. Juries, judges, police officers and politicians in the South nearly all supported, or turned a blind eye to, intimidation, threats and violence against those who made any attempt to disturb the status quo of white domination and strict segregation.

Little Rock, Arkansas, 1957

Events at Little Rock, Arkansas, in 1957 highlight the reasons for the lack of desegregation in southern schools. When nine black students were enrolled at Central High School, they were met on arrival by a white mob shouting abuse and threatening to lynch them. The students, led by Daisy Bates, president of the state's NAACP, expected to be protected and escorted into school by state troops who had been sent to safeguard law and order (so said the Arkansas state governor, Orval Faubus) but in fact were blocked by those troops.

A photograph of one student, 15-year-old Elizabeth Eckford, who was harassed and abused in a frightening manner, appeared on the front of national newspapers, both in the US and abroad, and shocked liberal opinion. Events such as these showed the US in a highly unfavourable light, not at all the image of freedom and democracy that the country preferred to portray.

With the eyes of the world on Little Rock, Eisenhower was forced to act, to show that the Constitution was being upheld and address Soviet propaganda. He sent in 1200 paratroops to escort the students into school. This action infuriated southern opinion (we are being 'occupied', said Faubus) and the troops could not protect the black students from bullying and other forms of intimidation once they were inside the school.

Nevertheless, the students remained at school while the civil rights campaigners could claim to have won a huge victory, forcing Eisenhower to set a precedent for Presidential intervention as well as favourable publicity – outside the South, at any rate.

Central High became a largely black school within a few years, as the victory encouraged the flight of many middle-class, white families to the suburbs in order to enrol their children in white schools. This 'white flight', which also occurred in northern cities, led to *de facto* economic segregation replacing the *de jure* segregation of Jim Crow.

Figure 4.3: As she walked into Central High School, Little Rock, Elizabeth Eckford was racially abused and spat on and there were shouts of 'Lynch her!'.

Why was Orval Faubus so admired following the Little Rock Crisis?

Despite a victory for desegregation in Little Rock, segregation remained in the schools of the Deep South for several more years. Governor Faubus became even more popular for his stand on racial segregation and was emulated by politicians in neighbouring states, indeed in Virginia the whole school system was shut down in 1958 and 1959 as part of Senator Harry Byrd's 'Massive Resistance' campaign.

By the end of the 1950s, very few schools in the Deep South were desegregated. It would take new tactics and broader support to pressurise the federal government into ending segregation in the South.

SOURCE 4.1

In July 1958 Faubus won nomination for a third term as governor with an unprecedented 69% of the vote. In September, the Supreme Court ruled unanimously that integration must proceed in Little Rock. But Faubus continued to fight, closing down the schools altogether a few days later. He then helped a small group of segregationists to set up the Little Rock Private School Corporation, to which he attempted to lease the public (state) schools on a segregated basis. In a Gallup Poll taken in late 1958, Americans selected Faubus as one of their ten most admired men. During 1958, Little Rock's public (state) schools were closed. Nearly half of the city's white students enrolled in private schools. Most of the black students in Little Rock did not attend school.

Adapted from Williams. J. 1987. **Eyes on the Prize: America's Civil Rights Years, 1954–1965.** *New York, USA. Viking Press.*

4.3 What was the significance of the Montgomery Bus Boycott, 1955–56?

The story of the Montgomery Bus Boycott is probably better known than any other event in the history of the civil rights movement. The traditional, 'heroic' view, put simply, was that a tired woman refused to give up her seat on a bus and that a brilliant young preacher subsequently led the grateful masses to victory and freedom. Historians now view the boycott differently. This section will provide a brief, factual survey of the boycott, and then examine the reasons for its success and assess its significance in advancing black civil rights.

An outline of the boycott

On 1 December 1955, in Montgomery, Alabama, 42-year-old **Rosa Parks** climbed aboard one of the city's segregated buses and sat behind the white section. When the bus filled up, the driver ordered her to give up her seat to a white man. Parks refused and was arrested.

On the day of her trial blacks boycotted the buses. In Montgomery 30 000 black people usually travelled by bus, providing most of the bus company's income. On this day, they walked.

> **Rosa Parks (1913–2005):**
>
> Parks joined the NAACP in Montgomery in 1943. She became branch secretary, worked on voter registration campaigns and ran the NAACP Youth Council. During the boycott, she was forced out of her job in a store and suffered death threats. Parks later moved to Detroit and worked for the African American congressman John Conyers from 1965 to 1988. She was awarded the Presidential Medal of Freedom in 1996.

Local black leaders, including many church ministers, decided to prolong the boycott after their initial success. They set up the Montgomery Improvement Association (MIA) to coordinate it and invited a young Baptist minister, **Martin Luther King**, to lead it.

> **Martin Luther King (1929–68):**
>
> King was brought up in Atlanta, Georgia, where both his father and grandfather were Baptist ministers, and he encountered racial discrimination and segregation on a daily basis. He went to theological college and later completed a PhD. In 1953, he married Coretta Scott, a fellow black activist from the South. King became convinced of the need for a mass movement against racial discrimination, founded on the Christian belief in reconciliation through love. He was also influenced by Mahatma Gandhi's success in India using non-violent mass action. King came to be seen as an icon of the civil rights movement and was an inspiration to millions, both black and white and he was awarded the Nobel Peace Prize in 1964. He was assassinated in 1968.

Their demands did not initially include the desegregation of Montgomery buses but did include:

- more courteous treatment of black passengers
- seating on a first-come, first-served basis with whites filling the bus from the front and blacks from the back
- the employment of some black drivers.

The bus company refused to compromise. They rejected all the demands for fear that 'the Negroes would go about boasting of a victory'. Besides, most whites thought the boycott would not last long. They did not think the blacks had the organisational ability to sustain it, and believed that they would start using the buses again once it rained. But the boycott did last: black people walked, shared lifts, cycled, hitchhiked.

Parks was fired from the white-owned store she worked for; bombs were thrown into black churches and cars; and, in January 1956, Martin Luther King's house – with his wife and daughters inside – was bombed. Yet the boycott continued.

In June 1956, the NAACP took the case to a federal district court, which ruled that the bus company's segregated transport was unconstitutional in the light of the recent Brown decision. The city of Montgomery appealed to the Supreme Court, which upheld the lower court's decision in November 1956.

In December, when the order became effective, Martin Luther King, E. D. Nixon and other local leaders took their first ride on a desegregated bus. The year-long boycott had more than achieved its goal.

Reasons for the success of the boycott

The bus boycott was not completely spontaneous. It was the result of years of grassroots activism and was sustained by a strong, well-organised black community in Montgomery. The community's leaders were no longer afraid to stand up for their rights, despite ongoing intimidation.

Foremost among them was E. D. Nixon, a railway porter who had been inspired by A. Philip Randolph. Nixon had helped to organise the Montgomery Voters' League in 1940, and led a march of 750 people to register to vote in Montgomery in 1944. For many years he was president of the NAACP's Alabama state branch.

Rosa Parks was an active member of the NAACP who had long campaigned against the injustice of segregated public transport and the insulting, abusive behaviour of Montgomery's bus drivers. She did not just get swept up accidentally in the historical events of 1955!

Jo Ann Robinson was a professor of English at all-black Alabama State College and president of the Women's Political Council, a group of 300 educated black women who had been campaigning for voter registration and the desegregation of the buses for several years. They had also persuaded the city authorities to employ black policemen.

When Parks was arrested, Nixon and Robinson's group knew this was the ideal case to challenge, particularly given Rosa Parks' status in Montgomery as a respectable, dignified, married woman.

Nixon and Robinson took responsibility for mobilising the blacks of Montgomery. Their years of experience gave them the knowledge of who to contact, and the skills to organise a citywide boycott.

Nixon called a meeting of church ministers, college professors and others whose leadership would be crucial. He persuaded them to announce the plans in their sermons on Sunday (the day before the boycott), to distribute leaflets and to persuade the black taxi companies to transport people at bus fare rates. Robinson and her colleagues stayed up half the night producing, and later distributing, thousands of leaflets to publicise the boycott.

SOURCE 4.2

The Southern practice of racial segregation or racial separation was the correct, self-evident truth which arose from the chaos and confusion of the period after the Civil War. Separation promotes racial harmony. It permits each race to follow its own pursuits and its own civilization. Segregation is not discrimination. Segregation is not a badge of racial inferiority, and this fact is recognised by both races in the Southern States. In fact, segregation is desired and supported by the vast majority of the members of both races in the South, who live side by side under harmonious conditions.

Adapted from a speech in the Senate by James Eastland, Senator for Mississippi, 27 May 1954.

QUESTION

What do you think Eastland was trying to achieve in this speech?

Extending the boycott

The one-day boycott was a huge success. Hardly any black people took buses. But to force the bus company to agree to their demands, they would have to extend the boycott. Nixon set up the Montgomery Improvement Association (MIA) to organise the extension of the boycott, and asked Martin Luther King to be president.

King addressed a mass meeting at the Holt Street Baptist Church on the evening of the initial boycott. Nearly 5000 blacks turned up for the meeting with most standing outside, listening on loudspeakers. Encouraged by their success, they voted unanimously to continue.

King immediately struck a chord with his listeners by simultaneously praising American democracy and appealing to Christian values, reminding his congregation of Jesus' call to love their enemies. His rhetoric soared over the crowd 'We are not wrong in what we are doing. If we are wrong, the Supreme Court is wrong. If we are wrong, the Constitution of the United States is wrong. If we are wrong,

God Almighty is wrong.' The impact of his speech was to inspire and galvanise the thousands who attended.

The boycott was sustained for over a year costing the bus company over $1 million. Evening meetings in churches were attended by thousands, and the ministers played a crucial role in sustaining the boycott. Abuse was hurled at black pedestrians and car pools were bombed, but this only strengthened the blacks' resolve.

When King's house was firebombed, thousands of blacks surrounded it, many with guns and knives, ready to take revenge. King came out and told the crowd to put away their weapons. 'We must love our white brothers no matter what they do to us. We must meet hate with love.' Whites had thought that they could break King and break the boycott. Instead they made him into a hero and a symbol of black resistance to the extent that historian Claybourne Carson describes King as a 'prophet'.

Bombings and the arrests of church leaders attracted huge publicity, both in America and abroad. Donations poured in and more cars were purchased for the car pools. Organised in a highly disciplined way, the pools enabled blacks to get to work all over the city. After more than a year – 381 days – the bus company backed down and segregation on Montgomery's buses was ended.

ACTIVITY

King has been criticised extensively for hypocrisy particularly in terms of his invocation of Christian principles being incompatible with his extra-marital affairs and the plagiarism of his PhD dissertation. Does it matter that King was not as pure as his popular image? Was it essential to the success of the movement that his failings were disguised?

Figure 4.4: Rosa Parks takes a front seat in a desegregated bus following the victorious boycott.

The significance of the boycott

The boycott was a local action, started and sustained by Montgomery's black population. There had been similar bus boycotts before, in Baton Rouge, Louisiana and elsewhere, but none had been sustained for so long or been so successful. Black solidarity remained firm in the face of intimidation and terror. That in itself instilled huge confidence and pride in the black community, and made African Americans more determined to continue their campaign. Furthermore, the boycott was successful in eliciting a Supreme Court ruling in the blacks' favour as well as a climb-down by the bus company.

Montgomery's black people had shown they could exploit their economic power as a weapon in their battle. They had also shown that organised collective action – local, popular and sustained – could achieve advances in civil rights. The boycott set a precedent, and over 20 other southern cities desegregated their bus transport after boycotts.

The boycott also brought Martin Luther King to the fore. The ground had been laid and the momentum established by others but, once he became the campaign's spokesman, his charisma and broad appeal allowed him to project the civil rights message far beyond Montgomery. His church, together with others, provided the organising centres for the boycott. His measured response to the bombing of his house curbed the hotheads who might otherwise have resorted to violence and it won nationwide respect, particularly among northern whites. This support would be crucial in the future, when bringing pressure to bear on the federal government.

ACTIVITY

List the reasons for the success of the Montgomery Bus Boycott. Use a Diamond Nine template to put them in order of importance, and justify your order in discussion with a partner.

The Southern Christian Leadership Conference (SCLC)

The Montgomery bus boycott also led to the formation of the Southern Christian Leadership Conference (SCLC) in January 1957. The SCLC was formed by King and other church ministers in order to leverage the power of the black churches, and mount sustained mass demonstrations against racial discrimination and segregation. Being based on the black churches, it was less vulnerable to state repression than the NAACP, which was a political organisation.

Those churches also provided meeting places, a stable base of support and a network of communications. Several of the SCLC leaders helped to develop the philosophy of peaceful confrontation, of non-violent direct mass action, which would be developed, taught and practised widely and successfully in the early 1960s. As historian Adam Fairclough argues, the SCLC 'not only out-sang, out-prayed and out-marched their oppressors, they also out thought them'.

In the late 1950s, President Eisenhower's government responded to increasing black pressure, and the need both to win the northern black vote and also improve America's international image, by passing two Civil Rights Acts. Both were diluted by Dixiecrats in Congress, notably James Eastland, but Eisenhower himself was less than enthusiastic.

The first act, in 1957, set up a Civil Rights Commission to monitor racial relations. The second, in 1960, imposed criminal penalties for public officials obstructing black voters (although they would be tried by all-white juries if in the South).

SOURCE 4.3

In 1958, to keep harmony within civil rights ranks, King hurried up to New York and had a long talk with the NAACP leaders, assuring them that SCLC's approach supported and supplemented theirs. While the NAACP focused on legal strategy, SCLC would concern itself with 'spiritual strategy' – with raising the moral conscience of America. As King repeatedly said, there was no single road to the promised land. Therefore, it was imperative that negroes advance on a united front along several parallel paths – one led by SCLC, another by the NAACP, still others by CORE and the Urban League.

Adapted from Oates, S. B. 1988. **Let the Trumpet Sound.** *Edinburgh, UK. Payback Press.*

ACTIVITY

With reference to its origins, purpose and content, assess the values and limitation of Source 4.3 to a historian studying the SCLC.

As the 1950s drew to a close, white supremacist groups still dominated the South. There was an increase of only 3% in the number of black people added to the electoral registers as a result of Eisenhower's two Civil Rights Acts. Many cities ignored the Supreme Court rulings and continued to enforce segregation in schools and other public facilities.

In Montgomery itself, schools, cinemas, parks, hospitals, restaurants and hotels remained segregated and, after the end of the bus boycott, there were further attacks on King's house and four black churches were bombed. The SCLC failed to enlist massive, grassroots support and Ella Baker, its executive director, complained that the organisation was failing to 'develop and use our major weapon – mass resistance'.

Theory of Knowledge

Changing interpretations:

In an article from January 2005 entitled 'Paradoxes of King Historiography' for the *Organization of American Historians Magazine of History*, Claybourne Carson discussed the changing interpretations of Martin Luther King. These interpretations have seen him lauded as the 'Great Man' who saved black Americans, then denigrated for his failings, recontextualised as someone who was merely the figurehead of a grassroots movement, and diminished as inferior to the firebrand Malcolm X. What does this say about how historians interpret the people they study, and how do you see King?

Paper 3 exam practice

Question

'The primary importance of the Montgomery Bus Boycott was that it led to the emergence of Martin Luther King as a leader of the civil rights movement.' To what extent do you agree with this statement?
[15 marks]

Skill

Writing an introductory paragraph

Examiner's tips

Once you have planned your answer to a question (as described in the exam practice sections of Chapters 2 and 3), you should be able to begin writing a clear introductory paragraph. This needs to set out your main line of argument and to outline *briefly* the key points you intend to make (and support with relevant and precise own knowledge) in the main body of your essay. Remember: 'To what extent…?' and 'Examine…?' questions clearly require evaluation and analysis of opposing arguments – and a judgement. If, after writing your plan, you think you will be able to make a clear final judgement, it's a good idea to state in your introductory paragraph what overall line of argument or judgement you intend to make.

This question requires you to assess the importance of the Montgomery Bus Boycott in leading to the emergence of Martin Luther King as a leader of the civil rights movement and, above all, to make a judgement about how important King's emergence was in comparison to all the other factors.

For this question, you should:

* assess what King contributed to the success of the boycott
* assess what other local leaders contributed
* consider what was achieved by the black community as a whole
* make a judgement about what was most important about the boycott, both at the time and for the future.

Setting out this approach in your introductory paragraph will help you keep the demands of the question in mind. Remember to refer back to your introduction after every couple of paragraphs in your main answer.

Common mistakes

A common mistake (which might suggest to an examiner that a candidate hasn't thought deeply about what's required) is to fail to write an introductory paragraph at all. This is often done by candidates who rush into writing *before* analysing the question and writing a plan. The result may well be that they focus entirely on the importance of Martin Luther King in the boycott, an approach that may neglect other ways in which the boycott was important. Even if the answer is full of detailed and accurate own knowledge, this will not answer the question, and so will not score highly.

Sample student introductory paragraph

Martin Luther King was to be the pre-eminent leader of the civil rights movement and, for that reason alone, his emergence as a leader of the boycott was important. He inspired and helped to unite Montgomery's blacks in a prolonged and ultimately successful boycott. However, the boycott was started by, and based on, the organising ability and experience of, people such as E. D. Nixon and Jo Ann Robinson, as well as the example of Rosa Parks. The Montgomery Bus Boycott was also important because it showed that popular, well-organised and sustained action could force the city authorities to back down, and thus it served as an example to civil rights activists elsewhere. King's emergence was important, especially as he was able to attract wide support from white America but, without collective, mass action, the boycott would not have succeeded and been so significant in the advancement of African American civil rights.

EXAMINER'S COMMENT

This is a good introduction, as it shows a good grasp of the question and sets out a clear and logical plan that is clearly focused on the demands of the question. It shows a sound appreciation of the importance of individuals – King included – and of mass action in the success of the boycott, and it explicitly demonstrates to the examiner what the main line of argument is going to be. This indicates that the answer – if it remains analytical, and is well supported – is likely to be a high-scoring one.

Activity

In this chapter, the focus is on writing a useful introductory paragraph. So, using the information from this chapter, and any other sources of information available to you, write introductory paragraphs for at least two of the following Paper 3 practice questions.

Remember to refer to the simplified Paper 3 mark scheme given in Chapter 11.

Paper 3 practice questions

1 Examine the rise of the African American civil rights movement in the years from 1945 to 1960.

2 Discuss why schools were not immediately desegregated after the verdict in the Supreme Court case *Brown versus Topeka Board of Education* in 1954.

3 To what extent was the Montgomery Bus Boycott the major turning point in the campaign for African American civil rights in the 1950s?

4 Compare and contrast the role of the Supreme Court and the role of the Federal government in the advancement of civil rights for African Americans in the 1950s.

5 Evaluate how much the lives of African Americans in the South changed in the 1950s.

The peak of
the campaign
for civil rights,
1960–65

5

Introduction

This chapter examines the most intensive period in the campaign for African American civil rights in the US. It starts with the explosion of student activism in 1960 in the form of sit–ins and Freedom Rides. It then explores the development of many different forms of direct, popular action, such as the SCLC campaign in Birmingham, Alabama, the 1963 March on Washington and the SNCC-led Freedom Summer of 1964. These campaigns culminated in the passing of the pivotal 1964 Civil Rights Act and 1965 Voting Rights Act.

TIMELINE

1960 **Feb:** Sit-in movement begins in Greensboro, North Carolina

Apr: Student Nonviolent Coordinating Committee (SNCC) formed

1961 **May:** Freedom Rides begin

Nov: Desegregation in interstate travel enforced

1962–64 SNCC voter registration campaign in Mississippi

1963 **Mar–May:** 'Project Confrontation' in Birmingham, Alabama

Jun: John F. Kennedy's TV address refers to civil rights as a 'moral issue'

Aug: March on Washington

Sep: Murder of four African American girls in a church in Birmingham, Alabama

Nov: Assassination of President Kennedy

1964 **Jun–Aug:** Freedom Summer

Jul: Civil Rights Act passed

1965 **Jan:** Martin Luther King joins voter registration campaign in Selma, Alabama

Feb: Killing of Jimmie Lee Jackson leads to the Selma–Montgomery march

Mar: 'Bloody Sunday'

Aug: Voting Rights Act passed

Overview

• The student sit-ins of 1960 and the formation of the Student Nonviolent Coordinating Committee (SNCC) reinvigorated the civil rights movement.

• The Freedom Rides of 1961 and the violence they provoked led to federal intervention.

• The SNCC launched a sustained campaign for the right to vote in Mississippi from 1962 to 1964.

• The SCLC campaign in 1963 in Birmingham, Alabama attracted national and international attention, forcing Kennedy to commit his administration to reform.

• The March on Washington in 1963 was huge and peaceful but had little immediate impact.

• The Freedom Summer of 1964 in Mississippi highlighted the strength of white supremacist feeling in the South.

• The 1965 campaign for voter registration in Selma, Alabama, speeded up the passing of the 1965 Voting Rights Act.

5.1 Why were sit-ins and Freedom Rides launched in 1960–61?

On 1 February 1960, four smartly dressed black students walked into a Woolworth's store in Greensboro, North Carolina. They bought several items and then sat down at the whites-only lunch counter and asked to be served. They were refused but continued to sit reading the Bible and carrying on with their studies, until closing time. The next day, 29 students followed their example and, on the third day, all but two of the 65 seats were occupied.

The students were pushed, kicked and punched by young whites. They had ketchup poured over them and cigarettes stubbed out on their bodies, but they did not retaliate. When the police arrived, the students were arrested for trespass but were replaced by others and on this and succeeding days, white mobs arrived to abuse them and caused a disturbance.

The sit-ins were a gift to the media and news of them spread fast, first to other campuses and then to other cities. Soon, similar sit-ins were taking place in the cities of several neighbouring southern states, notably in Nashville, Tennessee. By August 1960, 70 000 students – both black and white – had followed the example of the Greensboro four, and over 3600 had been arrested. The Greensboro students provided the spark that launched a new wave of protest.

The rise of the sit-ins and their impact

The actions of the first four students were not completely spontaneous. They had been inspired by Brown in 1954 and then waited six years for something more and the frustration made them determined to take some form of non-violent direct action to further the cause of civil rights. They had read about Gandhi's passive resistance against British rule in India, had heard King's speeches, and knew of the Montgomery Bus Boycott and similar actions. Theirs was not the first-ever sit-in; such tactics had been tried before. However, it was their idea to do something in Woolworth's, in Greensboro, and their example reignited the civil rights movement, bringing it back to the grassroots and away from leaders like King and hierarchical groups like the NAACP. Their example spread across the South. Soon there were 'wade-ins' on whites-only beaches in Florida and 'read-ins' in whites-only libraries.

Figure 5.1: Students sit quietly while white people pour food over their heads at a Woolworth's lunch counter in Jackson, Mississippi, May 1963.

At the beginning of the 1960s, the civil rights movement seemed to have lost momentum. Six years had passed since the Brown decision of 1954 and the teens of 1954 had not seen widespread desegregation of schools in the South, nor of cafes, restaurants, hotels, cinemas, parks or swimming pools. Church organisations and the SCLC continued to hold rallies and train people in the art of non-violent direct action, but only modest changes were achieved in the South. What progress was being made was the gradual, slow progress favoured by Eisenhower.

Many young people from the black universities in the South were growing impatient, especially when they learnt of fellow blacks in African countries gaining their independence. When Vice-President Nixon was invited to attend independence celebrations in Ghana in 1957, he asked a black guest what it was like to be free. The guest replied: 'I wouldn't know. I'm from Alabama.'

Theory of Knowledge

History and independence movements:

The student leader, John Lewis, said: *'We identified with the blacks in Africa. They were getting their freedom, and we still didn't have ours in what we believed was a free country.'* Lewis saw the civil rights movement in the US as part of a wider process of civil rights that included decolonisation in Africa, but was he correct? How do the names we give to events or combinations of events become the historical reality of textbooks? You might consider the origins of terms like 'Cold War', 'Industrial Revolution' or the recent 'Arab Spring'.

Another reason that the sit-ins started at this time was because there was a growing national movement, fuelled by the media. In Philadelphia, a young church minister called Leon Sullivan formed a new organisation to target retail stores that refused to employ blacks, yet which relied on black customers. In the first few months of 1960, about a quarter of a million black Americans joined 'Don't buy where you can't work' boycotts. Martin Luther King later invited Sullivan to speak at the SCLC conference. Activists in the North and South sang the same protest songs, listened to similar music and read similar magazines. In the words of the song by Bob Dylan (see 8.3, Music), the times – they were 'a-changing'.

At first, the NAACP was critical of the sit-ins, preferring to continue the more orderly route of taking legal action. The SCLC also feared that the students were too confrontational. They hoped the students would come under the wing of their elders, however without families to think of or jobs to lose the students could afford to be more radical. Nevertheless, both the NAACP and SCLC, as well as the Congress of Racial Equality (CORE), offered support in finance, legal aid and training, which the students accepted. Television, now widespread in American homes, helped to publicise the campaign, seemingly confirming the TV news axiom 'if it bleeds it leads'.

Journalists flocked to report the disturbances that took place in and outside stores across the South. Most Americans, especially whites, may not have approved of the sit-ins, but it was very clear which party were in the right. Even the segregationist editor of a North Carolina newspaper contrasted the smart dress and peaceful, dignified behaviour of the students with the 'ragtail rabble, slack-jawed, black-jacketed, grinning fit to kill' white mobs who taunted them.

Nashville, Tennessee

One of the other cities where students started sit-ins was Nashville, Tennessee on 13 February 1960. Meanwhile, older black people began to boycott the main city stores – this in a city where blacks spent $50 million annually. Although a boycott was a less confrontational form of action, it could have huge economic impact, as the boycott of city buses had done in Montgomery. The students who sat-in at the lunch counters in Nashville were arrested by the police, only to be replaced by waves of more students who arrived to take their places. Two students produced 'Rules of Conduct' for the sit-ins. These insisted that the students should be friendly and courteous, stay non-violent following King's Montgomery example, sit straight and face the counter, and not retaliate, leave or laugh.

The protesters followed these rules and did not hit back, even when they were spat at and punched. Many had role-played the abuse they received beforehand in preparation. The students adopted a policy of 'Jail, no bail', refusing to pay bail so that the police would have to keep them in prison. As the prisons filled up, bail was reduced to $5, but the students still refused to pay. Many of them had to be released as there was not enough room for them. Three weeks later, the Nashville bus station served blacks at the lunch counter and, in May, the city centre stores decided to desegregate their lunch counters. However, it was to be another four years before Nashville desegregated its hotels, cinemas and fast-food outlets.

Although the gains in Nashville may have been modest, they were repeated in many other cities in the South. The disruption caused by the sit-ins and the economic effects of consumer boycotts hit businesses. Woolworth's profits fell drastically and, within a year, they desegregated the lunch counters in all their stores across the South.

The Student Nonviolent Coordinating Committee (SNCC)

One of the most significant results of the sit-ins was the formation of the Student Nonviolent Coordinating Committee (SNCC). This originated in April 1960, two months after the Greensboro sit-in. **Ella Baker**, one of the few leading female figures in the SCLC, asked student leaders to attend a meeting in Raleigh, North Carolina. Most of those attending came from black colleges in the South, but there were also some northerner supporters, including whites. Baker challenged the students to find bigger targets, 'bigger than a hamburger or even a giant-sized Coke'. Baker, alongside the historian Howard Zinn, became a long-term adviser to the SNCC.

Ella Baker (1903–86):

Baker joined the NAACP in 1940 and helped set up new branches. Keen to mobilise the black community as a whole rather than rely on lawsuits, she left the organisation in 1946. She campaigned against segregated schooling and police brutality in New York, raised funds for the Montgomery Bus Boycott, and worked for the SCLC. She urged the founding of the SNCC in 1960, and campaigned extensively for voter registration.

Figure 5.2: Ella Baker, who championed many grassroots campaigns during her long career as a civil rights activist.

Martin Luther King also spoke at the meeting in Raleigh, but Baker steered the students towards setting up a completely independent organisation. She made a remark directed at King when she advised them to adopt 'group-centred leadership' rather than a 'leader-centred group' and later famously said of King, 'Martin didn't make the movement, the movement made Martin.'

The students did not need much prompting: they were idealistic, committed and proud of what they had achieved. The SNCC, formed at the end of the meeting, was to remain highly democratic, with no obvious leader emerging. Also, it was far less male-dominated than the SCLC: many women were to play leading roles including Diane Nash who had led the Nashville movement. SNCC activist James Lawson criticised the NAACP for its 'overreliance on the courts' and 'futile middle-class technique of sending letters to the centres of power'. This was an early sign of the splits that would plague the civil rights movement but in the meantime the movement now had the 'shock troops' needed to exploit the successes of 1954 to 1956.

KEY CONCEPTS ACTIVITY

Perspectives: The historian Clayborne Carson saw the sit-ins as spontaneous and owing little to existing civil rights organisations. Yet historian William Chafe saw them as 'an extension of, rather than a departure from, traditional patterns of black activism'. Using your understanding of this section and any other resources available to you, write a couple of paragraphs to explain the interpretation you most agree with.

Freedom Rides, 1961

In May 1961, 13 CORE volunteers, seven black and six white, set off on a bus journey from Washington, DC, to New Orleans, repeating the 1947 'Journey of Reconciliation'. They planned to sit together, rather than in the segregated black and white sections of the bus. When they stopped at bus terminals, they planned to ignore 'White' and 'Colored' signs in toilets, waiting rooms and restaurants. Blacks would go to 'White' toilets and vice versa. The inspiration for these 'Freedom Rides' was **James Farmer**, leader of CORE. He wanted to test a 1960 ruling of the Supreme Court that banned segregation in interstate transport.

Farmer's intention was to create crises at bus terminals in the South by provoking the extremists, which would in turn attract publicity and, he hoped, force the federal government, now led by the dynamic young President John F. Kennedy (JFK), to intervene. Farmer claimed this was not civil disobedience as the riders were not disobeying any law, instead they were claiming their legal right to sit together and to use desegregated facilities.

James Farmer (1920–99):

As a boy, Farmer had seen his father, a college professor, humiliated by whites. He went on to found CORE in 1942, and pioneered the sit-in technique during the Second World War. He organised the Freedom Rides, and was one of the speakers at the March on Washington in 1963.

As the bus arrived in Anniston, Alabama, it was firebombed by a mob of 200. When the riders staggered out of the bus to avoid the harmful effects of the smoke, they were beaten up. When a second bus arrived, the police stood by as thugs ordered the black riders to sit at the back. They refused. When two white riders attempted to intervene, they were beaten up. One of them, a retired professor, spent the rest of his life in a wheelchair as a result.

When those who were not hospitalised travelled on to Birmingham, Alabama, the police chief 'Bull' Connor told the local Ku Klux Klan leader that they would give the Klansmen 15 minutes before they intervened. Alabama's Democrat Governor John Patterson was unsympathetic too: 'When you go somewhere looking for trouble, you usually find it.'

QUESTION

What does Source 5.1, following, suggest about the relationship between the civil rights activists and the Kennedys?

SOURCE 5.1

The Kennedys meant well but they did not feel it. They didn't know any blacks growing up – there were no blacks living in their communities or going to their schools. But their inclinations were good. I had the impression that Bobby was doing what needed to be done for political reasons. He was very conscious of the fact that his brother had won a narrow election victory and he was afraid that if they antagonised the South, the Dixiecrats would cost them the next election. And he was found to be very, very cautious and very careful not to do that. But the Civil Rights Movement changed the situation in the South, so it became dangerous for him not to do anything.

Adapted from an interview with James Farmer, the first director of CORE, by C. David Heymann for his book **RFK: A Candid Biography of Robert F. Kennedy**, *1998, New York, USA, E. P. Dutton.*

For Kennedy, the Freedom Rides were 'a pain in the ass'. The president was about to meet the Soviet leader, Nikita Khrushchev in Vienna, and the last thing he wanted was to allow Khrushchev to take the moral high ground. Besides, Kennedy depended on some very powerful southern Democratic senators to steer his legislation through Congress. If the federal government intervened, it could alienate southern Democrats and divide his party. It was JFK's brother, Robert, the attorney general, who finally threatened to send in US marshals unless the local authorities agreed to provide protection for the riders.

Despite the beatings, the riders continued. When they arrived in Montgomery, they were attacked by Klansmen. Reporters and photographers were beaten too. When a large meeting, addressed by Martin Luther King, was held in the Baptist church in Montgomery, the building was surrounded by an angry mob who threw stones and homemade bombs in. With a very real danger that those inside could be burnt alive or, if they tried to escape, savaged by the mob, King phoned Robert Kennedy in Washington, who immediately ordered 400 US marshals from a nearby base to intervene.

Figure 5.3: The KKK firebombed this Freedom Ride bus in Anniston, Alabama, on 14 May 1961.

SOURCE 5.2

Testifying before a US Senate Committee in the 1960s, former US Attorney General Nicholas Katzenbach summed up the 'unique difficulty' in Mississippi and parts of Alabama and Louisiana of 'gathering information on fundamentally lawless activities'. Ku Klux Klan activities had the sanction of local law enforcement agencies, political officials and a substantial segment of the white population. The Klan drew its membership almost exclusively from that resentful part of society that looked on physical resistance as the necessary and suitable expression of whites at a time of challenge. Violence swelled Klan ranks and attracted a wider pool of supporters who saw the Klan as the only organisation that did anything to counter the black encroachment into their lives.

Adapted from Chalmers, D. M. 2003. **Backfire: How the KKK helped the Civil Rights Movement,** *Rowman & Littlefield.*

QUESTION
Does the explanation given in Source 5.2 excuse the federal government's failure to clamp down on the Klan?

The Marshals used tear gas to disperse the mob, the first show of federal force since Eisenhower sent paratroops to Little Rock in 1957. Robert Kennedy now hoped for a cooling-off period, but Farmer was determined to carry on: he did not want the riders to be seen as having given in to white violence. New riders joined the bus to replace those hospitalised and more than a thousand more activists, mostly black but also whites, including clergy, professors and trade union members, defied segregation on further Freedom Rides and in the bus stations. Again they filled the jails and the movement spread to the North: in Chicago, 2500 black people rode in 46 buses to City Hall with banners demanding better housing and jobs.

Eventually, in November 1961, Robert Kennedy ordered the Interstate Commerce Commission to enforce desegregation on their buses and in their bus terminals. Signs on the buses and in the toilets and waiting rooms had to be changed: the old ones (such as 'Whites Only', 'Black Waiting Room') were removed. The Supreme Court had originally ruled in 1946 that segregation on interstate transport was illegal, the federal government finally enforced the ruling 15 years later.

Campaigning for civil rights in Mississippi, 1961–63

The traditional interpretation of the civil rights movement emphasises the role of national leaders, such as Martin Luther King, Kennedy, Earl Warren or Thurgood Marshall. This is known as 'Great Man' history and it can lead historians to neglect the importance of local struggles and the role of 'ordinary' people. Nowhere is this grassroots movement more in evidence than in Mississippi in the early 1960s.

At this time, the state of Mississippi was the poorest in the US; 45% of its people were black, a higher percentage than in any other state. It had more beatings and lynchings than other states. Only 5% of Mississippi's blacks were registered to vote, and no black person had been elected to any office in the state since 1877, when Reconstruction ended. However, for most blacks, poverty was a far more pressing problem than voting. Most lived in small, isolated, rural communities like Money, Mississippi where 14-year-old Emmett Till had been murdered in 1955. Many had lost their jobs on the land with the increased use of chemical fertilisers and mechanisation and their children received only very basic primary school education.

Medgar Evers was the leader of the NAACP in Mississippi. He organised a voter registration drive, knowing that if blacks were registered to vote in Mississippi, they would have greater power. Making up nearly half the population of the state, they would be able to elect congressmen and local officials. However, the forces of white supremacy were both well organised and well financed.

Medgar Evers (1925–63):

Evers was born and brought up in Mississippi. Despite being a veteran of the Second World War, Evers was repeatedly prevented from registering to vote by a white mob with knives and guns. Refused entry to the whites-only University of Mississippi Law School, he worked for the NAACP, campaigning for desegregation and voter registration and investigating violent crimes against blacks. In 1963, he was murdered in front of his house while his family slept inside. President Kennedy insisted that he be buried in Arlington National Cemetery with full military honours.

Lawyers, judges and politicians were often members of the White Citizens' Council. Fear of unemployment deterred many blacks from attempting to register to vote; those applying had to give their employer's name, which meant, in the words of one activist, 'you would be fired by the time you got home'. The authorities employed informers and spies, and published racist articles in the newspapers. Not surprisingly, very few blacks were willing to risk registering to vote as, in addition, the only candidates were also racist whites.

In 1962, the local NAACP invited the SNCC to send in volunteers. These young activists would live alongside poor, rural blacks, developing local leaders according to local needs. This was very much the approach favoured by Ella Baker ever since the first student sit-ins in 1960.

This campaign would be one of many rural projects, part of a national movement financed by the Voter Education Project (VEP). The VEP was set up by Robert Kennedy in order to channel student energies away from the more highly publicised sit-ins and Freedom Rides, and relieve the federal government of the pressure to intervene.

SNCC volunteers went from house to house in the small towns encouraging people to register to vote. They organised literacy classes to help blacks pass the literacy and other tests that were imposed by the state authorities. Above all, they tried to help local blacks to overcome their fear: fear of losing a job, fear of being hurt, fear of being killed.

The local SNCC leader, Bob Moses, was knifed, shot at and imprisoned. The volunteers faced constant threats and had their phones tapped; those arrested were subjected to police beatings, while black churches and the houses of SNCC workers were firebombed by the Klan.

When the SNCC appealed to the federal government to intervene, the authorities in Washington insisted that law enforcement was a state responsibility. Besides, the Kennedy government was very reluctant to antagonise southern Democrats, several of whom, like James Eastland, held important positions in Congress by virtue of the longevity of their service. Robert Kennedy pressed the Federal Bureau of Investigation (FBI) to be more active but, under the leadership of its powerful, racist, boss, J. Edgar Hoover, it provided very little protection.

Not surprisingly, the voter registration campaign had little success; few new voters were registered and the VEP cut off funding in Mississippi. It would take a major crisis and nationwide publicity to force the federal government to throw its weight behind the campaign for civil rights. The SCLC campaign in 1963 in Birmingham, Alabama, did exactly this.

ACTIVITY

Watch the 2011 film *The Help* based on the novel by Kathryn Stockett. It is set in Mississippi during the civil rights movement of the early 1960s and it tells the story of three women, one white and two black, who come together to expose the evils of racism.

5.2 To what extent was the campaign in Birmingham in 1963 a turning point?

At his inauguration in 1963, the new governor of Alabama George Wallace vowed: 'I say segregation now, segregation tomorrow, segregation forever!' Martin Luther King saw Wallace as 'the most dangerous racist in America today'. Birmingham, the capital of Alabama, was the largest industrial city in the South and it was reputed to be 'the most segregated city in America'. It had a history of racial tension and police brutality, with a high rate of black unemployment and poor housing and the amount of Klan activity had led to the city being known as 'Bombingham' to its black citizens.

Fred Shuttlesworth and Martin Luther King

In 1956, after the state had banned the NAACP, the black Baptist preacher Fred Shuttlesworth established the Alabama Christian Movement for Human Rights. He worked closely with the SCLC to challenge segregation on buses and in schools in Birmingham. In retaliation, the Klan burnt his home and his church, and the police tapped his phones. When he enrolled his children at a white school near his home, a mob stabbed his wife and attacked him as police looked on. In 1963, he pleaded with Martin Luther King to come to Birmingham.

The time was right: a recent campaign in Albany, Georgia, had died out with no visible gain thanks to the sophisticated policing of Laurie Pritchett, the Chief of Police in Albany, and King and the SCLC had not made a major breakthrough since the Montgomery Bus Boycott. The movement was losing momentum and the non-violent approach of the SCLC was losing ground, especially in the North, to more militant black nationalists like Malcolm X. Above all, the government had done little, despite all Kennedy's promises to improve civil rights. A significant campaign to attract widespread media attention and boost support for civil rights was needed to put pressure on the president.

Birmingham was a suitable target for a new campaign because of its history of segregation and racial violence, and the groundwork had already been laid by Shuttlesworth and his movement. The Klan was known to be large and guaranteed to be violent in the face of public demonstrations. The public safety commissioner, Bull Connor, could also be relied on to resort to physical force which would attract widespread publicity and public outrage, and force the federal government to intervene. If civil rights actions could be successful here, in one of the biggest and most segregated cities, then perhaps Jim Crow laws throughout the South could be swept away.

Project Confrontation

King now devised 'Project Confrontation'. Its aim would be to desegregate businesses, such as large retail stores and force them to employ blacks and integrate their facilities for customers (blacks were not allowed to use the same toilets as whites, or try on clothes before buying them). The plan was for a peaceful march, from the Baptist church to the city centre, to disrupt traffic and carry out a very public boycott of city-centre stores on the busy shopping days leading up to Easter.

The demonstrators were met by police with batons and dogs. This show of force attracted media attention, which in turn attracted more marchers, more police violence and more publicity. Many were arrested, and then the state authorities secured a court injunction (a special court order) forbidding further protests.

With money for bail running out and some black businesses calling for a retreat by the demonstrators, King came under intense pressure to obey the injunction and call off the campaign. If he carried on, he risked losing the support of key allies, especially in Washington, and the long-promised Civil Rights Bill that Kennedy had now introduced might be undermined.

On Good Friday, King announced that he had received an 'injunction from heaven', calling on him to disobey immoral, man-made laws and carry on leading the demonstrations until 'Pharaoh lets God's people go'. He saw it as his duty as an American Christian to obey a higher law, God's law, as the evils of segregation and racial injustice were so great. He marched to City Hall, was arrested and put in solitary confinement.

'Letter from Birmingham jail'

A group of white clergyman now placed a big advertisement in the *Birmingham News*, in which they criticised Project Confrontation, saying it was illegal and led by 'outside agitators'. Reading a copy of the paper in his jail cell, King scribbled his response in the margins. He explained his non-violent philosophy, saying he was not an outside agitator but a dutiful Christian fighting 'injustice'. He wrote of how hard it was 'to explain to your six-year-old daughter why she can't go to the public amusement park that has just been advertised on television, and see tears welling up in her eyes when she is told that Funtown is closed to colored children'.

King also warned that if peaceful demonstrators were dismissed as 'rabble rousers', millions of people would instead turn to black nationalism and a 'frightening racial nightmare' would ensue.

Figure 5.4: Martin Luther King looks out through his cell window, Jefferson County Courthouse, Birmingham, Alabama, after being imprisoned there again in 1967, four years after his famous 'Letter from Birmingham jail'.

A week later, King was released on bail, but it seemed that the demonstrations might die out. There were not many more adult demonstrators willing to risk jail and its consequences for their jobs. Then an SCLC official had the idea of a 'children's crusade', for school students to take the place of their elders. After all, it was their future and they had no jobs to lose.

ACTIVITY

Use the internet to read both the white clergymen's statement and Martin Luther King's 'Letter from Birmingham jail'. What are the criticisms that the clergymen make? How does King answer them?

The Children's Crusade

In May, hundreds of children skipped school and gathered at the Baptist church. They watched an inspiring film about the sit-ins and then they set off, marching, singing and praying. They were arrested and sent to jail. Impressed by the children's bravery and shocked by police behaviour, many more adults joined the demonstrations. Television reporters came from all over the country.

With demonstrations continuing, Bull Connor now resorted to the use of high-pressure fire hoses, which knocked people over and threw them against walls. Pictures of this, and of police using German Shepherd dogs against teenagers, appeared on TV stations all over the US and in newspapers around the world, especially in the USSR. Millions were sickened.

With thousands jailed, sometimes 60 to a cell, and America's image at home and abroad severely damaged, the federal government was forced to act. Senior federal officials were sent to start talks between King and Birmingham businessmen. The latter were losing money because of the boycott and disorder. Under huge pressure from Washington, they gave in and agreed to desegregate their businesses, which included stores, cinemas and restaurants. Most importantly, the mayor and city council agreed to desegregate schools. King proclaimed a 'magnificent victory for justice'.

Figure 5.5: In May 1963, in Birmingham, Alabama, high-pressure fire hoses were used to disperse peaceful demonstrators.

Meanwhile, white extremists threw bombs into the house of King's brother and the hotel where King himself was staying. There were also attacks by blacks on white businesses and the police, and Kennedy prepared to send in federal troops before King was able to pacify the angry blacks with his call for non–violence.

The impact of the Birmingham campaign

In the next few months, 50 other cities in the South agreed to desegregation in order to avoid the chaos of Birmingham. In the summer of 1963, 100000 demonstrated across the US, against segregation, job discrimination and police brutality. Some of the biggest demonstrations were in northern cities such as Detroit and Philadelphia. Thousands were injured and imprisoned, and ten were killed.

Robert Kennedy hosted a meeting of black writers and other intellectuals, and was heavily criticised for his inaction. The writer James Baldwin warned in his essay 'The Fire Next Time' that if there was not 'total liberation' soon, there would be grave consequences. King told the president that black Americans were at 'breaking point'.

King and the other SCLC leaders had known how Connor would react to the Birmingham campaign and how the media would depict his reactions. As one SCLC member said: 'There never was any more skilful manipulation of the news media than there was in Birmingham.'

There was an upsurge in support for civil rights, and donations poured into the SCLC. An opinion poll in 1963 found that 42% of Americans thought race was the most pressing American problem, whereas only 4% had thought so a year earlier. For many Americans, black and white, Birmingham and the subsequent demonstrations and disturbances were a major turning point in the campaign for civil rights.

Figure 5.6: The iconic civil rights photograph of a young Walter Gadsden (left), Officer Dick Middleton and police dog Leo.

Theory of Knowledge

History and ethics:

The photograph in Figure 5.6, taken by Bill Hudson, has been credited with turning international attention to the side of the civil rights movement by the historian Diane McWhorter. However, the truth is not quite as straightforward. Research the reality behind the scene and then consider the ethics of how the photograph was used by the press.

In June 1963, John F. Kennedy had said in a televised speech that segregation was 'a moral crisis' that required action by the federal government. He went on to prepare a comprehensive Civil Rights Bill that would ban segregation in all public places and presented it to Congress. He had finally committed himself to the cause and broken with the southern Democrats.

ACTIVITY

Draw up a list of reasons why the Birmingham campaign can be seen as a turning point in the development of the civil rights movement. Then put them in order of importance. Discuss with a partner, or the class, why you have put them in this order.

5.3 How successful was the March on Washington in 1963?

Most civil rights activists, like the thousands of SNCC volunteers, worked on a local level. However, others wanted to take their case to a national audience and to the politicians in Washington. One of these was A. Philip Randolph, who had planned a 'March on Washington' as far back as 1941 (see 4.1, The development of black activism).

Martin Luther King and other civil rights leaders now approached Randolph with the aim of organising such a march in order to show mass support for, and put pressure on Congress to pass, the Civil

Rights Bill. 1963 would be the centenary of Lincoln's Emancipation Proclamation, and a march that ended with speeches in front of the giant Lincoln Memorial in Washington would be highly symbolic.

Roy Wilkins of the NAACP was initially not keen, fearing that such a demonstration might not persuade Congress, while **John Lewis** of the SNCC would have preferred mass sit-ins in Washington. However, a compromise was reached, to which all the main civil rights leaders agreed, for a national protest. Two of the main demands would be for jobs and freedom, but passing the Civil Rights Bill was the priority. The director of the march was the 74-year-old Randolph, and Bayard Rustin, a long-term member of the NAACP, was the key organiser.

John Lewis (b. 1940):

Lewis participated in the Nashville sit-ins, the Freedom Rides and the voter registration campaign in Selma. He was co-founder of the SNCC, and he spoke at the March on Washington. He was also director of the Voter Education Project (VEP).

Organising the march

At first, President Kennedy – like most Americans – was opposed to the march. He feared that many more congressmen might oppose his bill if they felt they were being forced to pass it under threat. However, when he realised that all the key civil rights leaders were determined to go ahead, Kennedy decided to stamp his mark on the march and make sure it increased support for his Civil Rights Bill. The following agreements were made with the organisers:

- the date would be set for a Wednesday, not a weekend
- the organisers would try to attract as many whites as possible, including church and trade union leaders
- demonstrators would be encouraged to dress conservatively
- they would arrive by train and bus in the morning and depart the same day
- detailed programmes would outline the day's events
- the 'march' would consist of a short walk with speeches at the end.

DISCUSSION POINT

John Lewis complained that the march was becoming a 'march in, not on Washington'. What do you think he meant? Which of the agreements listed above do you think were the result of federal government demands? Explain why.

Bayard Rustin and a team of organisers spent weeks planning the march. Hundreds of volunteers were recruited to act as marshals, and it was agreed with the authorities that white police would be stationed around the edges to deter any white extremists. Hundreds of drinking fountains, toilets and First Aid stations would be set up (Washington in August is very hot and humid). A New York church agreed to send 80 000 cheese sandwiches.

The march was to be the first time that America (and the world) had seen such a massive black protest, so it had to be well organised. Congress was worried that there might be too many black protesters in one place, while Rustin was worried that there might be too few (under 100 000), and Robert Kennedy felt that a low turnout would not be good for the president as it was his Civil Rights Bill that needed support.

Rustin and King brought in Protestant ministers, Catholic priests and Jewish rabbis to be at the front of the march, as well as musicians including Bob Dylan to entertain the crowds before and during the speeches. The churches organised over 2000 'freedom' buses and 30 special trains. Police leave was cancelled, federal troops were to be on standby and liquor stores were closed.

The march, 28 August 1963: 'I have a dream'

In the event, the march passed off peacefully. A quarter of a million people attended, coming from Chicago, Detroit and New York as well as from Birmingham and other cities in the South. Most were middle class and black, but one quarter were white and there were clergy of all faiths. It was the biggest demonstration in US history. There were two hours of live music, mostly freedom songs (many of which were now popular among all classes and colours). Placards, all approved by the organisers, demanded 'Jobs for All', 'End Segregation' and 'Voting Rights Now'.

Figure 5.7: Martin Luther King at the March on Washington, 28 August 1963.

All the main civil rights leaders spoke. When John Lewis's speech was leaked the day before, there was enormous pressure on him to tone it down. The speech was critical of the Civil Rights Bill as too little, too late, and it spoke of marching through the South, 'leaving a scorched earth'. Randolph, the elder statesman of the movement, persuaded him to cut out the more inflammatory statements. Consequently, the sense of unity was preserved.

Although no women spoke, Randolph introduced the heroines of the movement such as Rosa Parks, Daisy Bates and Diane Nash. The white leader of the car-workers' union linked civil rights to the Cold War saying 'We cannot defend freedom in Berlin so long as we deny freedom in Birmingham.'

Last to speak was Martin Luther King. He evoked the memory of Lincoln and the Declaration of Independence in the famous 'I have a dream' speech, conveying his vision of an America where 'my four little children will one day live in a nation where they will not be judged by the color of their skin but by the content of their character'. A hugely passionate and charismatic man, King delivered a speech that was inspiring, spine-tingling and uplifting. At the end, there was a stunned silence – and then cheering and weeping.

The impact of the march

Most historians have seen the march as a resounding success. It was both peaceful and celebratory. It was broadcast live for three hours on US television and was widely covered in many other countries but not the USSR. Many Americans saw (some for the first time) blacks and whites united, marching together and saw that it was not threatening.

That evening, the TV networks all focused on King's speech in their news programmes and, from that point onwards, the American public saw King as the leader of the civil rights movement. However, this was not the case. The SCLC was only involved in a few campaigns. Local leaders did not need him. Some SNCC members mocked him as 'De Lawd'. Furthermore, many black militants were critical. **Malcolm X** described the march as the 'Farce in Washington… subsidised by white liberals and stage-managed by President Kennedy'.

> **Malcolm X (1925–1965):**
>
> Born Malcolm Little, a former thief, pimp and burglar, Malcolm X converted to Islam in prison and became a key figure in the Nation of Islam. A powerful preacher who criticised white America and advocated self-reliance and self-defence, he was accused by some of promoting anti-white racism and violence. He was assassinated by members of the Nation of Islam in 1965.

Nor did the march lead to a swift passing of the Civil Rights Bill. Many in Congress were not moved and southern Democrats were disappointed that Kennedy had supported the march. Malcolm X was correct when he claimed that no one in Congress changed their mind about the bill as a result of the march. In the South, segregationists remained as entrenched as ever. Less than three weeks after the march, a bomb was thrown into a church in Birmingham, killing four young black girls at Sunday School. This event shocked and sickened millions. Angry blacks rioted in Birmingham, attacking white shops and the police. The FBI launched a huge investigation, but it was not until 1977 that three members of a Ku Klux Klan splinter group were convicted.

However, an even greater shock was the assassination of President Kennedy in November. His successor, Lyndon B. Johnson, skilfully appealed to Congress to pass the bill as a tribute to the memory of Kennedy, and Johnson used all his years of experience as a senator to steer the Civil Rights Bill through Congress. It was eventually passed in July 1964 (see 6.3, Johnson and the Civil Rights Bill, 1964 and 6.3, The impact of events in Birmingham, 1963).

DISCUSSION POINT

There has been wide-ranging debate among historians on Martin Luther King's role within the civil rights movement. Some, such as Manning Marable, have played down his importance. Others, such as Steven Lawson, have said that we should 'not lose sight of the reality that King's presence had an enormous impact on how the movement progressed and was received'. How do you see the significance of King's role?

DISCUSSION POINT

The March on Washington received huge television coverage, but what was actually achieved? The historian Robert Cook believes 'it was a major triumph for the civil rights movement'. On the other hand, Manning Marable wrote that 'even the SCLC and NAACP experienced a bewildering sense of "What Next?" after the March' as, although it had been a clear success in terms of numbers, it had not led any segregationists to change their minds. Which view would you most agree with?

5.4 What was the Freedom Summer, 1964?

The 1964 Civil Rights Act banned segregation in schools and all public places, and incorporated measures for enforcement, but it did little to remove the obstacles that prevented blacks from voting. In Mississippi, the SNCC had campaigned since 1962 to increase voter registration among rural blacks (see 5.1, Campaigning for civil rights in Mississippi, 1961–63). This campaign was the most sustained and intensive of the whole civil rights movement, and it carried on despite intimidation, bombing, killing and lack of federal government support.

Then, in the summer of 1964, Bob Moses decided that a much bigger operation was needed, and more publicity was required in order to force the federal government to act. He called for hundreds of northern volunteers to come to Mississippi during their university vacation in order to get blacks to register to vote and to run summer schools for their children.

The majority of these students were white and many were from privileged backgrounds. Several went on to hold high office, such as governor of California and mayor of New York. Moses realised that attacks on whites would attract far more publicity than attacks on blacks, which were commonplace and often went unreported. Most of the volunteers came from liberal Democratic families. One volunteer said: 'I'm going because the worst thing after burning churches and murdering children is keeping silent.' Six hundred of these volunteers headed south for Mississippi's 'Freedom Summer'.

For white Mississippians, and especially the 6000-strong 'White Knights' of the KKK, this was an invading northern army. The state police force was doubled in size and more guns and gas masks were brought in. Meanwhile, on the civil rights side, the churches continued to teach their members how to register to vote and behave non-violently in the face of attack, and 'Freedom Schools' were set up to teach children about black history and literature.

'Mississippi Burning'

In June, the students received a week's training and were warned: 'You may be killed'. The Klan targeted three of the first volunteers: a black Mississippian and two whites from New York. When the three men went to investigate the burnt-out remains of a black church in Neshoba County, they were arrested.

The police took them in for questioning (on speeding charges) and informed the local Klan. When the volunteers were released, they were followed by three vehicles and no more was seen or heard of them. There was a national outcry.

President Johnson ordered a huge investigation and sent 200 sailors to help trawl the river and swamp where the bodies of the volunteers were thought to have been dumped. Thousands were questioned by FBI agents in what was codenamed 'Mississippi Burning'. The bodies were found a month and a half later.

Eighteen people were implicated but the state refused to prosecute. In 1967, the deputy sheriff and six others were convicted, albeit of the lesser charge of conspiring to violate the civil rights of the victims. Even so, this was the first time a Mississippi jury had convicted Klansmen in connection with the death of a black man.

Figure 5.8: Neshoba County deputy sheriff Cecil Price (right) and Edgar Ray Killen (left) appear in confident mood as they await the verdict in their trial for murder in 1967.

Despite the continuing violence, the work went on. The students organised black voter registration, wrote press releases and taught black children in Freedom Schools. For these volunteers, it was a transforming experience, a summer that changed them forever. According to activist Fannie Lou Hamer, many black Mississippians came to see that some 'white folks are human'.

That summer, three more civil rights workers were killed and eighty were attacked. There were numerous bombings but none of the white racists were convicted. Three thousand black children attended Freedom Schools, but only 1600 of their parents succeeded in registering to vote. Fear still prevented most from even making the attempt.

Theory of Knowledge

History and film:

The 1988 film *Mississippi Burning* is based on the search, by FBI agents, for the murderers of the three civil rights workers during the Freedom Summer of 1964. Research the reliability of the film and consider what use a film like this can be to students of the civil rights movement.

DISCUSSION POINT

The historian Adam Fairclough wrote that, for three years, 'Mississippi became the most sustained, intensive project of the entire Civil Rights Movement'. What justification is there for this view?

5.5 Why did Martin Luther King go to Selma in 1965 and what was achieved?

Voter registration in Selma, Alabama

Alabama, like neighbouring Mississippi, was a highly segregated society and the Civil Rights Act made little immediate difference. Schools, buses, hotels, restaurants, parks and swimming pools remained strictly segregated. In white neighbourhoods, the roads were paved. In black neighbourhoods, there were dirt roads.

In Dallas County, where the town of Selma is situated, only 1% of blacks were registered to vote. The registration office was only open on two Mondays per month, and the hours were very irregular: the office often opened late, shut its doors for long lunch hours and closed early. Even if applicants did turn up when the office was open, they were subject to long delays and had to answer lengthy questionnaires that included detailed questions on the Constitution. Even the slightest mistake meant disqualification. The registrar had the final say and he would always ask the question: 'Does your employer know y'all are here?' Intimidation kept most black people away.

In 1963, the SNCC had organised a voter registration campaign. Not surprisingly, it led to job dismissals and beatings, especially when photographs of applicants appeared in the newspapers. The organisers were accused of being 'communist agitators'. When the authorities banned public gatherings of more than three people, even an orderly queue of a few people became illegal. Not surprisingly, little progress was made.

In January 1965, local SNCC activist Amelia Boynton invited Martin Luther King to come to Selma. King saw Selma as a 'symbol of bitter-end resistance to the Civil Rights Movement in the Deep South'. A successful campaign would be a fitting tribute to the four girls killed in Birmingham the previous year.

Selma had other attractions, too. It already had a large, well-organised local campaign and hundreds of people attended its meetings. Furthermore, the sheriff, Jim Clark, was a hot-tempered racist, like Bull Connor (see section 5.1), who could be relied upon to act violently and attract the media.

King and other SCLC leaders were confident that they could provoke the kind of crisis that would attract the publicity needed to pressurise the federal government into passing a Voting Rights Act. Such a law, giving the federal government powers to override state authorities, could demolish all the obstacles that prevented blacks from voting.

Violence and imprisonment

In January 1965, King and SNCC leader John Lewis led a march to the courthouse in Selma where voter registration took place. At first, the sheriff herded the marchers peacefully into line but, the next day, he shoved a woman and the photograph appeared in the New York Times the next day. A week later, he elbowed a middle-aged woman, who hit him back before she was clubbed in return. Again, the photograph appeared in the press the next day.

Every day, a new wave of demonstrators arrived at the courthouse, singing 'Ain't Gonna Let Nobody Turn Me Around', and every day hundreds were arrested for gathering without a permit. As planned, King was one of those arrested.

The prisoners shared a broken toilet and slept on concrete floors. The floors were deliberately flooded and the heating was turned off, but the prisoners sang and clapped, all of which was reported in the press. Just as he had done in Birmingham, King wrote a letter from jail.

He sent it to the *New York Times* in the form of an advertisement. One of the sentences was written out in capitals: 'THIS IS SELMA, ALABAMA. THERE ARE MORE NEGROES IN JAIL WITH ME THAN ON THE VOTING ROLLS.'

At a nearby church in Selma, Malcolm X made a speech in which he warned whites that many blacks were less patient than King – in other words, the alternative to King was more threatening. Although Malcolm X was seen as a critic of King, he was, in effect, encouraging the non-violent approach to civil rights.

The demonstrations continued and, by February, 3000 protesters were in jail in Selma. Even the black teachers, normally the most conservative of the black professional classes, were persuaded to march – that, in turn, encouraged many more, especially their students. A federal judge now intervened, barring the registrar from using complicated registration tests and ordering him to enrol 100 per day when the office was open. Meanwhile, the violence continued: when the campaign was extended to a neighbouring county, state troopers smashed heads and ribs and shot dead a black army veteran, Jimmie Lee Jackson, who was trying to protect his mother from a beating.

The outrage caused by this event led to the decision to organise a march from Selma to Montgomery, the state capital, a distance of 87 km (54 miles) which would symbolically return King to where he began a decade earlier.

Bloody Sunday, March 1965

The march took place on Sunday 7 March and was led by the SCLC and SNCC. King was keen to be seen to work with the SNCC, which had done all the initial groundwork in Selma. Also, the leaders of both organisations wished to show a united front in order to strengthen their case for a Voting Rights Act.

More than 500 people set off, but they were blocked at the Edmund Pettus Bridge leading out of town by state police with batons and gas masks. The marchers were ordered to 'turn around and go back to your church'. Two minutes later, the police charged. Men and women, young and old, were mown down and gassed. Police on horseback then charged into the fleeing, falling demonstrators. Five women were left unconscious and 57 people were taken to hospital for treatment.

Most significant of all, as far as the organisers were concerned, the press and TV cameras were present in large numbers. Television programmes were interrupted to show scenes from what became known as 'Bloody Sunday', and 50 million viewers saw the violence and heard Sheriff Clark racially abusing the demonstrators.

A nationwide outcry followed. Thousands of petitions were sent to President Johnson, demanding action. Demonstrations took place in more than 80 cities across America. Over 100 senators and congressmen spoke out in favour of voting rights.

Figure 5.9: Police attack demonstrators in Selma, Alabama on Bloody Sunday, 7 March 1965.

In order to keep up the momentum and maintain the pressure on the federal government, King called upon religious leaders, of all denominations, to join him in 'a ministers' march' to Montgomery two days later. When the 1000 black and 450 white marchers reached the town bridge, they were again met by state police. They stopped to pray and then agreed to turn around and walk back.

Many accused King of a climb-down, but there was no loss of momentum or of publicity because that evening a white mob attacked three clergymen and one of them, a white northern minister called James Reeb, was so badly beaten that he died in hospital. The assailant (who had 26 arrests for assault) was found not guilty, amid rumours, circulated by Sheriff Clark, that the murder had been staged by a civil rights worker in order to win sympathy for the cause.

The response of the federal government

The impact of the murder of a white minister was massive. The outrage was such that President Johnson was forced to address Congress. In his televised speech, watched by 70 million people, he spoke with far greater passion than ever before. He said of the marchers: 'Their cause is our cause' and 'the Selma protest is a turning point in American history'.

He ended his speech, with the words of the most popular freedom song: 'We shall overcome' and so identified himself with the campaign.

Johnson's speech brought tears to King's eyes as he watched on television. Two days later, Johnson presented his Voting Rights Bill to Congress.

When the Democrat governor of Alabama, George Wallace, tried to ban the proposed march from Selma to Montgomery, on the grounds that it would disrupt traffic and cause disorder, a federal judge overrode him and gave authorisation for the march to go ahead. Johnson sent 2000 troops to protect the marchers, as well as planes and helicopters to deter bombers and snipers.

Not all of this was due to King. The situation in Washington was changing for a number of reasons. The mass media was now hugely supportive of the civil rights campaign, southern Democrats were no longer as strong in the Senate, black voting power in the north was greater, and as the historian Mary Dudziak powerfully argues, the Cold War context meant that the US government had to act in order to maintain America's image as the home of liberty and democracy.

Nevertheless, the Selma campaign put the voting rights issue right at the top of the political agenda, and opinion polls showed that there was widespread support for reform; indeed the historian Stephen Oates describes it as both the movement's finest hour and King's finest hour.

Figure 5.10: Young men march from Selma, Alabama to Montgomery, Alabama to demand the right for black people to vote.

The march from Selma to Montgomery

At its third attempt, the march set off on Sunday 21 March, two weeks after Bloody Sunday. Now there were 3000 marchers, led by King and including A. Philip Randolph and long-standing NAACP leader Roy Wilkins. There were church leaders representing Protestants, Catholics and Jews. Priests and nuns, preachers and rabbis marched together.

Along the road the usual abuse was hurled at the marchers and hate leaflets were dropped from a plane, but troops and army vehicles prevented outright violence. The marchers covered about 16 miles a day, singing and clapping for much of the time, and slept in camps on the side of the road overnight.

Volunteers drove out from Selma with supplies of food and drink. The Alabama legislature declared that the marchers were conducting wild interracial sexual orgies at their camps. SNCC leader John Lewis said, 'All these segregationists can think of is fornication and that is why there are so many shades of Negroes.'

On the last night, many celebrities (film stars and singers, black and white) turned up to show their support. A makeshift stage was erected and singers, comedians and actors entertained the marchers. Next day, there were rumours of snipers out to shoot King as he entered Montgomery, so a dozen similarly dressed black men, of similar height, were sent to the front of the march to surround King and act as decoys.

In the centre of the state capital, King made a characteristically uplifting and optimistic speech to 25 000 people, the biggest civil rights gathering in southern history. But there was still a white backlash: a white mother of five from Detroit, Viola Liuzzo, was shot dead at the wheel of her car as she gave a lift back to Selma to some of the marchers. An Alabama state jury acquitted the murderers who were all members of the Klan.

Most historians credit King with the success of the Selma march and the comparative speed with which the Voting Rights Act was subsequently passed. Yet Manning Marable criticises King for what happened on the second march. King had secretly agreed with the federal government that the marchers would not confront the police but would turn back at the bridge. SNCC leaders were furious and walked back into Selma singing 'Ain't Gonna Let Nobody Turn Me Around'. According to Marable, they felt betrayed, and one critic denounced King as an 'accomplice of the white power structure'. How far can this judgement be justified?

The Voting Rights Act, 1965

The march put great pressure on both the two main political parties, while opinion polls showed 75% in favour of a Voting Rights Act. In August 1965, Johnson finally signed the act in, in a ceremony held in the same place that Lincoln had signed the Emancipation Proclamation in 1861. The act banned the use of literacy and other tests for voter registration, and it gave the federal government the right to send in federal registrars if too few blacks were registered. This brought Alabama, Georgia, Louisiana, Mississippi and South Carolina under federal supervision.

The full, longer-term effects of the Voting Rights Act will be examined in the next chapter.

Paper 3 exam practice

Question

Evaluate the importance of non-violence in the African American civil rights campaign in the years 1960 to 1965. **[15 marks]**

Skill

Avoiding irrelevance

Examiner's tips

Do not waste valuable writing time on irrelevant material. If it is irrelevant, it will not gain you any marks. This problem can arise because:

- the candidate does not look carefully enough at the wording of the question (see Chapter 1)
- the candidate ignores the fact that the questions require selection of facts, an analytical approach and a final judgement; instead, the candidate just writes down all that they know about a topic (relevant or not), and hopes that the examiner will do the analysis and make the judgement
- the candidate has unwisely restricted their revision (for example, if a question crops up on the use of non-violence, rather than the expected one on the role of Martin Luther King, the candidate tries to turn it into the question he or she wanted!).

Whatever the reason, such responses rarely address any of the demands of the question asked.

For this question, you will need to:

- cover the use of non-violence in several campaigns during the relevant period (1960–65)
- assess the actual results of non-violence as well as of other policies, methods and tactics
- provide a judgement about whether the use of non-violence was the most important reason for the improvement in civil rights, or whether any other factors were more important.

Common mistakes

One common error with this type of question is for candidates to write about material they know well (such as Martin Luther King's belief in non-violence), rather than material directly related to the question (the use of non-violence in specific campaigns).

Another mistake is to present too much general information, instead of material specific to the command terms (material that enables evaluation).

Finally, candidates often elaborate too much on events outside the dates given in the question (see the guidance in Chapter 2).

Sample paragraphs of irrelevant focus/ material

The use of non-violence was crucial in improving civil rights in the early 1960s. Demonstrators were repeatedly attacked by white police and onlookers but they refused to hit back.

Martin Luther King had developed his theory of non-violence over many years. He was a committed Christian who believed in love and reconciliation and he was influenced by Mahatma Gandhi, who had organised massive demonstrations against British rule in India. Gandhi lived a simple life and dressed like an Indian peasant, which appealed to millions of Indian people because it showed he was very humble. Martin Luther King was also very humble, although he was not a Hindu like Gandhi. King had studied the Bible and the writings of many Christian philosophers before he became a church minister, and he believed in non-violence even when his house was bombed. His children could have been killed. In his final years, he criticised the use of military violence in Vietnam and said that more government money should be spent on peaceful, poor American citizens than on killing Vietnamese.

[There then follow two more paragraphs on the theory of non-violence before the candidate even begins to discuss its use in the campaign for civil rights from 1960 to 1965.]

EXAMINER'S COMMENT

This is an example of a weak answer. It starts off reasonably well, giving an indication of the candidate's belief in the importance of non-violence and how it works. There are a couple of lines on Martin Luther King's belief in non-violence that are relevant and helpful but then the essay loses its focus and veers off course, giving unnecessary detail on the life of Gandhi and King's criticism of the Vietnam War in the late 1960s.

The section marked in blue in the answer is irrelevant, and will not score any marks. In addition, the candidate is using up valuable writing time, which should have been spent on providing relevant points and supporting knowledge.

Activity

In this chapter, the focus is on avoiding writing answers that contain irrelevant material. Using the information from this chapter, and any other sources of information available to you, write an answer to one of the following Paper 3 practice questions, keeping your answer fully focused on the question asked. Remember: writing a plan first can help you maintain this focus.

Remember to refer to the simplified Paper 3 mark scheme given in Chapter 11.

Paper 3 practice questions

1   Compare and contrast the contributions of King and Kennedy to the civil rights movement in the years 1960 to 1965.

2   Evaluate the importance of southern opposition in obstructing African Americans from gaining their civil rights in the years from 1960 to 1965.

3 'The campaigns in Birmingham and Selma were the main reason why civil rights legislation was passed in 1964 and 1965.' To what extent do you agree with this statement?

4 Discuss the role of the SNCC, in the years from 1960 to 1965, in helping African Americans to gain their civil rights.

5 Examine the reasons for, and nature of, the role played by the media in the civil rights movement between 1960 and 1965.

6

The achievements of the civil rights movement by 1968

Introduction

This chapter weighs up the impact of the civil rights legislation of 1964 and 1965 in the US, fi nding that it had signifi cant eff ect in the South but far less in the cities of the North and West, where violence erupted. Martin Luther King's campaign against segregated housing in one of those cities, Chicago, had only limited success. The chapter assesses the achievements of King and of Presidents Kennedy and Johnson, and suggests that King's role was vital in winning over white America and the federal government, and that Johnson was far more committed and effective in addressing civil rights than Kennedy.

TIMELINE

1964 Jul: Civil Rights Act

1965 Aug: Voting Rights Act; riots in Watts district, Los Angeles

1966 Jun: James Meredith undertakes 'March against Fear'

Jul: Martin Luther King's Chicago campaign

1968 Poor People's Campaign

Apr: Assassination of Martin Luther King; Fair Housing Act

KEY QUESTIONS

- How successful was the civil rights legislation of 1964–65?
- Why was Martin Luther King less successful after 1965?
- Who achieved more for civil rights – Martin Luther King or the federal government?

Overview

- The Civil Rights Act of 1964 banned segregation in public places. Its impact was significant in the South but was less so in the North.
- The Voting Rights Act of 1965 swept away the obstacles that had prevented blacks from voting in the South.
- Both acts were more effectively implemented than any previous civil rights legislation since the Civil War.
- Martin Luther King attempted to address residential segregation in Chicago but achieved only limited success.
- King's assassination deprived the civil rights movement of its most effective spokesman.
- King's key contributions were to represent black America to white America, and particularly the federal government and to have kept the movement peaceful for so long.
- President Kennedy was reluctant to commit his government to reform, but was converted by the impact of events in Birmingham.
- President Johnson used his vast experience and political skill to steer major civil rights legislation through Congress.

6.1 How successful was the civil rights legislation of 1964–65?

The Civil Rights Act, 1964

The Civil Rights Act of 1964 virtually wiped out Jim Crow laws in one stroke. It banned segregation in schools, hospitals, hotels, restaurants, libraries and all other public accommodation. Businesses that employed more than 100 people were forbidden from practising racial discrimination and, within three years, this would apply to smaller businesses as well.

It established the Equal Employment Opportunity Commission, a permanent agency to investigate claims of racial discrimination. The Supreme Court moved quickly to uphold the act, in order to pre-empt any suggestion that it was unconstitutional.

Much racial segregation and discrimination had been illegal for many years, but now this was to be enforced by the federal government rather than state government. Black Americans would no longer have to file suits in the law courts to stop segregation. It was now the responsibility of the federal government to ensure that there was no segregation, and legal action was more likely to be quick, effective and unaffected by local bias.

There were also other ways in which the government could act: one of the most effective was by withdrawing federal funds from any school or business that failed to integrate. In the next two years, Johnson's government used federal funds to support educational authorities in the South in integrating their schools. By September 1965, 88% of school districts in the South had complied.

Unemployment among blacks remained higher than among whites, but a prosperous black middle class emerged in the 1960s. This may have happened anyway through measures such as the 1944 GI Bill which allowed returning black and white soldiers to have a free university education, but it was partly a result of better educational and economic opportunities that were enhanced by the Civil Rights Act and the federal government's greater willingness to enforce it.

The anger of northern blacks was evident in the urban riots of the mid 1960s, such as the Watts riot of 1965. These perplexed southern whites, who only saw evidence of improvement for blacks, especially as they began only five days after the Voting Rights Act was signed. Even in what had been the two most racist states, Alabama and Mississippi, nearly two-thirds of towns had desegregated their public accommodation (such as hotels, restaurants, libraries and parks) by the end of 1965.

By 1970, opinion polls suggested that the majority of southerners accepted the integration of public accommodation in the South. Great improvements for blacks undoubtedly took place, and whites adjusted to many of the changes brought about by the civil rights movement relatively easily. Even interracial marriage became far more accepted, particularly after the aptly named 1967 Supreme Court case *Loving versus Virginia*.

The one issue on which white attitudes were definitely not more liberal in the late 1960s was housing, expectations remained that black and white areas should be distinct and separate. This was particularly evident in Chicago during Martin Luther King's campaign in 1966. It was certainly one of the causes of inner-city bitterness and anger that led to unrest in the cities of the North and West in the mid to late 1960s.

After King's assassination and the subsequent riots in 1968, Congress provided the first real protection against racial discrimination in housing. The Fair Housing Act of 1968, which made it illegal to discriminate in the buying, selling and renting of residential property, was the final significant piece of 1960s civil rights legislation. It was a fitting tribute to King, who had worked so hard in the area in his final years.

Johnson knew that legislation alone could not ensure equality:

SOURCE 6.1

You do not take a person who, for years, has been hobbled by chains and liberate him, bring him up to the starting line of a race and then say, 'you are free to compete with all the others', and still justly believe that you have been completely fair… This is the next and the more profound stage of the battle for civil rights.

Extract from Lyndon B. Johnson's Commencement Address at Howard University 'To Fulfil These Rights', 4 June 1965.

QUESTION

What implications does the statement by Lyndon B. Johnson in Source 6.1 have for future federal policy?

Johnson favoured positive discrimination (or 'affirmative action') to help blacks. However, he came up against a white backlash that followed the riots in the mid 1960s, which showed the limits of the civil rights legislation of 1964 and 1965.

Neither Act had made much difference to the lives of black people in the ghettos of cities such as New York, Chicago, Los Angeles and Detroit. The blacks in these cities had been free to vote for many

years but remained stuck in poor housing, with poor schools and high
unemployment. In practice, they were no less segregated after the
legislation of the mid 1960s than they were before.

ACTIVITY

Writing about the impact of the civil rights legislation in the
South, the historian Manning Marable wrote: 'Jim Crow was
legally finished, yet black workers and sharecroppers were still
victims of bombings, lynchings and rapes... Black southerners had
the electoral franchise [from 1965] but what of economic security,
housing and the right to live without fear?' Why was economic
equality so much more difficult to achieve than political equality?

The Voting Rights Act, 1965

The Voting Rights Act of 1965 ensured that blacks were not prevented
from registering to vote and thus finally enforced the 15th Amendment
of 1870. In states where less than half of the adults had voted in the
1964 election, the law automatically suspended the use of literacy and
other tests. If too few blacks registered after the tests were suspended,
the federal government was empowered to send in federal registrars:
in this way, Alabama, Georgia, Louisiana and Mississippi were soon
brought under federal supervision. John Lewis said that the act was 'as
momentous as the Emancipation Proclamation'.

Within a month, 60% of Selma's blacks were registered and across the
South as a whole, the percentage of blacks who were registered to vote
rose from 35% in 1964 to 65% by 1969. The figures for four states in the
South are shown in Source 6.2:

SOURCE 6.2

Percentage of blacks registered to vote:

Year	Alabama	Georgia	Louisiana	Mississippi
1964	19.3	27.4	31.6	6.7
1968	61.3	60.4	60.8	67.5

Source: Marable, M. 1991. **Race, Reform and Rebellion.** *University Press of Mississippi, USA. p. 82.*

The whole tone of electoral politics therefore changed in the South: there were no more open declarations of race hatred and white supremacy by politicians whose electorate was now often 50% black, and for the first time since reconstruction black candidates became a feature of voting cards.

Voting power also brought political power. In just four years, from 1965 to 1969, the number of blacks elected to public office in the South increased six-fold. There was also a huge increase in the number of blacks elected to public office across the whole of the US. The act seemed to reinforce the change in public life throughout America.

SOURCE 6.3

Number of blacks elected to public office:

Year	In the South	In the whole of the US
1965	Less than 100	300
1970	500	1400

Figures from Sitkoff, H. 1982. **The Struggle for Black Equality.** *Hill & Wang, New York. p. 229.*

By 1977, more than 2000 blacks held office in the 11 southern states of the old Confederacy. They included two congressmen, 11 state senators, 95 state representatives, 67 mayors and 18 police chiefs. In 1979, former

SNCC worker Marion Barry became mayor of Washington, DC, while the cities of Los Angeles, Detroit and Atlanta also elected black mayors.

6.2 Why was Martin Luther King less successful after 1965?

After the Voting Rights Act was passed, Martin Luther King turned his attention to major Northern and Californian cities and to the very different challenge of desegregating the urban ghettos there. He and his SCLC colleagues decided to focus on Chicago. However, in the two years preceding King's Chicago campaign many of the ghettos had exploded in two summers of rioting.

Riots in Watts, Los Angeles, 1965

Five days after President Johnson signed the Voting Rights Act, a riot erupted in the black ghetto of Watts, Los Angeles, triggered by an arrest for drink-driving in which a black woman was roughly handled by the police. A crowd gathered, blows were exchanged, and stories spread of a woman having been beaten up by the police.

This was a city in which 65 blacks had been shot and killed by police in the previous two and a half years. There followed five days of rioting, often accompanied by chants of 'Burn, baby, burn!' The Watts riots were eventually suppressed by police and National Guardsmen, but 34 people, mostly black, were killed, 4000 were arrested and $40 million worth of damage was done.

It was described as the work of a mindless minority. Yet it was not mindless: most of the properties destroyed were white-owned stores that were thought to charge excessive prices for their goods. Like millions of others, Martin Luther King was shocked. He flew to Los Angeles to try to calm the situation, only to be heckled by teenagers who told him to 'go back where you came from'.

Figure 6.1: Buildings aflame in Watts during the five nights of rioting in the summer of 1965.

The severity of the Watts riots showed, very starkly, what little effect the recent civil rights legislation had on the lives of many urban blacks. The huge ghettos in the cities were far bigger than in any city in the South and economics led to segregation as whites moved to the growing suburbs.

About 4 million blacks had left the South for cities in the North and West between 1940 and 1965. In Watts, much of the old industry had declined, leading to high unemployment that was six times higher in Watts than the city average. New factories were being built on the outskirts of Los Angeles, but public transport (in a city where the majority, but not the poorest, had cars) was completely inadequate, making it difficult to travel to the suburbs where most of the new jobs were available. There was massive overcrowding, partly because a vast amount of land had been given away to the LA baseball team for a new stadium.

Many of the black residents, having migrated from the rural South, were poorly educated, either because they had only received a very basic schooling or because inner-city schools were overcrowded and inadequately resourced. The sewers stank in the hot summers because there was not enough water pressure to flush the toilets. In addition, there was no hospital in the area.

Martin Luther King in Chicago in 1966

This pattern of urban poverty and deprivation was replicated in many northern cities and, during the Selma campaign, Martin Luther King had vowed to march until 'Negroes and whites live side by side in decent, safe and sanitary housing'. In 1966, King and other SCLC leaders decided to target the city of Chicago.

This was a huge challenge. Selma had 15 000 black residents, Chicago had over 700 000 in a city of 3 million people. Most blacks voted for the Democratic Party, which was headed by Mayor Richard Daley. One of Chicago's congressmen was a black Democrat and, like some other black leaders, he did not welcome the SCLC. After all, King and his colleagues were southerners, used to campaigning in the very different conditions of the South. Nevertheless, a number of local black community leaders were keen for the SCLC to come to Chicago and inject new energy into their campaign for improved housing, education and increased employment opportunities.

In January 1966, King moved his family into a run-down apartment in one of Chicago's ghettos, keen to show that he was prepared to live alongside ghetto dwellers and share the same deprived conditions that they had to put up with. The landlord immediately brought in repair men fearing the media scrutiny, leading some of King's colleagues to joke that the best way for King to improve housing in Chicago would be to move from building to building all over the city.

King took reporters around rat-infested, unheated housing, and he led marches and demonstrations to put pressure on private landlords and city authorities. At one particular meeting, Mayor Daley promised to improve and integrate housing. Meanwhile, Daley's police showed great restraint: Daley was not going to invite adverse publicity for his city, as Bull Connor had done in Birmingham in 1963.

Nevertheless, some of the marches and demonstrations provoked disturbances, and many people attributed this violence to King's arrival. Many black businessmen as well as whites in Chicago and other northern cities were far less sympathetic to King than they had been in Selma or Birmingham. After all, black people in Chicago and New York were not deprived of the vote or subjected to attacks by the KKK like they were in the South.

March in Cicero neighbourhood

Yet King was still determined to highlight the existence of segregated housing and of all-white neighbourhoods. Many publicly funded housing projects were either all-black (in the ghetto) or all-white. In the field of private housing, King knew that estate agents steered black homebuyers away from white areas and that, if black families did move into all-white neighbourhoods, they came up against verbal and often physical abuse. He planned to lead a march into an all-white area, knowing that it would show up race hatred, attracting publicity and perhaps violent opposition, hoping that this might shame majority opinion into pressurising the authorities to enforce change.

The march, by black and white activists, would take place in Cicero, a white working-class Chicago neighbourhood. As expected, it provoked a hostile response from residents who feared that a black influx into their neighbourhood would lead to lower house prices and increased crime. The marchers were met by bottles and rocks and cries of 'apes' and 'savages'. King himself was hit by a rock and, of course, it made the national press. He later said that he 'had never seen, even in Mississippi, mobs as hostile and as hate-filled'.

King and the SCLC succeeded in highlighting the problems that faced black people living in the inner-city ghettos. Their campaign also showed why many urban blacks, especially among the younger generation, were attracted by appeals for Black Power (see Chapter 7). Blatant racism and the feeling of being hemmed into ghettos with poor, damp housing, overcrowded schools and high unemployment were fuelling the movement for Black Power. King understood the appeal of the movement and he praised Black Power's emphasis on self-esteem and black pride. Nevertheless, he remained constant in his philosophy of non-violence and for integration, which supporters of Black Power challenged.

King also recognised that the Chicago campaign had achieved little. Some concessions had been won and Johnson offered $4 million as a favour to Daley for improved housing. Operation Breadbasket, headed by a young SCLC recruit, Jesse Jackson, succeeded in putting consumer pressure on businesses to employ more blacks. However, Mayor Daley and the city authorities did not live up to their promises once King had left Chicago.

Above all, unlike in Birmingham and Selma, the federal government did not intervene. They felt no need to do so, as there were no TV pictures of police brutality. More significantly, Mayor Daley was one of the key figures in the national Democratic Party, and in the next mayoral elections he secured 80% of the black vote anyway.

DISCUSSION POINT

How much was achieved by the SCLC campaign in Chicago? Should the SCLC's expectations of the campaign have been different for a city in the North?

The Poor People's Campaign, 1968

Despite Chicago, King continued to speak out about the extent of inequality in American society and the lack of opportunities for all poor people, both black and white. Increasingly, he criticised the whole capitalist system; not just the federal, state and city authorities, but the landlords making profits out of substandard housing and the inner-city store owners charging excessive prices. Most significant of all, he became an outspoken critic of the Vietnam War, pointing out that 'it is estimated that we spend $500 000 to kill each enemy soldier, while we spend only fifty-three dollars for each person classified as poor'. (Later, he would go so far as to call the US 'the greatest purveyor of violence in the world today'.)

This antagonised President Johnson and Congress, who had spent billions on programmes to tackle poverty. It also alienated the majority of white Americans, who withdrew their support for civil rights following riots in several northern cities in the summers of the mid 1960s.

Although the broad coalition of civil rights groups was falling apart, King joined others in planning for a massive demonstration in Washington, DC, in 1968. He was the only black civil rights leader capable of attracting the wide range of support needed to carry the non-violent campaign of civil disobedience forward.

The Poor People's Campaign, as it came to be called, would involve the poor, both black and white, urban and rural, setting up camp right in the heart of the capital. The aim was to pressurise Congress into giving $30 billion of federal funds to economically depressed areas.

Figure 6.2: Martin Luther King (second-right) on the balcony of a Memphis motel on 3 April 1968. He was shot on the same balcony the next day.

King's assassination, April 1968

At the end of March, King was asked to lend his support to a strike by black garbage collectors, who were demanding equal treatment to their white counterparts, in Memphis, Tennessee. There he delivered a last and almost prophetic speech. The next day, 4 April, he was shot dead by a lone white racist.

The assassination of King led to a wave of rioting in over 100 American cities. The shock of the assassination also led Congress to pass an act to promote more integrated housing, although this only had a limited impact. The Poor People's Campaign soon came to an end, and the civil rights movement split further as the SCLC struggled to cope.

It had already achieved its main aims, of ending legal segregation and discrimination, and many of the most prominent white supremacists had left office or died, so it had lost its main targets and its unity of purpose. Now it had also lost its voice and its most charismatic leader.

Theory of Knowledge

History and commemoration:
Martin Luther King's birthday has been a public holiday in the US since 1986. How do you think it should be commemorated? What purpose does the commemoration serve for students of history? Does King deserve it, given that all US presidents only get a single-day public holiday to commemorate them?

6.3 Who achieved more for civil rights – Martin Luther King or the federal government?

The achievements of Martin Luther King

As the last section showed, King achieved far less in the last three years of his life than he had in the period from 1960–65. Historian Harvard Sitkoff wrote: 'despite good intentions, he had little success in desegregating the North, alleviating the misery of the impoverished or promoting world peace'. Another historian, Clayborne Carson, believes: 'If King had never lived, the black struggle would have followed a course of development similar to the one it did.' Yet it is hard to see the civil rights legislation of 1964 and 1965 being passed without him.

In the eyes of the vast majority of Americans, both black and white, King was the most effective leader of the civil rights movement. Even Ella Baker, who criticised the fact that so much praise was heaped on him rather than on the thousands of civil rights workers all over America, admitted that his contribution to the movement was massive.

King led by example, showing great courage and stamina in the face of opposition, assaults and threats of assassination. He had many spells in prison, often in harsh conditions. He was a superb communicator, both with other civil rights leaders and with the general public. With his unrivalled ability as a preacher and his appeal to Christian values, above all to the redemptive power of love, suffering and forgiveness, he captured his black audiences. With his appeal to American values, such as the belief in liberty, justice and democracy, he inspired millions, both black and white. In 1963 he was *Time* magazine's Man of the Year and in 1964 he was awarded the Nobel Peace Prize.

There were other, more militant activists, such as Malcolm X, who were well known, but it was King who, for more than a decade, attracted the national media. Thus, until the mid 1960s, it was the non-violence, the carefully planned confrontations, the positive role of religion, and the faith in the all-important role of government that was emphasised in the press and on television.

Many African American leaders had contacts in government. The NAACP continued, successfully, to bring cases to the Supreme Court, and its leaders, such as Roy Wilkins, regularly had access to officials in the White House and lobbied Congress. The SNCC kept in touch with the Justice Department, particularly attorney general Robert Kennedy, in the early 1960s. Black politicians such as New York Congressman Adam Clayton Powell pushed for legislation within Congress. But Martin Luther King undoubtedly had the greatest influence in Washington and, ultimately, that was crucial to the passing of the civil rights legislation of the mid 1960s.

The breakthrough legislation of 1964 and 1965 could not have been achieved without the work of thousands of activists campaigning at local and regional levels such as the SNCC in Mississippi. They constituted the nationwide core of support for civil rights, without which King and the other leaders could not have exerted such force on the federal government. What King did with such great skill was to present the local dramas to a national audience. In playing the media, he was as skilled as any politician and far better than most.

Once he and the SCLC had selected a campaign, they used non-violence in order to provoke violence ('creative tension', King called it). They also learned from their mistakes in Albany and adapted their tactics so they worked in subsequent campaigns in places such as Birmingham and Selma when the police subjected the demonstrators to violence. This was captured on television and shown nationally and internationally, thus forcing Kennedy and then Johnson to act. The role of these presidents and of the federal government will now be examined.

KEY CONCEPTS QUESTION

Significance: 'The movement made Martin, Martin didn't make the movement.' To what extent do you agree with Ella Baker's perspective on Martin Luther King's importance to the civil rights movement?

KEY CONCEPTS ACTIVITY

Significance: Ella Baker's famous quote about Martin Luther King is a tacit criticism of the 'Great Man' view of history originally put forward by Thomas Carlyle who said, 'The history of the world is but the biography of great men'. Research historians' opinions on King and his significance – you might start with Peter Ling, Godfrey Hodgson, Manning Marable, Clayborne Carson, Howard Zinn, Mary Dudziak and Taylor Branch.

President Kennedy's role in civil rights

In this section, the contributions made by Presidents Kennedy and Johnson to the achievement of African American civil rights will be considered. In the popular view, typical of the hundreds of books published on the 50th anniversary of Kennedy's death in 2013, Kennedy has been portrayed as a champion of civil rights. Closer examination suggests his legacy is not as clear cut, presenting another challenge to 'Great Man' history.

When campaigning for the presidential election in 1960, John F. Kennedy said segregation was immoral and damaged America's international image. He promised that he would abolish segregation in housing projects funded by the federal government.

During the campaign in October 1960, when Martin Luther King was sentenced to four months of hard labour in prison in Atlanta, Kennedy telephoned King's pregnant wife to express his sympathy, while his brother Robert called the judge and managed to secure King's release. The increase in black support that this earned him may have made all the difference in the November election, which Kennedy won by the closest of margins. Certainly, black Americans had high hopes for the new, young president.

Figure 6.3: President John F. Kennedy urges Congress not to permit segregation, Washington, DC, 8 March 1961.

At first, John F. Kennedy gave the impression he would be a great champion of civil rights. He maintained contact with several leaders of the civil rights movement, especially King. He appointed more African Americans to official positions than any previous president, including five black federal judges, one of whom was Thurgood Marshall. He also set up the Equal Opportunities Commission.

However, Kennedy also appointed some segregationists to judicial positions in the South: one of them referred to black people in court as 'chimpanzees'. He had promised, before his election, to get rid of segregation in federal housing projects 'at the stroke of a pen' – but it was only after two years and the receipt of thousands of pens from protesters that he passed what was a very weak measure.

Kennedy and the Freedom Rides, 1961

As stated in Chapter 5, Kennedy was reluctant to intervene on behalf of the Freedom Riders. Like Eisenhower before him, he believed it was up to state authorities to maintain law and order and, therefore, to protect the riders. Also, Kennedy did not want to alienate southern Democratic voters who he would need to win a second term.

Eventually, he was forced to intervene when the attacks on the riders intensified and were directed at whites as well as blacks. However, he did not publicly support the actions of the riders or protest against their imprisonment. Instead, the Kennedy administration established the Voter Education Project to fund programmes to increase the number of registered black voters. They hoped that this might divert attention away from the disorder created by the rides, increase the number of Democratic voters and avoid alienating white southern Democrats.

The impact of events in Birmingham, 1963

All in all, Kennedy's government did comparatively little for African American rights in its first two years in power. The events of 1963, particularly the campaigns initiated by the SCLC, would force Kennedy's hand. The incidents in Birmingham, Alabama, were given extensive, nationwide publicity and Kennedy himself said he felt 'sick' when shown the photographs of police dogs attacking peaceful civil rights marchers, many of whom were teenagers.

With public opinion increasingly calling for federal intervention, Kennedy faced mounting pressure. This pressure did not only come from within the US. The secretary of state (foreign minister) referred to white supremacy as 'the biggest single burden that we carry on our backs in foreign relations'. The prime minister of Uganda, supported by several other black African leaders, sent an open letter to Kennedy in which he condemned the attacks on 'our own kith and kin'.

In June, Kennedy sent a Civil Rights Bill to Congress. It guaranteed equal access to public buildings, schools and jobs. It also threatened a loss of federal funds for state and local agencies that continued to practise segregation and discrimination. Kennedy had finally come out strongly in support of civil rights.

The March on Washington, 1963

Civil rights leaders knew they had to maintain the pressure on the federal government if Congress was to pass Kennedy's bill. Kennedy was opposed to the march but he told his advisers: 'If we can't stop it, we'll run the damn thing'. The climax of the march was changed from the Capitol building, where Congress met, to the Lincoln Memorial, where marchers could be cordoned off on three sides by water.

Other changes were also made. It was even said that government officials planned to play 'He's Got the Whole World in His Hands', a civil rights song, through the loud speakers, if any speech became too inflammatory. In effect, the Kennedy government converted the demonstration from a protest against federal inaction into a rally in favour of its own Civil Rights Bill. However, when the president was assassinated three months later, the Civil Rights Bill was still stuck in Congress.

On balance, Kennedy was reluctant to give overt support to the civil rights movement. He made symbolic gestures, such as appointing many more black officials than any previous president had and resigning from a segregated country club, but he only committed himself to major legislation when faced by the pressure of events at home, such as in Birmingham, and, to a lesser extent, abroad.

President Johnson's role in civil rights

Lyndon B. Johnson, Kennedy's vice-president, succeeded him as president. Already a highly experienced politician (he had been Texas senator for 15 years), he was determined to push through Kennedy's civil rights legislation. He had his own vision of a 'Great Society' and of 'an end to poverty and racial injustice'.

Johnson had started his working life teaching Mexican Americans and he saw the damage that poverty, prejudice and poor schooling could do. He knew that racial tension discouraged business investment and that desegregation would bring economic improvement to the South. He supported the Supreme Court ruling in the *Brown* case in 1954, and was one of the few southern politicians who had not signed the Southern Manifesto. Even if it meant alienating southern Democrats, Johnson was determined, as a tribute to Kennedy, to pass his Civil Rights Bill.

Johnson and the Civil Rights Bill, 1964

After years of experience in the Senate, Johnson was skilled at negotiation. He made deals in order to get his bill passed through Congress. He needed Republican support as he knew many southern Democrats would vote against the bill. The Republican leader in Congress was promised federal money for a project in his home state of Ohio.

Outside Congress there was increased public support for civil rights, and a wide cross-section of religious leaders – Protestant ministers, Catholic priests and nuns, and rabbis – lobbied Congress.

In July 1964, the Civil Rights Act was passed. Stronger than Kennedy's bill, it banned segregation in all public places. The Equal Employment Opportunities Commission was pushed forward to monitor and enforce progress. And it was backed up by rulings in the Supreme Court, thus pre-empting any challenges about its constitutionality.

The FBI's dirty tricks

Not all branches of the federal government were as supportive of civil rights as the president and Congress. The director of the Federal Bureau of Investigation (FBI), J. Edgar Hoover, saw Martin Luther King as a communist sympathiser (some civil rights workers had undoubtedly been members of the Communist Party).

In Kennedy's time, Hoover had received permission from Robert Kennedy to tap King's phone. (Both Kennedys believed they had to be seen as being strongly anti-communist. Also, they suspected that Hoover knew of JFK's extra-marital affairs, which could be seen as a security risk and therefore subject to investigation.) Hoover had also bugged the hotel rooms in which King had stayed.

When King was awarded the Nobel Prize in 1964, Hoover called him 'the most notorious liar in the country'. The FBI sent King a parcel of recordings (supposedly of illicit sexual behaviour) from his hotel rooms, with an unsigned note recommending suicide.

Figure 6.4: President Lyndon Johnson (right) with J. Edgar Hoover.

Johnson and the Voting Rights Act, 1965

After the passing of the Civil Rights Act, Johnson turned to his advisers and said: 'we have delivered the South to the Republican Party'. Indeed, in the presidential elections of November 1964, the southern states of Alabama, Georgia, Louisiana, Mississippi and South Carolina all turned against the Democrats. However, Johnson won every other state except Arizona in a landslide victory in which he gained 94% of the black vote. Johnson was now in a far stronger position, with Democratic majorities in both houses of Congress.

Johnson prepared a Voting Rights Bill to ensure that the 15th Amendment was finally enforced and black people were able to vote in every state. Meanwhile, the civil rights campaigners kept up the pressure. In Selma, Alabama, Martin Luther King led a voter registration drive in one of the most racist regions in America (see section 5.5). With thousands of demonstrators in prison, violence escalating and support for voting reform increasing, Johnson addressed Congress to call for an end to black disenfranchisement.

Just as events in Birmingham in 1963 had forced Kennedy's hand, so now Selma forced the pace over voting reform. The Voting Rights Act was passed in August 1965. The act swept aside all obstacles to voter registration, and its effect was immediate. On 14 August, in Selma, 381 black people were enrolled by federal registrars.

Johnson's record on civil rights

Although increasingly preoccupied with the war in Vietnam, Johnson continued to support civil rights after 1965. He used federal funding to speed up school desegregation in the South, and his Higher Education Act of 1965 provided extra funding for poor black colleges.

It was largely due to Johnson's government that the number of black college students increased fourfold in the 1960s. However, he came up against a growing white backlash after the Watts and other riots, while King's Chicago campaign showed how strong northern white racism was. Even white liberals demanded that black people 'quiet down' and 'accept' the gains they had made.

The Kerner Commission, which was set up by Johnson to investigate the causes of the urban riots, blamed white racism – especially in the police – for much of the violence. Rather depressingly, its conclusion echoed *Plessy versus Ferguson*, saying that: 'Our nation is moving toward two societies, one black, one white – separate and unequal.' Nevertheless, the verdict of many black people and of most historians has been favourable in assessing Johnson's record on civil rights.

When Johnson died and his body lay in state in Washington, 60% of those who paid their respects were black. The NAACP activist Clarence Mitchell declared that Johnson had 'made a greater contribution to giving a dignified and hopeful status to Negroes in the United States than any President including Lincoln, Roosevelt and Kennedy.'

In putting the role of the federal government in context, the historian Steven Lawson wrote:

SOURCE 6.4

The federal government made racial reform possible, but Blacks in the South made it necessary. Had they not mobilised their neighbours, opened their churches to stage protests and sustain the spirits of the demonstrators, and rallied the faithful to provoke a response from the federal government, far less progress would have been made. Thus, the real heroes of the civil rights struggle were the Black foot soldiers and their white allies who directly put their lives on the line in the face of often overwhelming odds against them. Federal officials were not heroes yet they proved essential for allowing the truly courageous to succeed.

Lawson, S. and Payne, C. 1998. **Debating the Civil Rights Movement, 1945–1968.** *Lanham, USA. Rowman & Littlefield. p. 42.*

QUESTION

Does Source 6.4 give a fair assessment of the significance of the role of the federal government in the civil rights movement?

The second discussion point in this chapter asked you to consider the 'Great Man' theory of history in relation to King. Steven Lawson's interpretation (Source 6.4) strongly emphasises the role of the 'Black foot soldiers and their white allies', the thousands of ordinary people who collectively made up the civil rights movement and forced the federal government to act. As Lawson says, it was the actions of these grassroots protesters that made civil rights reform 'necessary', and the government that made it 'possible'.

ACTIVITY

The last few sections have focused on the roles of Presidents Kennedy and Johnson in the 1960s. In order to deepen your understanding of the role of the federal government as a whole, and over a longer period, read the following interpretations (Sources 6.5 and 6.6) of the civil rights movements and decide which one you think is more accurate.

SOURCE 6.5

The American South had a long tradition of racial oppression but, during the civil rights movement, the weight of federal institutions – the presidency, the judicial system, the media, the American sense of fair play – were finally brought to bear on the problem, leading to remarkable changes in southern race relations.

Adapted from Lawson, S. and Payne, C. 1998. **Debating the Civil Rights Movement, 1945–1968.** *Lanham, USA. Rowman & Littlefield. p. 99.*

SOURCE 6.6

Right now, all over the nation, the struggle for negro equality is expressing itself in marches, demonstrations and sit-ins. It seems very clear to me that these people are protesting against something more than the denials and humiliations that they have suffered. They are protesting about the failure of the legal system to respond to the legitimate grievances of our citizens. They are protesting because the very procedures supposed to make the law work justly have been changed into obstructions that prevent it from working at all.

Adapted from a speech given by Robert Kennedy to the Missouri Lawyers Association on 27 September 1963.

QUESTION

Compare and contrast the views expressed in Sources 6.5 and 6.6 about the role of the federal institutions in addressing civil rights.

Summary

The period from 1964 to 1968 saw huge strides made in the fight for African American civil rights as the landmark legislation of 1964 and 1965 finally ended the influence of *Plessy versus Ferguson* and the last remnants of Jim Crow. The achievement required a concerted effort by both President Kennedy in introducing the 1964 Civil Rights Act before his death and President Johnson in pushing it through, but it also required a final push on the part of the civil rights activists. However, the achievement of legal and political rights was always the easy part of the campaign; it should not be forgotten that the March on Washington was for both 'Jobs' and 'Freedom'.

Legal and political freedom had been attained with enormous effort, but it had been relatively cheap to provide. The cost of addressing economic inequality was far greater and proved beyond the scope of King's influence and strategy, faced as he was with a backdrop of increasing US involvement in Vietnam and increasing frustration on the part of his fellow movement members.

Paper 3 exam practice

Question

To what extent were the interventions of Presidents Kennedy and Johnson the most important reason for the passing of the civil rights legislation of 1964–65? **[15 marks]**

Skill

Avoiding a narrative-based answer

Examiner's tips

Even once you have read the question carefully (and so avoided the temptation of including irrelevant material), produced your plan and written your introductory paragraph, it is still possible to go wrong.

By 'writing a narrative answer', history examiners mean providing supporting knowledge which is relevant (and may well be very precise and accurate) *but* which is not clearly linked to the question. Instead of answering the question, it merely **describes** what happened.

The main body of your essay/argument needs to be **analytical**. It must not simply be an 'answer' in which you just 'tell the story'. Your essay **must address the demands/key words of the question**. Ideally, this should be done consistently throughout your essay, by linking each paragraph to the previous one, in order to produce a clear 'joined-up' answer.

You are especially likely to lapse into a narrative answer when answering your final question – and even more so if you are getting short of time. The 'error' here is that, despite all your good work at the start of the exam, you will lose sight of the question and just produce an account, as opposed to an analysis. Even if you are short of time, try to write several analytical paragraphs.

Note that a question that asks you the extent to which you agree with a statement expects you to come to judgements about the success or failure or the relative importance of a factor or individual, or the accuracy of a statement. You need to provide a judgement on the views expressed in the statement. Very often, such a question gives you the opportunity to refer to different historians' views (see Chapter 7 for more on this).

A good way of avoiding a narrative approach is to refer back to the question continually, and to use the wording of the question in your answer. That should help you to produce an answer that is focused on the specific aspects of the question – rather than just giving information about the broad topic or period.

For this question, you will need to cover the following reasons for the passing of the civil rights legislation:

- the roles of both Kennedy and Johnson
- the role of Martin Luther King, for example in the March on Washington and in the Birmingham and Selma campaigns
- the importance of sit-ins, Freedom Rides and other grassroots activism in mobilising support and putting pressure on the federal government.

You will then need to make a judgement in your conclusion.

Common mistakes

Every year, even candidates who have clearly revised well, and therefore have a good knowledge of the topic and of any historical debate surrounding it, still end up producing a mainly narrative-based or descriptive answer. Very often, this is the result of not having drawn up a proper plan.

The following extracts from a student's answer show an approach that essentially just describes the roles of Kennedy and Johnson, without any analysis of whether they were the most important reason for the passing of the legislation.

Sample paragraphs of narrative-based approach

This example shows what examiners mean by a narrative answer – it is *not* something you should copy!

President Kennedy was very important in passing civil rights laws because he supported Martin Luther King. For instance, he rang his wife when she was pregnant and King was in jail. He appointed many black people to positions in his government, and he sent troops to Montgomery at the time of the Freedom

Rides. He said he was sickened by the sight of police dogs attacking peaceful demonstrators in Birmingham. He went on television and sent a Civil Rights Bill to Congress. If he had not been killed, he would have persuaded Congress to pass the Bill.

President Johnson achieved even more. He was a very experienced politician and, although he came from the South, he supported civil rights. He pushed the Civil Rights Bill through Congress by persuasion and arm-twisting. Then, in 1965, after Bloody Sunday, he also went on television and said he would make it possible for all blacks to vote. He passed the Voting Rights Act.

[The rest of the essay continues in the same way – there are plenty of accurate, relevant facts about the actions of Kennedy and Johnson, and there is some reference to the campaigns in Birmingham and Selma, but there is no attempt to answer the question by examining the role of other people or assessing whether Kennedy and Johnson were most responsible for passing the legislation.]

Activity

In this chapter, the focus is on avoiding writing narrative-based answers. Using the information from this chapter, and any other sources of information available to you, try to answer one of the following Paper 3 practice questions in a way that avoids simply describing what happened.

Remember to refer to the simplified Paper 3 mark scheme given in Chapter 11.

Paper 3 practice questions

1   Examine the impact of the civil rights legislation of 1964–65 in improving civil rights for African Americans?

2   Compare and contrast the roles of Martin Luther King and the federal government in the African American civil rights movement in the 1960s.

3 Discuss the impact of grassroots campaigners on the civil rights movement.

4 To what extent do you agree that the civil rights legislation of 1964–65 had a major impact on African American civil rights in the South but made little difference in the North?

5 Evaluate the impact of Martin Luther King on the campaign for African American civil rights after 1965.

The growth of Black Power in the 1960s

7

Introduction

This chapter examines why splits occurred in the civil rights movement in the US in the mid 1960s, in particular why some members of the SNCC (Student Nonviolent Coordinating Committee) became disillusioned with the non-violent, integrationist approach. It then evaluates the career and importance of Malcolm X. Finally, it discusses the meaning of Black Power.

TIMELINE

1959 TV documentary *The Hate that Hate Produced* brings Malcolm X to national attention

1963 Malcolm X suspended by Nation of Islam over comments on John F. Kennedy's assassination

1964 **Mar:** Malcolm X leaves Nation of Islam

Mar: Mississippi Freedom Democratic Party (MFDP) ignored at Democratic Party convention

1965 **Feb:** Malcolm X assassinated in New York

1966 **May:** Stokely Carmichael elected chairman of SNCC

Jun: Meredith March and emergence of idea of 'Black Power'

Oct: Black Panthers founded in Oakland, California

KEY QUESTIONS

- What caused the civil rights movement to change?
- How significant was Malcolm X?
- What were the consequences of the Black Power movement?

Overview

- Disillusionment set in among some SNCC members during the Freedom Summer of 1964.
- The SNCC and CORE (the Congress of Racial Equality) became more militant, distancing themselves from King and the mainstream civil rights movement.
- Malcolm X voiced the anger and bitterness of many urban blacks in the North.
- The impact of Malcolm X, as a black leader, was second only to that of Martin Luther King.
- 'Black Power' emerged in 1966 and was particularly associated with the name of Stokely Carmichael. It emphasised black racial pride and, for some, armed self-defence.

7.1 What caused the civil rights movement to change?

Even at the height of its success, in 1963–65, the civil rights movement was showing signs of strain and a lack of unity. This became particularly evident during the Mississippi Freedom Summer of 1964 (see 5.4).

Disillusionment and the Freedom Summer of 1964

The Mississippi Freedom Summer campaign of voter registration caused some division among civil rights workers. In particular, the involvement of over 900 northern, white, student volunteers, was resented by some SNCC field workers. They saw the students as 'fly-by-night freedom fighters', privileged whites who were only there for the summer.

For the SNCC workers and the black population of Mississippi, the bombings and lynchings would continue. Some objected that the white student volunteers took over many of the responsibilities that local blacks had done, undermining black self-confidence and perpetuating the stereotype of black inferiority. Some SNCC workers began to criticise the integrationist approach and the requirement for blacks and whites to work together.

Furthermore, as white violence against blacks continued, some SNCC workers decided to carry guns. They were beginning to lose faith in non-violent protest; they now felt that violence should be met with violence. Despite President Johnson's promises, the FBI was not doing enough to protect civil rights workers and the black population. What deepened the disillusionment of many SNCC workers, however, was what happened to the Mississippi Freedom Democratic Party (MFDP).

The treatment of the Mississippi Freedom Democratic Party, 1964

Elections were to be held in 1964, and President Johnson hoped to be elected in November and receive a mandate for change. But first he would have to be chosen as the Democratic Party's candidate.

The process of selecting the candidate would culminate in the national convention in Atlantic City, New Jersey. Each state would send a delegation (group of representatives) of its party members and they would then vote to approve the nomination of Johnson to contest the presidency on behalf of the Democratic Party. Not surprisingly, all of Mississippi's 68 delegates were white, so the SNCC and other activists established the Mississippi Freedom Democratic Party (MFDP) in order to provide an alternative to the official delegation. 80 000 members were enrolled and the MFDP's delegation, containing blacks *and* whites, was then freely elected. Claiming to be the truly democratic delegation, it demanded its right to represent the state's Democratic Party at the convention, challenging the legitimacy of the Dixiecrats.

The MFDP delegation backed Johnson as their candidate, but Johnson was worried about losing white support right across the South if he supported the MFDP. He expected to be chosen as presidential candidate, and the last thing he wanted to spoil his victory was a race row. Besides, he was confident that America's blacks would vote for him in the election anyway. His Civil Rights Act had just passed Congress, while his War on Poverty programme would help millions of poor black people.

The War on Poverty had been 'declared' by Johnson during his State of the Union address on 8 January 1964. It contained a range of measures on healthcare, education and welfare that attempted to create a 'Great Society'. Though the focus of the legislation wasn't exclusively on black people they made up a substantial proportion of the those in poverty and research suggested this was 19% of the population.

Eventually, the MFDP was pressured into agreeing that the all-white Democrats should be the official delegation, in return for the compromise solution of two members of the MFDP being given non-speaking, non-voting seats at the convention.

Worse still, from the point of view of many activists, was that Martin Luther King and other SCLC leaders agreed to the 'compromise', confident that the continuing non-violent campaign and the policy of working with, not against, the Democratic government in Washington would bring more reform.

For many SNCC activists, especially those who had suffered violence in the Freedom Summer, this was a betrayal. One SNCC worker described it as 'the end of innocence'. Many in the organisation lost faith in the Democratic Party, in white liberals and in Martin Luther King.

DISCUSSION POINT

Re-read the section on the Mississippi Freedom Summer of 1964 in Chapter 5. What conclusions do you think the SNCC would draw from their experience in Mississippi?

The SNCC and CORE become more militant

One of those SNCC workers who became increasingly disillusioned and radical was **Stokely Carmichael**. In 1965, he led a voter registration drive in Lowndes County, Alabama. Four-fifths of the population in this remote rural area was black, but racial discrimination and white terror were widespread and the 1964 civil rights legislation had made little difference. Impressed by the militancy of local black leaders, Carmichael persuaded them to set up their own organisation, the Lowndes County Freedom Organization (LCFO), determined to meet white violence with armed resistance. All of its members were black and its symbol was a snarling black panther.

Stokely Carmichael (1941–98):

Born in the West Indies, Carmichael graduated from all-black Howard University in Washington, DC, in 1964. He became an SNCC worker and organised voter registration drives in the South and by 1966 had been arrested 27 times. He criticised the non-violent, integrationist approach to civil rights before becoming SNCC chairman in 1966. He popularised the term 'Black Power', which had threatening connotations for whites compared with the non-violence of King.

Meanwhile, CORE was active in campaigning for voter registration in Louisiana. Their meetings and demonstrations were patrolled and protected by the Deacons for Defense and Justice. Mostly made up of black army veterans, the Deacons were the first organised, armed black group in the South. The LCFO and the Deacons provided links from the rural South to the militant black nationalism that was emerging in the North and used the speeches of the recently assassinated Malcolm X to justify their stance.

Figure 7.1: Stokely Carmichael – who popularised the term 'Black Power' – in 1968.

By the time of the Watts riots in August 1965, the SNCC and CORE were becoming less committed to non-violence and integration with whites. In the South, the bombings and lynchings continued; SNCC worker Julius Lester expressed what many felt: 'The days of singing freedom songs and the days of combating bullets and clubs with love are over.'

While the NAACP and the SCLC felt that the federal government was finally delivering on its promises, the SNCC was distancing itself both from the former two and the Democratic government. Furthermore, increasing opposition to US involvement in the Vietnam War was causing more divisions in the civil rights movement. In July 1965, the SNCC declared that blacks should not 'fight in Vietnam for the white man's freedom until all the Negro people are free in Mississippi'.

The only civil rights leader who could maintain any kind of unity between the different organisations was Martin Luther King. However, non-violent protest could only be sustained by hope and optimism, and in the North, by the mid 1960s (as King discovered in Chicago), bitterness and disillusionment were widespread.

The historian Adam Fairclough quotes a student in Harlem, New York, who told visitors from Mississippi: 'Turning the other cheek is a load of trash. Up here we understand what snake is biting us.' Fairclough says: 'This was the language of Malcolm X, not Martin Luther King.'

7.2 How significant was Malcolm X?

No black leader, apart from Martin Luther King, had greater impact on America in the late 1950s and early 1960s than Malcolm X. No black leader instilled more fear in white America and no black leader more eloquently voiced the anger and despair of urban blacks, especially the young, more effectively than Malcolm X. Yet, when he was killed in 1965, he left behind no programme or plan of action, no mass-based, lasting organisation to carry on his work. So how significant *was* he?

In contrast to King, Malcolm X had a disrupted, insecure and unhappy childhood. Brought up in the Midwest, his father was a Baptist lay preacher and follower of Marcus Garvey (see section 3.4) but was killed when Malcolm was six. The cause was said to be a tram car accident, but Malcolm later believed it was the work of white racists. His family broke up and he was sent to a foster home. Malcolm was a bright child but, in a formative moment, when he said he wanted to become a lawyer, he was told by his English teacher that this wasn't a realistic goal because of his colour.

At 15, he was expelled from school and went to live with his half-sister in Boston. He took the usual jobs of unskilled blacks in the ghetto – shoe-shine boy and waiter – before drifting into a life of drugs, pimping and gambling. In 1946, he was jailed for burglary.

Prison changed him. He read a lot, especially on the history of black people in America, and he converted to the Nation of Islam (NOI), a black American religious organisation often referred to as the Black Muslims. His reading and his new faith gave him a sense of purpose, and also the conviction that all his personal failures and family tragedies were caused by white racists. Released from prison in 1952, he called himself Malcolm X, with the X representing the African name he never had. He launched himself into preaching and recruiting people to the NOI, becoming a favourite of the Nation's leader, Elijah Muhammad.

He portrayed himself as the spokesman of the oppressed black masses, especially in the urban ghettos: 'I'm one of those 22 million black people who are the victims of Americanism.' He criticised the 'so-called Negro leaders' and their policy of non-violent integration with white people: 'the black man in America will never be equal to the white man as long as he attempts to force himself into his house'. He said that the only way to overcome 300 years of domination by 'white devils' was for black Americans to take control of their own lives, to rely on self-help, and to defend their own communities. Black people should stop 'begging' the system for 'jobs, food, clothing and housing'.

In expressing the anger and frustration of urban blacks, he made some extreme statements: he predicted racial warfare and a 'day of slaughter for this sinful white world'. Lashing out at black Christian leaders, he said, 'churches should be bombed and preachers killed'.

The Hate That Hate Produced

In 1959, a television documentary about the Nation of Islam was shown. *The Hate That Hate Produced* showed how the anti-black feelings of white supremacists had led to the backlash represented by people such as Malcolm X who was interviewed. The NOI was portrayed as a virulently racist army of black fanatics. When challenged about teaching 'racial hatred', Malcolm X said he was not teaching 'hatred but the truth, that the "black man" has been enslaved in the United States by the "white man"'.

The media spotlight focused on the threat of violence but also on X himself who came over as measured, intelligent, tall and handsome. Very few whites learnt of the Black Muslims' success in rescuing and rehabilitating poor blacks from lives of crime and persuading them to embrace such traditional American values as hard work, discipline and self-respect. As a result of the programme the group's membership doubled to 60 000 within weeks.

Malcolm X never came up with any specific programme, partly because the NOI claimed to be a religious organisation rather than a political one. What he did was to instil a sense of racial pride in urban blacks, teaching and preaching about African history and the emerging nations of black Africa. He urged blacks to set up their own businesses and to defend their neighbourhoods against police brutality and white thugs.

Theory of Knowledge

History empowerment and ethics:

The Nation of Islam teaches a very different perspective on both black history and Islam which could be seen as both racist and religiously intolerant. Should they be held to the same ethical standards as the segregationists?

Figure 7.2: Malcolm X with Muhammad Ali. The two met in 1962 and Malcom X became Ali's spiritual advisor.

Malcolm X and the civil rights movement

On the surface, Malcolm X was utterly different from the mainstream civil rights leaders (indeed, historian Peter Ling feels Malcolm X does not even count as a leader). Malcolm X opposed others' non–violent approach, and asked how you could have a revolution by turning the other cheek or putting children in the front line, as King had in Birmingham. He criticised the policy of working with whites to persuade the federal government to pass reform and described the

March on Washington as the 'Farce in Washington' – an event that was taken over by Kennedy's government to keep the blacks compliant.

Even when the Civil Rights Act was passed, he claimed it made no practical difference, especially to blacks in the ghettos. He was probably right: most urban blacks were still trapped by inadequate housing, poor schools and high unemployment. Malcom X talked of black separation, not integration, but failed to provide any coherent programme. He did not believe, however, that there could be a separate black state within the USA.

Malcolm X was heavily criticised by civil rights leaders. James Farmer, the founder of CORE, said: 'Malcolm has done nothing but verbalise.' However, Farmer did respect Malcolm X (who had outclassed him in a public debate), while Roy Wilkins, the NAACP leader, acknowledged that he 'helped us enormously by cataloguing the wrongs done to Negroes in such powerful language'. After his Malcolm's death, King sent a telegram to Malcolm's wife stressing how 'he had the great ability to put his finger on the existence and root of the problem'.

Indirectly, X supported the mainstream civil rights movement by pressurising its leaders to be bolder, while his radicalism made the traditional civil rights movement seem responsible and moderate by comparison. He undoubtedly scared some whites into believing that, if they did not accept the demands for civil rights, then the alternative of a black uprising would be much worse. Certainly, King used the threat of this 'nightmare' to pressurise white opinion into supporting civil rights.

Departure from the Nation of Islam, 1964

In March 1964, Malcolm X left the NOI. He was suspended by Elijah Muhammad for comments over the death of JFK, but had also come to disagree with the Nation's non-political stance, believing it should be politically active. Malcolm X was also outraged to discover that Muhammad had fathered children by different mistresses. Other leaders in the group resented Malcolm X's popularity and high profile.

Malcolm X certainly felt freer to act once he had left the NOI. He made a pilgrimage to Mecca, spoke internationally and set up the Organization of Afro-American Unity and Muslim Mosque Inc to give himself a new independent platform. However, he was killed before either group could have an impact. He advocated voter registration drives and the election of black candidates for public office, like the mainstream civil rights leaders. Unlike other leaders, he said that urban blacks should set up all-black community schools and called for the setting up of Rifle Clubs so that blacks could defend themselves and their families against police brutality and the violence of white vigilantes. He compared the presence of white police in the ghettos to an occupying army under colonial conditions.

In his final months, Malcolm X made overtures to the civil rights movement and no longer saw all whites as 'devils'. He praised the action in Selma of King and other civil rights leaders. We will never know how he would have developed further as a leader because, in February 1965, Malcolm X was assassinated by members of the NOI.

Malcolm X and Martin Luther King

Not surprisingly, Malcolm X has often been compared with and contrasted to Martin Luther King. There were undoubted similarities between the two men. Both were powerful speakers and gifted debaters. Both were fearless, despite death threats, in championing the rights of black people. Both believed that black people should be proud of their identity, should assert themselves, and should confront white racism.

However, the historian Manning Marable has pointed out that, while King saw himself primarily as an American, Malcolm X saw himself primarily as a black man. King showed blacks were prepared to protest non-violently (and even die) to realise the American ideals of 'life, liberty and the pursuit of happiness', as promised in the Declaration of Independence. Malcolm X, in contrast, claimed that the oppressed had a natural right to armed self-defence.

ACTIVITY

A month after Malcolm X's death, SCLC leader Bayard Rustin wrote: 'Malcolm is not a hero of the movement, he is a tragic victim of the ghetto.' What did he mean? How far do you agree? Divide the class into two sides in order to hold a debate.

Historians and the legacy of Malcolm X

Malcolm X taught a generation of, mostly young and poor, urban blacks to acknowledge the psychological damage that 300 years of slavery and white domination had caused. In its place, he instilled a positive sense of black identity. He was the most forceful supporter of black nationalism since Marcus Garvey. His ideas of racial pride and of African American control of black institutions expressed and shaped the changing beliefs of young, black activists. Many of those activists, especially from the SNCC and CORE, came to believe that insisting on interracial cooperation did not lead to the end of anti-black violence, whether in the rural South or urban North. For them, in the words of the historian Harvard Sitkoff, 'the struggle for desegregation [would become] a battle for self-determination'.

The Autobiography of Malcolm X, an account of his life and beliefs, was published a few months after his death. The book explored his feelings of rejection and his search for his identity, and it had and continues to have a huge impact on young black Americans as witnessed by the frequent references to Malcolm X in popular culture, notably rap music.

ACTIVITY

Draw a table like the one below, and make notes to compare Malcolm X and Martin Luther King. Use this book and your own research in the library or on the internet.

	Martin Luther King	Malcolm X
Background		
Religious beliefs		
Goal		
Methods		
Achievement		
Place in history		

Now write an answer to the following question. 'Compare and contrast the goals, methods and achievements of Martin Luther King and Malcolm X.'

John Lewis, the least militant of the SNCC leaders, acknowledged Malcolm X's ability to voice 'the aspirations, bitterness and frustrations of the Negro people more than any single personality' while King's colleague Bayard Rustin, who criticised much of Malcolm's message, said: 'he brought hope and a measure of dignity to thousands of despairing ghetto Negroes'. Among historians, Peter Ling argues that Malcolm X was not even a civil rights leader but a beneficiary of the mass media; the most recent biography of X, by Manning Marable, concludes that his most important contribution was that he 'represented the most important bridge between the American people and more than one billion Muslims throughout the world'.

7.3 What were the consequences of the Black Power movement?

'Black Power' was a nebulous term – it meant different things to different people. For some, the slogan 'Black is Beautiful' characterised Black Power, for others it was the image of the young, armed, black militant. Not surprisingly, it has been portrayed in different ways by historians. This section will examine how the Black Power movement emerged, its consequences and how it has been interpreted.

SOURCE 7.1

King was able to understand 'Black Power's' appeal just as he was able to appreciate how the hopelessness of ghetto life gave rise to the civil disturbances that had rocked American inner cities each summer since 1964. His empathy did not alter the fact that the idea of 'Black Power' limited his options after 1966. King did not believe that the slogan 'Black Power' could be fleshed out into a genuinely satisfactory programme of action, and it was certainly not a sound strategy with which to reverse the authoritarian measures and trends he already detected in the nation. Its inflammatory tone added to the always fraught task of leadership.

Adapted from Ling, P. 2002, **Martin Luther King Jr.**, *London, Routledge.*

QUESTION

What concerns were about the Black Power movement are highlighted in Source 7.1?

Until the mid 1960s, both the SNCC and CORE were committed to the non-violent, interracial struggle for civil rights. With the passing of legislation in 1964 and 1965, their stated goal of enshrining civil rights in federal law had been achieved. In the year following the death of Malcolm X, both organisations were seeking a new direction, new tactics and a new goal. Several developments led to a new phase of the movement and indeed the emergence of new leaders:

- the urban race riots, particularly in Watts, Los Angeles, in 1965
- the increasing American involvement in, and opposition to, the Vietnam War
- the assassination of Malcolm X
- the murder of Sammy Younge, an SNCC organiser, killed in Alabama in 1966 for using a 'whites only' toilet at a service station
- the need to develop a strategy for furthering black civil rights in the northern cities.

The SNCC was divided, but it was the fiery and proactive Stokely Carmichael who was elected as its new leader. In CORE also, a moderate leader was replaced by a militant one, Floyd McKissick. Both men, but especially Carmichael, grabbed the headlines and thrust their way into the national consciousness during the 'Meredith March'.

The Meredith March, June 1966

In 1962, James Meredith had been the first black student to attend the University of Mississippi. In June 1966, he planned to 'March Against Fear' from Memphis, Tennessee, to Jackson, Mississippi. He reckoned that the 350-km (220-mile) walk would take him 450 000 steps, one for each unregistered black voter in Mississippi. However soon after he entered Mississippi, Meredith was ambushed and hospitalised by shotgun pellets fired by an unemployed white man. Civil rights leaders felt that they should complete the march rather than let white racists think they had won. It was the last time the leaders of the SCLC, CORE and the SNCC would come together.

Stokely Carmichael wanted the march to be protected by the Deacons for Defense and Justice, and for it to be an all-black march. King agreed to armed protection, but he had his way on the inclusion of white supporters – otherwise he would have refused to participate. Carmichael craved publicity and he knew there would be far less media coverage if King left the event.

'Black Power! Black Power! Black Power!'

From the start of the march, the divisions between the groups were clear for all to see. When King preached non-violence, the militants proclaimed 'white blood will flow'. The singing of 'We Shall Overcome' was drowned out by chants of 'We Shall Overrun'. Then, in the town of Greenwood, Carmichael was arrested for pitching his tent in the grounds of a school.

Released on the same day, he seized the opportunity to grab the limelight by leaping on to the back of a truck and shouting: 'This is the 27th time I've been arrested and I ain't going to jail no more!' He called for 'Black Power!' and repeated his call. Soon the crowd were screaming back 'Black Power! Black Power! Black Power!' It was not the first time the term had been used, but it was the first time it was adopted as a slogan in the campaign for civil rights. And it was to spread like wildfire in the days and weeks ahead.

Martin Luther King and Black Power

King recognised that, in promoting racial pride, 'Black Power' represented a 'psychological call to manhood' and that it helped to overcome feelings of insecurity and inferiority. But he could not agree with its implication of violence, nor its exclusion of white liberals from the struggle for racial justice.

He believed it would do more harm to blacks than to whites, that it would isolate the black community and give 'the impression we are talking about black domination rather than black equality'. But Carmichael fed the media frenzy and he urged blacks to 'build a power base… so strong that we will bring whites to their knees'. At the end of the march, McKissick declared: '1966 will be remembered as the year we left our imposed status as Negroes and became Black Men. 1966 is the year of the concept of Black Power.'

ACTIVITY

Watch the 2013 film *The Butler* and the 2015 film *Selma* and discuss the perspectives employed in the films to bring out the stories of the civil rights movement. How do they deal with black involvement and white involvement in the movement?

The impact of Black Power

Viewed positively, Black Power was a logical extension of the civil rights movement. Legal equality had been achieved; now there was an opportunity to unite and organise in order to exploit this new political and economic power. With a heightened sense of self-reliance and self-confidence, black people set up new local organisations demanding 'community control' over police forces and ghetto schools and the teaching of black history.

Black businesses appealed to the new sense of racial pride and catered for the new market in African clothes, 'soul' music and African literature. Equating 'black' with 'beautiful', many African Americans adopted 'Afro' hairstyles while in 1968 James Brown sang 'Say it loud – I'm black and I'm proud' and the first Miss Black America beauty pageant was held. In fostering a new sense of self-confidence, Black Power helped to banish the belief, born of slavery and maintained by years of white supremacy, that blacks were inferior.

However, this positive, peaceful sense of black identity had to compete with calls to 'pick up the gun'. The rhetoric of violence and of separatism selectively quoted from Malcolm X was threatening to most whites, while being opposed by many black leaders.

Roy Wilkins said Black Power was 'the father of hatred and the mother of violence'. When Carmichael talked of 'building a movement that will smash everything Western civilisation has created' and urged black students to 'fight for liberty by any means necessary', he alienated most of the white public and many blacks, which also served to slow the donations that the SNCC depended on.

Figure 7.3: US medal winners Tommie Smith and John Carlos at the Olympic Games in Mexico in 1968, raising their black-gloved fists. They said they did so to show black unity and that they bowed their heads out of respect for Martin Luther King and Malcolm X.

Carmichael and other militants were accused of encouraging the violence and rioting that blighted so many cities in the 'long, hot summers' of the mid 1960s. Black Power came to be associated, in the minds of many whites, with the violence seen on the streets of the northern cities, which in turn alienated President Johnson.

In the South, away from the ghettos where 'Black Power' had most appeal, protest remained in the form of boycotts, demonstrations and voter registration campaigns, in an atmosphere that was now far less threatening of white violence – something that would have been unimaginable ten years previously.

The Black Panthers

Inevitably the media focused on the violent, not the peaceful, image of Black Power. This was typified by its fascination with the Black Panther

Party, a group described by the historian Hugh Pearson as 'little more than a temporary media phenomenon'. Taking its symbol of the black panther from that of the Lowndes County Freedom Organization, which Carmichael had helped to set up, the party was founded by Huey Newton and Bobby Seale in Oakland, California, in October 1966.

Its initial aim was to monitor the behaviour of the Oakland police ('the military arm of our oppressors') – its arrests of, charges against and treatment of Oakland's black residents. The Panthers favoured armed revolt and openly displayed their firearms. Dressed in their black berets and black leather jackets, the Panthers conveyed a cool, hard-edged image that appealed to many young men in the ghettos. Despite never having a membership in excess of 10 000 they received extensive negative media coverage.

Less widely reported were their free breakfast programmes for school children, free health clinics and ambulance service. Most whites only knew what they saw and read in the media. The head of the FBI, J. Edgar Hoover, said the Panthers were 'the greatest threat to the internal security of the country', but they were easily infiltrated by the FBI's COINTELPRO (COunter INTELligence PROgram), a covert FBI programme aimed at watching and disrupting domestic political organisations, and the police. Hundreds were arrested and nearly 30 killed in ambushes and shoot-outs. By 1970, most of their leaders were dead, imprisoned or forced into exile.

Figure 7.4: Militant members of the Black Panther Party march down 42nd Street en route to a news conference at United Nations Plaza. The conference had

been called to protest the murder trial of Black Panther 'defence minister' Huey P. Newton. A Panther spokesman said the party had formed a 'working alliance' with the Student Nonviolent Coordinating Committee in hopes of establishing a 'mass revolutionary black party'.

Interpretations of Black Power

The historian William Van Deburg took the view that Black Power had huge psychological benefits: 'By decolonising [black people's] minds, cultivating feelings of racial solidarity, and contrasting their world with that of the oppressor, black Americans came to understand themselves better.' He also pointed out that Black Power produced an outburst of creative work in art, music, literature and fashion. However, SCLC veteran Andrew Young said Black Power 'was a dead end. Its supporters could trigger polarisation but not genuine social change.' The historian Clayborne Carson concluded that the Black Power movement 'promised more than non-violence but delivered less'.

DISCUSSION POINT

What are the meanings of the quotations by Van Deburg and Young in the paragraph above? What is your view of their interpretations? In what ways did Black Power 'promise more than non-violence'? Can you find examples of the influence of Black Power in art, music, cinema, literature and fashion from the late 1960s to the early 1980s?

KEY CONCEPTS QUESTION

Continuity: To what extent had the lives of African Americans changed in the period from 1950 to 1968?

KEY CONCEPTS ACTIVITY

Continuity: It is important not to get carried away with the major events of national and international significance when studying the civil rights movement. Draw up a table with headings 'Political', 'Economic' and 'Social' and try to find areas where change was not achieved.

Summary

Chapters 4 to 7 have shown how black Americans, aided by sympathetic whites, battled against deeply entrenched disenfranchisement, discrimination and segregation. In the decade after the Brown decision, they largely conquered it. They paid a huge price in suffering but they won full legal rights as citizens. As the historian Harvard Sitkoff wrote: 'Although the civil rights movement did not bring all the results it promised, it has given African Americans the resources and the strengths necessary to continue the struggle.'

The black civil rights movement achieved a huge amount of change in the political status of African Americans and yet their economic and social status was still similar by the end of the 1960s, with lower paid jobs and poor quality education and housing the norm. Perhaps the most significant achievement of the movement was to bring black perspectives into the mainstream for politicians and the media and hence for the wider population. As such the black presence in popular culture underwent enormous change in the 1970s and subsequently with musical forms such as disco, soul, rap and RnB alongside an increased interest in black history in universities and use of black characters in films and advertising. This 'soft power', a contrast to the 'hard power' of political involvement and economic influence is a key part of the requirements for groups seeking to improve their status.

QUESTION

What parallels are there with the 'soft power' wielded by the other groups covered in this book?

Paper 3 exam practice

Question

Evaluate the impact that Malcolm X had on the development of the civil rights movement in the 1960s. **[15 marks]**

Skill

Using your own knowledge analytically and combining it with awareness of historical debate

Examiner's tips

Always remember that historical knowledge and analysis should be the core of your answer – aspects of historical debate are desirable extras. However, where it is relevant, the integration of relevant knowledge about historical debates and interpretations, with reference to individual historians, will help push your answer up into the higher bands.

Assuming that you have read the question carefully, drawn up a plan, worked out your line of argument/approach and written your introductory paragraph, you should be able to avoid both irrelevant material and simple narrative. Your task now is to follow your plan by writing a series of linked paragraphs that contain relevant analysis, precise supporting own knowledge and, where relevant, brief references to historical debate interpretations.

For this question, you will need to:

- explain what Malcolm X stood for and achieved
- examine his impact on the civil rights movement both during his lifetime (so, up to 1965) and afterwards
- assess whether he strengthened or damaged the movement, changed its direction and focus or caused it to fracture, consistently analysing the extent of his impact
- finally, make a judgement about how lasting or beneficial his impact on the movement was.

Such a topic, which has been the subject of much historical debate, will also give you the chance to refer to different historians' views.

Common mistakes

Some students, being aware of an existing historical debate (and knowing that extra marks can be gained by showing this), simply write things like: 'Historian x says… and historian y says…' However, they make no attempt to **evaluate** the different views (for example, has one historian had access to more or better information than another, perhaps because he or she was writing at a later date?); nor is this information **integrated** into their answer by being pinned to the question. Another weak use of historical debate is to write things like: 'Historian x is biased because she is American.' Such basic comments will not be given credit – what's needed is explicit understanding of historians' views, and/or the application of precise own knowledge to evaluate the strengths and weaknesses of these views.

Remember to refer to the simplified Paper 3 mark scheme given in Chapter 11.

Sample paragraphs containing analysis and historical debate

Most historians would agree that, long before the Black Power movement emerged in the mid 1960s, Malcolm X voiced the anger and frustration of young, urban blacks, especially in the North. Even the more moderate civil rights leaders acknowledged this contribution to the movement. Bayard Rustin went so far as to say that he had brought hope to despairing young blacks in the ghettos.

It can be argued that Malcolm X's criticism of the integrationist, non-violent approach of Martin Luther King and the SCLC helped the mainstream civil rights movement by pressurising the moderates to be bolder and by persuading public opinion and Congress to pass the Civil Rights and Voting Rights Acts in order to avoid the more militant campaign – even uprising – that Malcolm X's rhetoric appeared to threaten.

However, his justification of armed resistance by blacks went against the grain of non-violence that most groups within the civil rights coalition subscribed to. In this way, he encouraged the splits in the movement that emerged after his death in 1965. He also criticised the integrationist approach of mainstream civil rights organisations.

As the historian Manning Marable has pointed out, Malcolm X saw himself primarily as a black man claiming the black man's right to armed self-defence, whereas King and most other civil rights leaders stressed that they were

Americans striving to achieve the American ideals of life and liberty. Malcolm X thus alienated white opinion and lessened the chances of achieving further civil rights legislation.

[The writer has already made use of one historian's view showing how Malcolm X's impact led to a weakening of interracial support for civil rights. Later, this essay incorporates the more favourable view of another historian who sees the contribution of Malcolm X and the later Black Power movement as contributing to the evolution of the civil rights movement after the legislation of the mid 1960s had outlawed desegregation.]

Malcolm X left no lasting programme or organisation to carry on his work. What he did leave was added self-confidence and assertiveness among many urban blacks. Much of this had a very positive impact in the form of self-help organisations, some of which were formed during his lifetime and even more of which were to emerge under the umbrella of Black Power. As the historian Howard Sitkoff wrote, the battle for desegregation became the battle for self-determination. In other words, with segregation banned, it was now for blacks to unite and organise themselves in order to exploit their political and economic power.

EXAMINER'S COMMENT

This is a good example of how to use historians' views. The main focus of the answer is properly concerned with using precise own knowledge to address the demands of the question. The candidate has also provided some brief but relevant knowledge of historical debate, which is smoothly integrated into the answer. However, there is no attempt to evaluate the views of the historians mentioned.

Activity

In this chapter, the focus is on writing an answer that is analytical and well supported by precise own knowledge, and one which – where relevant – refers to historical interpretations and debates. Using the information from this chapter, and any other sources of information available to you, try to answer one of the following Paper 3 practice questions using these skills.

Paper 3 practice questions

1   To what extent, did the civil rights movement in the USA become more radical between 1965 and 1968?

2   'Martin Luther King did far more to improve the lives of African Americans than Malcolm X did.' To what extent do you agree with this statement?

3   Compare and contrast the role of Black Power with that of non-violence in addressing the problems of the ghettos.

4   Discuss the reasons for the fracturing of the civil rights movement after 1965.

5   To what extent was the work of the National Association for the Advancement of Colored People (NAACP) the most important reason for the improvement in civil rights for African Americans from its founding in 1909 to 1968?

8 | Youth protest movements in the Americas

Introduction

This chapter deals with the development of youth protest in the Americas, and focuses on the US in particular with key events from other countries in the final section. It examines the situation of young people in the US at the end of the Second World War, and assesses whether they can be accurately defined as a group. The chapter then seeks to address why youth protest movements emerged in the 1960s and 1970s America, the nature of the grievances and aims of the protesters, and how successful the various movements were in achieving these aims. Finally, it will look at how youth culture changed in the post–war period before addressing the effect of these changes elsewhere in the two continents.

TIMELINE

1960 Apr: Student Non-Violent Coordinating Committee (SNCC) formed after sit-ins begin

1962 Jun: Port Huron Statement issued by Students for a Democratic Society (SDS)

1964 Berkeley and Yale students begin to protest against Vietnam War

1967 Jul: First 'Summer of Love' in Haight-Ashbury area of San Francisco draws 100 000 hippies

Dec: Youth International Party (Yippies) founded

1968 Jan–Jun: 221 demonstrations take place on US campuses

1969 Jun: Stonewall riots in New York against persecution of LGBT (lesbian, gay, bisexual and transgender) community

Aug: Woodstock Festival takes place in upstate New York

1970 May: Four students shot dead in anti-war protests at Kent State University

Sep: Charles Reich publishes *The Greening of America*

KEY QUESTIONS

- Why did youth protest emerge in the Americas after the Second World War?
- What were the goals of the young protesters in the 1960s and 1970s?
- How did youth culture change in the 1960s and 1970s?
- How successful were the youth protests of the 1960s and 1970s in achieving their original goals?
- How did youth movements influence politics in Canada and Latin America?

Overview

- The post-war growth of university education and the 'baby boom' (increased birth rate) created a new demographic of wealthy, young intellectual liberals.
- Some of these joined the SNCC and took part in black civil rights protests in the early 1960s, learning the key techniques of successful media-friendly protest.
- Youth dissent initially lacked a clear focus and involved protest in favour of women's rights and civil rights, and protest against university policies, environmental damage and the government.
- Youth protest was closely entwined with the counter-culture – the growth of rock and folk music, the widening availability of drugs, and a more liberal attitude to sex.
- Youth protest finally came together around opposition to the Vietnam War.

8.1 Why did youth protest emerge in the Americas after the Second World War?

'Upward mobility on a rocket ship' was how the economist Frank Levy described the post-war American experience. US industries soon adapted war production techniques to produce consumer goods that quickly became seen as necessities. The US economy grew at a rapid rate, with Gross National Product (GNP) leaping 36% in the 15 years up to 1960, while average incomes grew even faster, at 43%. This formed an enlarged middle class and reduced the need for young people to go straight into the workforce after school. As a result, the American teenager – of the type portrayed in the 1985 film *Back to the Future* – was born. These teenagers often received allowances (regular amounts of money) from their parents, and found employment in the growing service sector, so they had money while at high school. These young people were encouraged to aspire to a college education to guarantee their share of the American dream.

DISCUSSION POINT

In 1931, historian James Truslow Adams coined the phrase 'the American Dream' in his book *The Epic of America*. He defined it as 'that dream of a land in which life should be better and richer and fuller for everyone, with opportunity for each according to ability or achievement. It is not a dream of motor cars and high wages merely, but a dream of social order in which each man and each woman shall be able to attain to the fullest stature of which they are innately capable, and be recognised by others for what they are, regardless of the fortuitous circumstances of birth or position.' Why is the 'American Dream' an important concept in US history?

Figure 8.1: Michael J. Fox (far left) as Marty McFly in *Back to the Future*. Made in 1985, the film featured a 1980s teenager transported back to the 1950s.

Theory of Knowledge

History and economics:

The philosopher and economist Karl Marx believed that history was a series of class struggles between capitalists and their workers (whom he called the proletariat) and that the two groups would always be in tension because the capitalist owners exploited the workers. Does the growth of teenage workers in the 1950s support or negate his hypothesis?

Education

The size of the education sector in the US exploded after the Second World War. Before US entry into the war, the average grade reached by Americans was 8. (Grade 8 is the end of middle school, reached at the ages of 13 to 14. High school runs from Grade 9 to Grade 12, ages 15 to 18.) Thirty years later the average grade was 12, and 50% of young people of college age went on to higher study, with over 20% graduating. The expansion of post-high-school provision was also spectacular, with many new institutions created and others significantly expanded to accommodate the influx of students.

Student life in the growing universities centred around lectures, fraternities, sororities and sports, with social issues largely ignored. However, as the 1960s began, the election of John F. Kennedy stimulated youth interest in politics. Kennedy seemed to be the embodiment of hope, from his New Frontier programme – an ambitious plan to address both poverty and environmental issues – to his promise to put a man on the moon by the end of the decade. As a result, students became more politicised.

Left-leaning groups, such as the Students for a Democratic Society (SDS formed in 1960), began to gather support, but many more engaged with the civil rights demonstrations that were taking place throughout the South, most notably the sit-ins of 1960–61 and the Freedom Rides of 1961 (see Chapter 5). Even more signed up to Kennedy's 1961 initiative, the Peace Corps, which proposed to send young Americans out into the world to help the poor and to become less insular in their thinking, the ambition of which seemed to embody the new spirit of youth engagement.

However, although there was a rise in political engagement among young people, they were by no means a majority . Just 12% of students identified themselves as part of the 'New Left' movement in 1970, so in terms of numbers they were far less substantial than the black civil rights movement or even the Native Americans rights groups.

What the youth protesters did have on their side was the prestige that came from attending an élite university, and the ability to express themselves in the language of the ruling class. Many attended some of the most notable universities in the country, such as Yale, Stanford and Berkeley – the traditional breeding grounds of wealth, privilege and the 'Establishment' (the people holding the power in US society).

For these students, the future corporate and political leaders of the nation, to be riding buses in the South in 1961 or marching with James Meredith in 1966 (see 7.3, The Meredith March, June 1966) was something new, and worthy of media attention.

8.2 What were the goals of the young protesters in the 1960s and 1970s?

At the start of the 1950s there were 3.6 million TV sets in the US; by the end of the decade there were 67 million and these TVs brought the images of protest from Montgomery and Little Rock (see Chapter 4) into the campuses.

TV showed a world of injustice and poverty that was alien to many students and challenged the American Dream. Students whose families had fled to the suburbs, which led to the creation of inner-city ghettos, were finally seeing what their families had tried to 'shield' them from, and they were outraged. They were outraged about racism, outraged about poverty, outraged about the use of pesticides portrayed in Rachel Carson's 1962 book *Silent Spring* and outraged that the powers that be – which they increasingly referred to as 'the man' – were doing nothing.

Later, these concerns would be joined by the resentment and, after 1969, fear of the draft, suspicion of the FBI, and a fear of 'globalism' (the post-war idea that the US had the right to project political influence on a global scale).

However, unlike their 1968 peers in France, Britain, Hungary or even in China (where a Mao-endorsed decade of youth protest, the Cultural Revolution, had begun in 1966), there were no specific goals for the youth protesters of the US in the 1960s. Instead, a generalised questioning of authority pervaded the discussion in coffee shops and on campus lawns.

It was only when the escalating conflict in Vietnam began seriously to threaten the liberty of male students that the war united student protest.

Figure 8.2: Vietnam War protesters, Kansas, 1967.

The attack on education

Initially, students concentrated their anger on the universities. Protests were inspired by the SDS, despite attracting a mere 200 delegates to its annual convention in 1963 and being poorly funded. Many students criticised depersonalised courses and teaching, and some blamed the universities for their expansion.

Often, for example in Harvard, this expansion had led to the eviction of poor local residents to make room for plush new offices and labs. Some students even began to question the whole process of schooling and the growth of the university system. Universities were seen as 'degree factories' churning out qualified young people who were then fit to work for 'the man' until they collected their pensions.

The writer **Paul Goodman** even opposed compulsory education, arguing: 'We have been swept aside on a flood-tide of public policy and popular sentiment into an expansion of schooling and an aggrandisement of school-people that is grossly wasteful of youth and effort and does positive damage to the young.' This opinion is shared by contemporary commentators such as the entrepreneur Peter Thiel.

> **Paul Goodman (1911–72):**
>
> Goodman was an American sociologist, anarchist and intellectual, whose 1960 book *Growing Up Absurd* inspired many of the student protesters with its vicious attack on the American system. He had also been involved in the new forms of therapy since the movement of the 1940s and 1950s, and was openly bisexual.

While Goodman was at the extreme end of the spectrum, the lure of being 'anti-Establishment' showed itself in a variety of ways. One of these was engaging with the direct-action tactics of the civil rights movement, particularly as they developed into the more aggressive tactics of Black Power (see Chapter 7). This confrontational approach, suggesting no solutions but demanding a change of direction, lent itself to the anti-Vietnam movement. On campus, students targeted the visible forms of 'the man', especially the Reserve Officer's Training Corps (ROTC).

The ROTC was a college-based officer commissioning programme run by the US armed forces. At many colleges, until the early 1960s, membership was compulsory for male students. Indeed, the success of students at the University of California in getting compulsory membership removed in 1962 could be seen as one of the first achievements of the student rights movement. Meanwhile, some students investigated the links between universities and defence contractors, and even the FBI and CIA – the latter were later exposed as having part-funding some of the activities of the National Student Association from the 1950s all the way up to 1967.

In hindsight, it is easy to dismiss this student radicalism as the work of a few hotheads. Militant protesters were often accused of coming from wealth and taking part in sanitised rebellion before rejoining the Establishment, affecting the disillusion that James Dean had captured in the 1955 film *Rebel Without a Cause*.

Environmentalism

Rachel Carson's 1962 book *Silent Spring*, which highlighted the damage caused by pesticides, started a fledgling environmental movement that seemed tailor-made for youth protest. The Washington University Professor of Plant Physiology, Barry Commoner, took the ideas further in his 1971 book *The Closing Circle*. Commoner had strongly opposed nuclear testing, and proposed the ideas of global warming long before they became commonly accepted. However, Commoner's socialist principles and criticism of nuclear technology at a time of Cold War tension did little for his popularity with the American political élite. He argued with other scientists about the priorities of the planet's problems – most notably with Paul Ehrlich, the author of 1968's *Population Bomb*. Commoner believed the misuse of technology was the greatest threat to the planet, Ehrlich the growth of population.

The environmental movement's greatest success in the period was the one-million-person Earth Day march, which took place in 1970 in New York, organised by Columbia University student Fred Kent. New York Mayor John Lindsay made Central Park available for the day. Since Manhattan was home to national TV stations like NBC and CBS, alongside print media giants like the *New York Times*, *Time* and *Newsweek*, coverage was widespread but the significance of Earth Day was numerical rather than political.

The scientific debate was lost on many Americans. The US birth rate was declining anyway, and food was getting cheaper (even though Ehrlich had pointed out that this came at a cost: the amount of the pesticide DDT found in the average mother's breast milk would make it illegal by the standards of the FDA – the Food and Drugs Administration). Nuclear power, widely used in Europe, seemed to offer cheap power and less dependence on oil.

It was not until the Three Mile Island disaster in Pennsylvania in 1979, when a malfunction led to a reactor meltdown, that nuclear power was questioned. Following the oil crises of 1973 and 1979, American people's attitudes to their energy supply started to become part of a national debate.

Support for other protest movements

While it was easy to criticise the more militant of the student protesters as a tiny minority, the scope of the protests should not be ignored. From support of the civil rights movement with the sit-ins, Freedom Rides and marches, to Earth Day 1970 and active protest for the women's movement and gay rights, and even support for Native American protests (though this was often vocal rather than physical), the student protesters committed themselves wholeheartedly to a series of high-profile campaigns that often involved physical danger. However, it was the anti-war protests that were the most obvious, and most successful, aspect of youth protest.

Vietnam

Protest against the Vietnam War began around 1964, and quickly developed into the most significant strand in youth protest. The early dissent, where 1000 Yale students marched in New York, was of little concern to the government. However, the largely uncensored media coverage given to the war, the creeping extension of the draft, and the escalating cost brought far more young people out against Johnson and Nixon in the ensuing years.

By 1965, 'teach-ins' of anti-war lectures and debates were being held in many universities. These passive but visible protests drew considerable support, with 20 000 attending at Berkeley from 21 to 23 May 1965, and an 8000-strong group of Berkeley students clashed with police in Oakland later that year. Though the protests were increasingly visible, Johnson was able to point to a petition signed by a quarter of Yale undergraduates who were in favour of the war, and it was all too easy to resort to the old excuse of blaming communist agitators.

The protests became harder to ignore when Norman Morrison, a 31-year-old Quaker, set himself on fire outside Secretary of Defence Robert McNamara's window at the Pentagon. McNamara later reflected: 'How much evil must we do in order to do good? We have certain ideals, certain responsibilities. Recognise that at times you will have to engage in evil, but minimise it.' This statement powerfully captured the Cold War pragmatism of the politicians that was in direct conflict with the attitude of the protesters and the spirit of the 1960s.

The protesters wanted the US out of Vietnam altogether, and wanted trials of the presidents who were responsible. First Johnson and then Nixon felt the force of their anger, and neither was helped by the anti-war efforts of celebrities. Jane Fonda, an Oscar winner in 1971, visited North Vietnam in 1972 with her soon-to-be husband **Tom Hayden**.

Tom Hayden (b. 1939):

Hayden was one of the founders of the SDS, after becoming disillusioned with the inactivity of the National Student Association. As president of the SDS he drafted the Port Huron Statement, which demanded disarmament, university reform and a more representative Democratic Party. He was frequently arrested during protests throughout the late 1960s. In the early 1970s he also made several trips to Vietnam and Cambodia as a peace activist with his future wife, the actress Jane Fonda.

Figure 8.3: Jane Fonda poses with an NVA anti-aircraft crew during her visit to North Vietnam in 1972, earning her the nickname 'Hanoi Jane'.

During the trip, Fonda was photographed on a Viet Cong anti-aircraft gun and made several radio broadcasts in which she denounced American political and military leaders as 'war criminals'. As the anti-war protest escalated and media interest in it grew, it began to siphon young men and women away from the civil rights movement.

The protesters detested the violence of the military against developing countries, but politicians felt trapped by the 1947 Truman Doctrine, which promised US help for any country threatened by communism and the Cold War paradigm of the 'domino effect' (that if one country turned communist, the countries surrounding it would follow). Both of these concepts had been instrumental in prompting the US to become involved in Vietnam in response to the overthrow of the French army by the Vietnamese Communist leader, Ho Chi Minh.

ACTIVITY

Free speech is a key part of the US Constitution, but when protesters spoke out against the war in Vietnam they were often accused of being anti-American. The actress Jane Fonda was subjected to extensive public criticism as a result of her visit to North Vietnam in 1972. How far do you think freedom of speech should be supported? Can you find any valid arguments against it in times of war or national emergency? Can you think of a contemporary example which would be as controversial?

ACTIVITY

Choose one of the goals of the youth protest movement and, using the information in this section and your own independent research, construct a manifesto of your demands. Include what you are angry about and what you think should be done to address this.

8.3 How did youth culture change in the 1960s and 1970s?

The economic and demographic changes, described in the previous section, account in part for the emergence of youth protest in the 1960s and 1970s. However, inspiration also came from a coming together of ideology, music and drugs that became known as the counter-culture.

The counter-culture

*[handwritten: → rejected convention + authority
media attention in "Happenings"
of 1966-7]*

The counter-culture was, in many ways, the culmination of 1960s protest and rebellion. It was popularised by a media that longed to criticise, but also glorified, the activities and styles of the young. Images of long-haired men in kaftans, tie-dyed shirts and sandals, shocked a nation that was accustomed to restraint. These 'hippies' (the word derives from the 1940s term 'hipster') favoured psychedelic music, the use of drugs such as marijuana and LSD and embraced sexual activity outside of marriage. For many among the older generation, it seemed as though society had broken down.

[handwritten: → contraceptive pill early 60s]

Rejection of the rat race

The US youth culture of the 1960s seemed to define itself in relation to the culture that it was seeking to replace. The New Left co-opted Freudian ideas, and referred to older people as 'repressed', trapped in the 'rat race', and fearful of what would happen if they stepped off the corporate treadmill.

The idea was adopted by the science fiction writer Philip K. Dick, whose 1968 book *Do Androids Dream of Electric Sheep?* – later filmed as *Blade Runner* – suggested a future religion called 'Mercerism', where followers would share the experience of walking up a never-ending hill, a comment on the monotony of life in the 'rat race'. In his 1960 book *Growing up Absurd,* Paul Goodman had asked whether 'grown-up citizens are concerned about the beatniks and delinquents… The question is why the grown-ups do not… draw the same connections as the youth.'

The sexual revolution

This conviction that 'repression' was at the root of society's problems led to a rejection of taboos. The licensing of the contraceptive pill in 1960 enabled women to take more control over their fertility, and so over their sex lives. Many young people abandoned conventional sexual relationships for the free love that was typified by the 'Summer of Love' of 1967.

Sexual taboos were challenged not only by the hippies, but also by the previously largely hidden gay community. The election of the openly gay Harvey Milk to a position on the San Francisco Board of Supervisors in 1978 was the culmination of a campaign for gay rights that had been ongoing since the Stonewall riots in New York in 1969, in which the LGBT community clashed with police, following a raid on the known gay bar, the Stonewall Inn.

Figure 8.4: The election of Harvey Milk.

Theory of Knowledge

History, morals and ethics:

The shift in ethical beliefs that occurred among many young Americans in the 1960s raises several interesting questions related to Theory of Knowledge. Can we say that the young people who adopted environmental issues, sexual freedoms and denounced homophobia were 'right'? In a related issue can it be argued that subverting a society's norms and rules is vital if that society is to be healthy? Is ethical knowledge therefore transient?

In straight circles, pornographic films and magazines became more popular. *Playboy's* best-selling issue came in November 1972 when over 7 million copies were purchased, and surveys suggested one in four male college students was a regular subscriber. *Hustler's* publisher, Larry Flynt, became an unlikely champion of free speech when, a regular fixture in the Supreme Court from 1974 onwards, he invoked his right to free speech as a defence of his publication.

The Kinsey reports on *Sexual Behaviour in the Human Male* (1948) and *Sexual Behaviour in the Human Female* (1953) had shown that Americans were not as conservative as many believed, but the increasing prevalence of sexual content in the 1960s and 1970s was a further challenge to the traditional values of an older generation.

Music

The sexual revolution was not merely a consequence of technological and social change, but could also be traced to the rise of popular music as a means of expression. Some Americans had feared the impact of Elvis Presley in the 1950s, and the onslaught of sexualised musicians in the 1960s continued this. Jim Morrison of *The Doors* was arrested in 1969 for lewd behaviour on stage, and the The Rolling Stones' 1965 hit '(I Can't Get No) Satisfaction' – a number 1 on the Billboard Chart – was overtly sexual.

But rock and roll was not just about sex. The 1960s also saw an explosion of protest songs. Malvina Reynolds echoed Carson's *Silent Spring* with her track 'What Have They Done to the Rain?', while Pete Seeger united environmentalism with hippy values in the track 'Where Have All the Flowers Gone?' However, the major figures in protest music were **Joan Baez** and **Bob Dylan**, both of whom performed at the 1963 March on Washington (see section 6.3).

Joan Baez (b. 1941):

Baez recorded a series of successful folk albums in the 1960s and 1970s, and was romantically involved with Bob Dylan. She was synonymous with the protest movements and sang 'We Shall Overcome' at the 1963 March on Washington. Baez refused to pay taxes in protest at the Vietnam War in 1963 and founded the Institute for the Study of Nonviolence in 1964, while encouraging resistance to the draft at her concerts. She travelled as part of a peace delegation to North Vietnam in 1972, and toured Chile, Brazil and Argentina in 1981, but was prevented from performing because of her strong views on human rights.

Bob Dylan (b. 1941):

Dylan's fiercely political lyrics were a sharp contrast to those of Elvis and The Beatles. He wrote a series of songs to commemorate deaths in the civil rights movement, and played at the March on Washington. His switch from acoustic to electric guitar outraged purists and his mumbling style alienated the older generation, but the principles he seemed to support, and his undoubted style, made him a hero and inspiration to many young musicians in the early 1960s. However, as early as 1964 – unlike Joan Baez – he began to withdraw from political protests, and even to renounce his association with some of the ideals espoused in his earlier songs.

Bob Dylan's songs were full of anger and hope, and spoke to those who saw the 1960s as an opportunity for society. Dylan, 'a phenomenon unto himself' according to historian Howard Zinn, would go on to write some of the most influential protest songs of all time. Songs such as 'The Death of Emmett Till', 'Hurricane' and 'The Lonesome Death of Hattie Carroll' provided a soundtrack to the civil rights movement. The influence of music was disputed, however. The folk singer Arlo Guthrie conceded that 'you don't accomplish very much singing protest songs to people who agree with you'.

Figure 8.5: Bob Dylan and Joan Baez.

SOURCE 8.1

Come mothers and fathers

Throughout the land

And don't criticize

What you can't understand

Your sons and your daughters

Are beyond your command

Your old road is rapidly agin'

Please get out off the new one if you can't lend your hand

For the times they are a-changin'.

Bob Dylan, 'The Times They Are A-Changin', 1964.

> **QUESTION**
>
> Why could 'vague' lyrics like those in Source 8.1 connect so easily with the very young people alienated by politicians whose key skill is meant to be communication?

As the significance of music to young people increased, so the size of concerts grew. In 1969, the extreme ends of the 'peace and love' generation were vividly illustrated. At Altamont in California, in December, 300000 gathered for a Rolling Stones concert which used Hells Angels (a notorious motorcycle club) as security; when the situation got out of hand, a black concert goer – Meredith Hunter – was stabbed to death after getting on stage with a revolver.

Four months earlier on the other side of the country, the legendary Woodstock festival took place in Bethel, New York. Here more than 400000 people spent three days sharing drugs and sex to a soundtrack provided by Jimi Hendrix, The Who, The Grateful Dead and Janis Joplin. Woodstock became a byword for the counter-culture, which was so different to the youth culture of the pre-war years.

Alternative lifestyles and the drug culture

Areas such as Haight-Ashbury in San Francisco became an alternative capital, where hippy men and women gathered to use marijuana and share free love. In 1967, 100000 hippies came together in Haight-Ashbury for the 'Summer of Love'. There was also a reaction against conventional modes of living, with some fleeing the city for rural communes.

The counter-culture lifestyle, celebrated in the 1978 novel *Tales of the City* by Armistead Maupin, was offensive to many hard-working, God-fearing Americans who had lived through the Depression. Meanwhile, the drug culture seeped into music with songs such as The Beatles' 'Lucy in the Sky with Diamonds', Jimi Hendrix's 'Purple Haze' and the Velvet Underground's 'Heroin', all of which were released in 1967.

Entrepreneurs

Sexual and political disaffection was partnered with a more indistinct concept of a 'generation gap'; the idea that the young people of the 1960s were different and would challenge the old order that their parents had so willingly accepted. The 'cultural revolution' inspired some of the most creative entrepreneurs and artists of modern times; for example, Steve Jobs (Apple), Ben & Jerry (ice cream) and Matt Groening (*The Simpsons*) all took the values and ideas of the 1960s and 1970s and allied them to the work ethic that traditionally defines the US to create inspiring products.

Charles Reich, the social historian whose 1970 book *The Greening of America* argued that the counter-culture heralded a new type of consciousness, which he labelled 'Consciousness III', based on personal freedom and the use of recreational drugs, declared:

SOURCE 8.2

The logic and necessity of the new generation — and what they are so furiously opposed to — must be seen against a background of what has gone wrong in America. It must be understood in light of the betrayal and loss of the American dream, the rise of the Corporate State of the 1960s, and the way in which that State dominates, exploits, and ultimately destroys both nature and man. Its rationality must be measured against the insanity of existing 'reason' — reason that makes impoverishment, dehumanization, and even war appear to be logical and necessary. Its logic must be read from the fact that Americans have lost control of the machinery of their society, and only new values and a new culture can restore control. Its emotions and spirit can be comprehended only by seeing contemporary America through the eyes of the new generation.

Reich, C. 1970. **The Greening of America.** *New York, USA. Random House. p. 4.*

QUESTION

What events support the assertions Reich makes in the passage in Source 8.2 about what has gone wrong in America by 1970?

The fact that serious scholars were writing works that were popular (*The Greening of America* topped the *New York Times* bestsellers list at the end of 1970) seemed to confirm the idea that youth culture was now both distinct and significant.

The rejection of science

The hippy ethos drew heavily on Buddhism and Hinduism, and one result of this was a rejection of the dominance of scientific progress. **Theodore Roszak** argued that the scientific and industrial revolutions of the last 100 years had merely facilitated the industrialisation of warfare and mass slaughter, at the expense of community and the human experience.

> **Theodore Roszak (1933–2011):**
>
> Roszak was an author and historian whose 1969 book *The Making of a Counter Culture: Reflections on the Technocratic Society and its Youthful Opposition* argued that American society resembled a 'world's fair in its final days, when things start to sag and disintegrate behind the futuristic façade'. In order to avoid this nightmarish future, Roszak argued for a less materialistic, less technocratic world.

Roszak's work tapped into a feeling that the changes in American society signalled more significant change in the world as a whole. Some of the communes of the early 1960s began to take on a more sinister aspect. These 'Doomsday Cults', which were based on the belief in an apocalyptic or catastrophic future, often ended disastrously, as with the Manson family murders of 1969 and the Jonestown Massacre of 1978 where cult leader Jim Jones caused the deaths of 900 of his followers.

Roszak's call for a rejection of materialism also reflected a continuity with the ideas of earlier American philosophers Ralph Waldo Emerson and Henry Thoreau, who had advocated self-reliance and a closer relationship with nature as far back as the 1850s. Roszak argued that Americans must seek to develop a 'new culture in which the non-intellective capacities of personality' dominate. Here, Roszak seems to foreshadow the theory of multiple intelligences put forward by Howard Gardner in 1983, which had a huge impact on education.

The swirl of ideas that were thrown up by the counter-culture confused and muddled intellectual debate for much of the 1980s, as psychology, sociology and computer science struggled to address the issues raised by those involved with youth culture in the post-war period.

Art

The art world reflected the anti-materialism of Roszak and youth protest, holding up a mirror to the American people who – in Norman Mailer's words – had become obsessed by the dollar rather than the frontier. Roy Lichtenstein and Andy Warhol elevated comic books and consumer goods to high art, in works such as the latter's Campbell's Soup Cans. Warhol, more than any other artist, understood the potential of art to comment on materialism. From his studio 'The Factory' to his comment that in the future everyone would enjoy '15 minutes of fame', Warhol satirised and justified the condition of America. Other critics bemoaned the fact that 'people no longer have opinions: they have refrigerators'.

Figure 8.6: Andy Warhol, who made images of celebrities, such as Marilyn Monroe, as well as Brillo boxes and soup tins, into high art.

Howard Zinn sees the changes that took place in the years from 1960 to the late 1970s as less about a 'generation gap' and more about the opening up of American society to new ideas and perspectives that could be embraced by anyone:

SOURCE 8.3

The new temper, the new behaviour, shocked many Americans. It created tensions. Sometimes it was seen as a 'generation gap' – the younger generation moving far away from the older one in its way of life. But it seemed after a while to be not so much a matter of age – some people remained 'straight' while some middle-aged people were changing their ways and older people were beginning to behave in ways that astounded others.

Zinn, H. 1980. A People's History of the United States. *New York, USA. Harper & Row Publishers. p. 298.*

QUESTION

Is the 'generation gap' still a reality today? If so, is it wider or narrower than in the 1960s and 1970s?

However, it was the young who seemed to lean to the 'new' more readily and in greater numbers, whether in sex, music, drugs, art or environmental activism. In addition, the media – always on the lookout for what would sell – led to a storm of changing fashions and fads. Youth culture began to move at an unprecedented speed.

ACTIVITY

Construct a table to show the perspectives of the young and older generation on the issues of education, the military, the environment, religion, politics, work, drugs, sex and music in the 1960s and 1970s.

8.4 How successful were the youth protests of the 1960s and 1970s in achieving their original goals?

Education

The persistence of the student protesters brought some changes on the campuses, not least in administrative areas and conditions in dormitories. New courses in black history and gender studies also reflected the changing times. In 1968, protesters at Columbia seized and held the president's office and the School of Architecture for several days. For the next three years, militant students seemed to be on every campus – storming buildings, abusing visiting speakers and battling with the police. There were 221 major demonstrations on university campuses in the first half of 1968 alone.

A need for change was obvious to both conservatives and reformers, but the increasingly uncompromising methods of the militants dismayed those who wanted to improve things. Slogans such as 'Don't trust anyone over thirty' and instances such as the 'Filthy Speech' movement at Berkeley only served to alienate those in authority who might have been willing to listen.

too radical
→ alienated

In addition, the Establishment found itself persuaded by the argument that this student protest was essentially a one-off. The 'baby boom' and the expansion of higher education meant that there were an unprecedented number of educated, wealthy college students, for some of whom revolt was a fashion. American universities would never again face this level of protest. The spiralling cost of a college education meant that those who successfully gained one immediately began having to repay their debt, and it quickly became obvious that radical militancy did not pay as well as law.

Environmentalism

more awareness + support.

lack of action → not successful

≠ Protection Agency

≠ ban on DDT.

While the environmental movement gathered support, it also alienated many mainstream Americans by its association with the hippy movement. The Three Mile Island nuclear disaster in 1979 did more to discredit nuclear power than any of the intellectual arguments between Commoner and Ehrlich. Meanwhile, the poor US record on environmental action suggests that the environmentalism of 1960s protest never effectively moved into the public consciousness. The politician and journalist Ralph Nader increasingly campaigned on an environmental platform in his five independent candidatures for president between 1992 and 2008. Although he had sufficient support from the children of the 1960s to ensure a media profile, he never had a realistic chance. The environmental protests of the youth movement in the 1960s and 1970s influenced the creation of the Environmental Protection Agency in 1970, and the 1972 ban on DDT can be traced back to the origins of Carson's work. However, it would be three more decades before environmentalism crossed over into the mainstream.

Civil rights

The issue of young people's involvement in the civil rights movement is covered in considerable detail in Chapters 4, 5 and 6. The following activity might be useful to draw your understanding together.

ACTIVITY

The key personalities in this chapter are far more debatable than in other chapters in this book, which might suggest that the absence of clear leaders is the main reason for the lack of clarity and arguable failure of youth protest. Plan an essay that answers the following question: 'To what extent was the absence of leadership the main reason for the failure of youth protest in the US in the 1960s and 1970s?'

Vietnam

From the small anti-Vietnam protests begun in 1964 by students at Yale and Berkeley, youth protest undermined the war effort with remarkable speed. By 1966, support for the war was eroding as Senator **William Fulbright** criticised bombing tactics, and other senators began to suggest that Vietnam was not the vital territory in the campaign against communism that Johnson believed.

J. William Fulbright (1905–95):

Fulbright was a southern Democrat senator for Arkansas, a signatory of the Southern Manifesto, and the longest-serving chairman in the history of the Senate Foreign Relations Committee. He had signed the 1964 Gulf of Tonkin Resolution, which led to escalated US involvement in Vietnam, but later became a critic of the war. In 1966 he published *The Arrogance of Power*, in which he attacked the interventionist nature of US foreign policy and its involvement in Vietnam in particular, providing vital political backing to the anti-war movement.

While the lessening support for the war was due in part to the protests, economic factors were even more significant. The threat of tax rises alarmed Republicans, while Democrats complained that the cost of Vietnam was eating into the Great Society budget.

Johnson and Vietnam

Johnson himself became a target, as the protesters made the war personal. Drawing on the images of women and children killed in raids on Vietnamese villages, the infamous chant 'Hey, Hey, LBJ, how many kids have you killed today?' haunted Johnson, forcing him to limit his public appearances.

The media proved to be a double-edged sword for the government. Reality intruded nightly on TV and in the haunting 1966 Simon & Garfunkel song '7 O'Clock News/Silent Night', which juxtaposes the Christmas carol with a sobering news bulletin from 3 August.

The John Wayne film *The Green Berets* was critically savaged for its overly positive interpretation of US foreign policy. Worse was to come when respected figures such as Martin Luther King began to condemn the war. Despite the cost to his relationship with Johnson, King accused the president of sending young black men to:

SOURCE 8.4

...guarantee liberties in Southeast Asia which they had not found in Southwest Georgia and East Harlem. So we have been repeatedly faced with the cruel irony of watching Negro and white boys on TV screens as they kill and die together for a nation that has been unable to seat them together in the same schools... I could never again raise my voice against the violence of the oppressed in the ghettos without having first spoken clearly to the greatest purveyor of violence in the world today – my own government.

Extract from Martin Luther King's 'Beyond Vietnam' speech, Riverside Church Meeting, New York, 4 April 1967.

QUESTION

How does King link the Vietnam War to civil rights in Source 8.4?

Meanwhile, military intake from the draft had risen from 5000 men per month in 1965 to 50000 per month in 1967. Into this tense atmosphere the student protesters charged. In Berkeley in 1967, protesters used smoke bombs against the police while 2500 of them tried to close the draft office. The protests grew until 8000 filled the streets, vandalising cars, trees and parking meters.

Many of the protesters were using marijuana, according to both police and newspaper reports. These were the 'shock troops' of the anti-war movement, willing to engage with the police and risk violence. More conservative – but still outraged – protesters met at rallies such as the 70 000-strong rally in Washington in October 1967. This was organised by the National Mobilization Committee to End the War in Vietnam, a short-lived coalition of anti-war activists formed in 1967, and it was known as 'The March on the Pentagon to Confront the War Makers'.

The events were described by novelist Norman Mailer in his Pulitzer Prize-winning book from 1968, *The Armies of the Night*. The peaceful nature of the protest broke down as radicals again attacked the strong government presence, which included National Guardsmen, paratroopers and federal policemen. This led to running battles outside the Pentagon and 625 arrests.

Student protest had an undoubted effect on key members of the government. Secretary of State Dean Rusk's son had a nervous breakdown brought about by the strength of his disagreement with his father. By 1965 the protests had made Vietnam the key issue facing the country; the annual Gallup poll on 'The public's view of the most important problem facing the country' had revealed desegregration as the issue for 1964, but Vietnam was the top issue for the next four years.

The media coverage made the military difficulties clear and there were also considerable economic pressures that eroded public faith in the government's war aims, such as when 1967 brought the first tax rises as a result of the war. By October, when the draft was introduced, 46% of those polled felt that the war had been a mistake. The same month saw draft cards being burned live on television. In a radical and highly symbolic act, 'bleed-ins' were organised, where donors gave blood for use by the Viet Cong.

The lack of progress was highlighted by TV reports and served to encourage the protesters belief in the futility of the war. The 1968 Tet Offensive fatally damaged the war effort, as Viet Cong troops temporarily occupied the US embassy in Saigon. The symbolism of this occupation of what was, legally speaking, American soil, when added to the strength of the North Vietnamese Army offensive, was a major shock to the US public. Meanwhile the financial figures were getting worse, with no end seemingly in sight.

The cost of the war was causing inflation to rise to its highest level since 1946. In 1965, the government deficit was $1.6 billion; by 1968 it was $25.3 billion. With Johnson already declaring that he would not stand for president again, protesters moved in for the kill. The Democratic Party conference held in Chicago in 1968 was descended upon by thousands of anti-war protesters. A pig was nominated for president by the Yippies, the American flag was symbolically lowered, and violence erupted as the police fought back. The conference was in chaos: 668 people were arrested and nearly 200 police officers were injured.

Nixon and Vietnam

The result for the Democrats was disastrous. Their candidate Hubert Humphrey was tainted by association with Johnson, and George Wallace, the racist governor of Alabama, took over 10 million votes as an American Independent Party candidate. Nixon rode to victory on a campaign promising peace with honour.   ⤳ safe hands

The Johnson presidency had been crippled by Vietnam. Sargent Shriver, who worked for both the Kennedy and Johnson governments, described the financial damage Vietnam did to Johnson's War on Poverty programme (see 7.1, The treatment of the Mississippi Freedom Democratic Party, 1964): 'Vietnam took it all away, every god-damned dollar. That's what killed the war on poverty.'

Between 1965 and 1973, $15.5 billion was spent on the Great Society compared with $120 billion on the Vietnam War. It is impossible to say with any certainty how successful the youth protests were in removing Johnson and the Democrats. Economic factors obviously played an enormous part, as did the intervention of Wallace, but the pressure on the president was sustained and vicious, and it changed the direction of Vietnam policy under Nixon.

Nixon's 'peace with honor' campaign involved troop withdrawals and an adjustment to the terms of the draft to save money and pacify protesters. This was a typical political calculation by Nixon who understood that the most vocal part of the anti-war movement were male college students threatened with the draft. The short-term effect was successful, with protests largely dissipating and Nixon enjoying an approval rating of over 70%. There were also signs of the changing power balance in American politics when Nixon addressed the nation:

SOURCE 8.5

And so tonight, to you, the great silent majority of my fellow Americans, I ask for your support… Let us be united for peace. Let us also be united against defeat. Because let us understand: North Vietnam cannot defeat or humiliate the United States. Only Americans can do that.

Extract from Richard Nixon's televised 'Silent Majority' speech, 3 November 1969.

KEY CONCEPTS QUESTION

Change: What does Source 8.5 suggest about how American politics had changed over the previous two decades?

The speech won universal acclaim and bought Nixon some time by linking the idea of opposition to the war with defeat for America. It also appealed to the 'silent majority', which struck a chord with the millions of Americans who had not protested, rioted or burned draft cards.

However, evidence that Nixon had covertly extended the war into Cambodia re-energised the protesters. In October 1969, the campuses were in uproar and the most widespread anti-war protest in American history took place. Protesters took to the streets in every major city and millions participated, across classes and age ranges.

Radical youths carried Viet Cong flags and burned the Stars and Stripes – perhaps the most symbolic non-violent gesture available – all the while chanting defeatist slogans. Nixon was forced to back down on an ultimatum he had delivered to Hanoi, but claimed that:

SOURCE 8.6

...to allow government policy to be made in the streets would destroy the democratic process. It would give the decision, not to the majority, and not to those with the strongest arguments, but to those with the loudest voices. It would reduce statecraft to slogans. It would invite anarchy.

Extract from Richard Nixon's letter to a university student, 13 October 1969.

To the cynical it seemed as though Nixon was suggesting that government policy should still be made in the boardrooms of giant defence companies. The protests continued. The 40-hour 'March Against Death' saw 40 000 individuals file past the White House, each bearing the name of an American soldier who had died in Vietnam. In a parallel to the 1963 March on Washington, on 14–16 November 1969, 500 000 mostly young people took part in the 'Mobilization' peace protest, the largest single anti-war demonstration in US history. Meanwhile, the revelations of military brutality from My Lai – where US soldiers raped, tortured and killed 500 Vietnamese civilians, mostly women, children and old men – gave the protesters even more ammunition. Many felt that the Vietnam War was now taking American youths and making them into murderers.

Kent State shootings

Perhaps the pivotal moment in youth protest occurred at Kent State University in May 1970, when four students were shot dead by the National Guard during a protest against the war. Some locals believed the National Guard had been justified in using lethal force, but the nationwide reaction was immediate and explosive. The governor of California – Ronald Reagan – closed all the state colleges, and Nixon was forced to offer to remove troops from Cambodia by June. Vietnam policymaking was being made in the White House and argued about on the street. Paralleling the police action against protesters at the 1968 Democratic Party convention in Chicago, at the Hard Hat riot of May 1970, 1000 students protesting the Kent State shootings were attacked by 200 construction workers; meanwhile, 100 000 pro-Nixon supporters marched in New York. It seemed as if the Nixon government was going to suffer the same fate over Vietnam that Johnson's had.

Figure 8.7: A shocked student reacts to the death of another student, during the Kent State University shootings, 1970.

Youth involvement in the war

While protests were occurring at home, it should not be forgotten that young people made up the bulk of the more than half a million American service personnel who served in Vietnam. The average age of the combat soldier in Vietnam was only 19. The drug use that had become increasingly commonplace in the US was rife in Vietnam as well. Some estimates suggest that 58% of soldiers smoked marijuana and over 20% took heroin. The army's own statistics seemed to confirm this – for example, in 1971 around 5000 US soldiers were treated for wounds but over 22 000 were treated for drug-related problems. The conditions in Vietnam made drug use an easy escape, but they also contributed to huge numbers of veterans being diagnosed with post-traumatic stress disorders. The pressures led the young soldiers to rebel; 83 officers were killed by their own troops during the war.

Many soldiers served their tour and then joined the anti-war coalition on returning to the US. This coalition was perhaps the most diverse protest movement in American history, including civil rights activists such as Martin Luther King and James Farmer, public figures such as

Dr Benjamin Spock and Jane Fonda, veterans such as **Ron Kovic**, draft-age students and their parents, as well as pacifists and leftists.

> **Ron Kovic (b. 1946):**
>
> Kovic is best known for his memoir of his time in Vietnam, *Born on the Fourth of July*, which was turned into an Oscar-winning film in 1990 in which Kovic was played by Tom Cruise. He was wounded in 1970 on his second tour and has been confined to a wheelchair ever since. After returning to the US he joined the peace movement and has been arrested 12 times for political activism in the anti-war movement. Kovic is symbolic of the blue-collar veterans who returned from Vietnam disillusioned by US action there.

The break-up of the movement

As the 1970s drew to a close, the loose ties that connected the disparate groups in the youth movement were visibly fraying. The group known as the 'New Left' were never a united political organisation in the way that left-wing parties were in Europe. Furthermore, the association of left-wing politics with communism from the McCarthy era had ensured that 'socialist' would remain an insult in the US for the next three decades. Most were essentially non-political activists who had issues with the relationship between government and big corporations rather than with capitalism itself. The remnants of the Black Power movement rejected the lack of focus of 'hippy' dissent, while those who had joined with the women's and gay rights movements were often accused of having a sexual agenda.

The Yippies

Some protesters went beyond militancy. Chief among these extremists were Jerry Rubin and Abbie Hoffman, the leaders of the Youth International Party, or Yippies. Founded on New Year's Eve 1967, the Yippies were stereotypically long-haired and anarchic and sometimes referred to as 'Groucho Marxists'. They had a talent for inventing slogans and overblown rhetoric. Rubin argued 'Fire is the revolutionary's god… Burn the flag. Burn churches. Burn Burn Burn', but his words lacked the potency of Malcolm X and Stokely Carmichael, and the Yippies were accused of indulging themselves and trivialising the idea of protest. As ever, it was easy for the media to give disproportionate coverage to the outrageous and to oversimplify the message – and, by doing so, bait the hard-working Americans whose understanding of their country had been shaken so badly throughout the 1960s and 1970s.

SOURCE 8.7

They [the youth protesters Goodman encountered] did not believe there was such a thing as the simple truth. To be required to learn something was a trap by which the young were put down and co-opted. Then I knew that I could not get through to them. I had imagined that the worldwide student protest had to do with changing political and moral institutions, to which I was sympathetic, but I now saw that we had to do with a religious crisis of the magnitude of the Reformation in the 1500s, when not only all institutions but all learning had been corrupted by the whore of Babylon.

Goodman, P. 2010. New Reformation: Notes of a Neolithic Conservative. *New York, USA. PM Press. p. 71.*

QUESTION

What does Source 8.7 suggest about Paul Goodman's opinion of youth protest?

The backlash against the counter-culture

In retrospect, it is easy to understand the alarm that electrified 'middle America' in the 1960s and 1970s. The vast majority of Americans were church-going, family oriented and conservative. They valued the work ethic and the democratic process, and were accustomed to a media that celebrated American achievements. In the early 1970s, the 'backlash' against the counter-culture began. Nixon's 'silent majority' of middle-Americans included blue-collar workers, conservatives and committed Christians who were angry and frightened by the domestic turmoil that seemed to be spreading through the country.

The 'silent majority' feared the consequences of the counter-culture would be a dilution or even a destruction of the American way, and a slide into communism. In the face of these concerns, millions began to lean towards the new Republicanism embraced by Nixon and, especially, Ronald Reagan in the 1980s.

SOURCE 8.8

In the 1960s, the New Left explicitly rejected Communism and grew influential enough to help stop the Vietnam War. But in the 1970s, the anti-war, civil rights, women's and other elements of a potential left-wing movement, instead of uniting, fractured into self-absorbed proponents of identity-politics. Meanwhile Richard Nixon seized on the alienation some working class whites felt for the counter-culture to position the Republican party as the champion of traditional American values: God, flag and country.

Hertsgaard, M. 2002. The Eagle's Shadow: Why America Fascinates and Infuriates the World. *New York, USA. Farrar, Strauss and Giroux. p. 163.*

QUESTION

The US is unique among the major industrial countries in never having developed an electorally competitive socialist political party. What does Source 8.8 suggest were the reasons for this in the period after the Second World War?

8.5 How did youth movements influence politics in Canada and Latin America?

Youth movements in Canada

In Canada the influence of the US was strong but there were also the issues of the legacy of British imperialism and the debate over independence for the French speaking state of Quebec. Two significant student organisations emerged in the late 1950s and 1960s, SUPA (Student Union for Peace Action) which emerged from the Campaign for Nuclear Disarmament and CYC (Company of Young Canadians).

SUPA was a decentralised organisation with roots in the universities and an ambition to change Canadian society as a whole but with no Canadian involvement in Vietnam and a much less hostile situation over ethnic minority rights the organisation became lost in ideological debates, losing members to CYC. The febrile atmosphere created by the social unrest in the US did, however, lead to the creation of the Front de libération du Québec (FLQ), who committed over 160 attacks between 1963 and 1970, killing eight people.

Many of the FLQ's members were in their late teens and early twenties, among them Pierre Vallières who wrote the 1968 book *Nègres blancs d'Amérique* (White Niggers of America) which drew parallels between the situation of French-Canadians in Quebec to that of African Americans in the US. In October 1970 members of the FLQ kidnapped the British trade commissioner and the Canadian minister of labour and vice-premier of Quebec, Pierre Laporte.

Laporte was killed, leading the Canadian prime minister Pierre Trudeau to suspend civil liberties while the hunt for the killers was carried out. Five of the six were caught by December and convicted. The events took the sting out of youth protest in Canada which never reached the heights of its southern neighbour. *+ never as strong as US*

In Central and South America, the prevalence of single-party states in the post-war period ensured that young people lacked the luxury of free speech that had benefited the youth protesters in the US. Nevertheless, youth movements did rise up in several Latin American states, where they were invariably met with violence.

Case study: Argentina

Youth protest in Argentina has a short but bloody history, as one might expect from a country blighted by unstable military regimes. In 1966, unrest by students and workers led to a military coup and subsequent dictatorship under General Juan Carlos Onganía. Onganía moved quickly to subdue student protest in 'La Noche de los Bastones Largos' (the Night of the Long Batons). University premises occupied by students and professors opposing the military regime were stormed, and 400 protesters were detained.

The fear of student action was evident in the tactics of subsequent military leaders, especially during the period known as the National Reorganization Process (1976–83) when many students joined the ranks of 'los desaparecidos' (the disappeared). A report by the National Commission on the Disappearance of Persons in 1983 estimated that of the remaining 9000 *desaparecidos*, around 21% were students.

Case study: Mexico

In Mexico in 1968, years of repression by the government exploded when students took to the streets to protest. The hosting of the Olympic Games, and the desire of the government to show Mexico in a positive light, led to a series of brutal crackdowns. As protests grew through the summer of 1968, the government became increasingly alarmed. When 10 000 protesters gathered at the Plaza de las Tres Culturas in Tlatelolco, a neighbourhood of Mexico City, police and the military – under orders from President Díaz Ordaz – opened fire. Estimates of the death toll range from 44 to 300, but the significance of the Tlatelolco Massacre was in the legacy of innocent young protesters mown down by a callous and unaccountable government.

Summary

The youth protest movement achieved little in concrete terms, certainly less than the African American civil rights movement. Some great music was produced, some brilliant entrepreneurs were inspired, and some other rights movements benefited from the idealism of youth both in the US and in the rest of the Americas. Even over Vietnam, while youth protest had contributed to the eventual withdrawal a cold political calculation of cost against military success could easily be seen as the most pressing reason for the exit. Successful revolutions need clear goals and effective leadership – the youth protest movement had neither.

not ete thre

ACHIEVEMENTS

1st ² ROTC membership removed in 1962

Paper 3 exam practice

Question

Examine the reasons for and effectiveness of youth protest movements in one country of the region in the period after the Second World War?
[15 marks]

Skill

Writing a conclusion to your essay

Examiner's tips

Provided you have carried out all the steps recommended so far, it should be relatively easy to write one or two concluding paragraphs.

For this question, we will work on the basis that you have chosen the US as the country. You will need to cover the following possible reasons for youth protest:

- the growth in higher education, which created an intellectual climate where protest could thrive
- the inspiration of other protest movements, such as those for African American civil rights and women's rights
- the influence of music and the cinema in terms of protest songs, giving 'outsider' figures a cult status, and making many liberally minded actors into celebrities
- the outrage caused by the Vietnam War and government action
- the threat to the environment highlighted by books such as *Silent Spring*
- the large numbers of young people in the US following the 'baby boom'
- the influence of the counter-culture and the sexual revolution, following the invention of the contraceptive pill and the increased availability of drugs.

In addition, you must make a judgement about how effective this protest was, you might look at effectiveness in the different areas protest was seen, civil rights (women, black, gay and native rights), environmental issues and anti-war protests or look at effectiveness in terms of attention garnered, political decisions influenced and the lasting legacy of protest.

This question requires you to consider an individual country, and to support your analysis with precise and specific knowledge – so you need to avoid generalisations. Also, a question that asks for an analysis of several reasons implicitly expects you to come to some kind of **judgement** about which reason(s) was/were most important.

Common mistakes

Sometimes, candidates simply rehash in their conclusion what they have written earlier – making the examiner read the same things twice! Generally, concluding paragraphs should be relatively short. The aim should be to come to a judgement/conclusion that is clearly based on what has already been written. If possible, a short but relevant quotation is a good way to round off an argument.

Sample student conclusion on why protests emerged

As has been seen, it is difficult to come to a single conclusion about why youth protest movements emerged in the US after the Second World War. Social factors were certainly vital: the growth in higher education and the increase in young people owing to the baby boom played a key part. There were also interconnected economic factors, with the increased wealth and leisure time of the young allowing them the freedom to protest and experiment. However, the main factor that drew on all the prevailing circumstances was the war in Vietnam. The ideals of the counter-culture, free love and the use of drugs were diametrically opposed to the campaign in Vietnam, which seemed to many to revolve around the killing of women and children. Hence, demonstrations swelled and the complex geo-political explanations for continued involvement did nothing to convince the protesters, who were fuelled by a heady combination of righteous indignation and self-interest. In terms of effectiveness withdrawal from Vietnam was a far more tangible success for youth protest than anything achieved by environmental activists or young people exclusively targeting rights but the argument that withdrawal from Vietnam was an economic decision remains compelling.

EXAMINER'S COMMENT

This is a reasonable conclusion as it briefly pulls together the main threads of the argument (without simply repeating or summarising them), but the judgement at the end is an example of a student 'sitting on the fence'.

Activity

In this chapter, the focus is on writing a useful conclusion. So, using the information from this chapter, and any other sources of information available to you, write concluding paragraphs for at least two of the following Paper 3 practice questions. Remember: to do this, you will need to do full plans for the questions you choose.

Remember to refer to the simplified Paper 3 mark scheme given in Chapter 11.

Paper 3 practice questions

1   Evaluate the reasons for opposition to the Vietnam War in the period 1964 to 1975.

2   To what extent were the goals of youth protest movements in at least one country in the region achieved by 1980?

3   'The greatest achievement of youth protest in the Americas was ending the Vietnam War.' To what extent do you agree with this statement?

4   Compare and contrast the methods employed in protesting against the war in Vietnam and in favour of African American civil rights.

5   Discuss the contribution of young people to protest movements in one country of the region.

9 | Feminist movements in the Americas

Introduction

This chapter deals with the rise of feminist movements in the Americas, and focuses in particular on the women's liberation movement in the United States. It will examine the origins of campaigns for women's rights in the period before the Second World War, and the impact of the war on the role and status of women. The chapter will also examine the goals of the movement and the extent to which these were achieved, as well as looking at opponents of women's rights and their influence on the resurgence of conservatism in the 1980s.

Links to the civil rights movement and youth protest will be explored, and the chapter will conclude with an examination of the cultural, political and economic legacy of feminist movements in the US. Feminist movements in other countries will be explored in the main sections of text and through a series of case studies.

TIMELINE

1920 Women given the right to vote

1923 Equal Rights Amendment introduced to Congress for the first time

1939–45 Seven million women take up factory jobs as men called up to army

1952 **Jul:** Death of Eva Perón in Argentina

1953 **Jan:** Simone De Beauvoir's *The Second Sex* published in US

1955 **Dec:** Rosa Parks protest sparks Montgomery Bus Boycott

1960 **Jun:** Birth control pill approved for marketing

1961 **Dec:** Presidential Commission on the Status of Women established

1963 **Feb:** Betty Friedan's *The Feminine Mystique* published

Jun: Equal Pay Act signed into law by Kennedy

1964 **Jul:** Title VII of Civil Rights Act prohibits sex discrimination in employment

1966 **Jun:** National Organization for Women (NOW) founded

1968 **Sept:** Radical feminists picket Miss America pageant in Atlantic City

Nov: Shirley Chisholm becomes first black woman elected to Congress

1969 **Apr:** Gloria Steinem publishes 'After Black Power, Women's Liberation' in *New York* magazine

1972 **Mar:** Equal Rights Amendment (ERA) passed by Senate (but fails to win ratification by a majority of state legislatures)

1973 **Jan:** *Roe versus Wade* decision gives women right to choose on abortion

1977 **Apr:** Mothers of Plaza de Mayo protest against regime in Argentina

1993 **Mar:** Janet Reno becomes US attorney general

Jun: Kim Campbell becomes first female prime minister of Canada

KEY QUESTIONS

• How significant was the issue of women's rights in the Americas before 1945?

• Why did the women's movement emerge in the Americas after the Second World War?

• What were the goals of the reformers in the women's movement?

• In what ways, and to what extent, did the role and status of women change as a result of the women's movement?

• How successful were the women's campaigns of the 1960s in achieving their original goals?

Overview

• After contributing prolifically to the war effort, many women were disappointed by the expectation that they should return to conventional roles after the Second World War.

• A second wave of feminism began nearly a decade after the end of the Second World War; these feminists were inspired by writers such as Betty Friedan and Germaine Greer.

• Technological changes, in particular the licensing of the contraceptive pill in 1960, enabled women to take more control over their fertility.

• Increasing pressure for legislative change led to a series of measures by the Kennedy and Johnson governments.

- Feminism took on a more assertive tone in response to the slowness of changes in measures such as pay and the Equal Rights Amendment (ERA).
- In 1973, the pivotal court case *Roe versus Wade* legalised abortion in the US.
- The period of liberalism in the late 1960s and early 1970s was followed by a backlash and return to 'family' values that saw the goals of protest become less coherent.

9.1 How significant was the issue of women's rights in the Americas before 1945?

Sister Juana Inés de la Cruz, a Mexican scholar and poet, could be seen as the mother figure of feminism in the Americas. Writing in the late 17th century, her poetry was filled with a sense of the injustices suffered by her gender. Her themes of the importance of education and the hypocrisy attached to women's sexuality would feature heavily in the feminist movements that followed nearly 200 years later. In one of her poems she poses the question, 'Who sins more, she who sins for pay? Or he who pays for sin?' Sister Juana is now largely forgotten and many feminist historians trace the contemporary origin of the movement to writers such as Mary Wollstonecraft in England, whose *A Vindication of the Rights of Women* (1792) was designed as a companion to Thomas Paine's *The Rights of Man* (1791).

First-wave feminism   US

In the 19th century and early 20th century, a movement that was later known as first-wave feminism emerged in the US. The first-wave feminists did not see themselves as such (the word 'feminist' only came into regular use after 1895), but their movement addressed inequalities in women's social and legal status. They focused on access to education, greater equality in employment and addressing the unfair laws surrounding marriage. The problems of working-class women, such as poverty and the lack of birth control, went largely unrecognised. In this way, there are clear parallels with the early stages of the civil rights movement, where the NAACP were sometimes criticised for concentrating on the middle class.

First-wave feminists, such as Elizabeth Cady Stanton, Alice Paul and Susan B. Anthony in the US, opened up higher education to women and gained the right for girls to participate in national examinations. They also smoothed the path to more women taking on roles in the professions, especially medicine. More significantly, they earned property rights for women through the Married Women's Property Act of 1870, and also gained some improvement in divorced and separated women's custody rights.

When it came to the question of the vote, however, like their sisters in Great Britain, they had failed to achieve any gains before the outbreak of the First World War. Paradoxically, in the US, women could be elected, but could not elect, indeed Jeannette Rankin had become the first woman to be elected to Congress in 1916, a full four years before the right to vote was established for women.

Between the wars

The First World War was a defining conflict, not least because it led to women taking on the roles of men who were away at war. This action went a long way to 'earning' women the vote in the UK and Canada in 1918, and in the US in 1920. With this achievement of political rights, the first wave of feminism seemed to die out; another parallel with the decline of the civil rights movement after the Civil Rights Act of 1964 and Voting Rights Act of 1965.

During the boom period of the 1920s, technological advances such as William Henry Hoover's upright vacuum cleaner introduced in 1926 improved the home lives of many women, and the growth of mass media and the consumer society led to the emergence of 'flappers' – young women who followed the new trends in fashion closely and were portrayed as intent on enjoying themselves and disregarding conventional standards of behaviour.

The growth in mass media also led to the emergence of female celebrities who created an aspirational environment for women in the US, among them was the future First Lady **Eleanor Roosevelt**, Jane Addams, who in 1931 became the first woman to win the Nobel Peace Prize for her work with the poor in Chicago, and Amelia Earhart, who was the first woman to fly solo across the Atlantic Ocean in 1932.

Eleanor Roosevelt (1884–1962):

Eleanor Roosevelt effectively created the modern role of the First Lady (the wife of the president), and became a committed supporter of civil rights. After her husband's death in 1945, Roosevelt continued to work for a variety of causes. As a politician, she was a delegate to the UN from 1945 to 1952 and chaired the committee that drafted the Universal Declaration of Human Rights and the committee on the Status of Women. As an activist and highly quotable speaker, she campaigned to enhance the status of working women, despite remaining opposed to the Equal Rights Amendment (see section 9.5).

The 1920s also saw the start of a long-running saga over the Equal Rights Amendment (ERA). This was a proposed change to the Constitution designed to guarantee equal rights for women. In 1923 it was put to Congress for the first time and then was introduced into every Congressional session between 1923 and 1970 but almost never reached the floor of either house for a vote. The problems over ERA were not just a case of the patriarchy asserting control. Historian Judith Sealander describes the debate as 'feminist against feminist' as those who believed in equality at all cost fought those who felt that women's rights deserved special protection rather than equality with men.

QUESTION

To what extent does the concept of civil rights have an agreed definition?

ACTIVITY

The original proposal for the Equal Rights Amendment split the feminist movement and it has continued to divide opinion. Research the opposition to ERA and consider whether any of its female opponents make a reasonable case.

9.2 Why did the women's movement emerge in the Americas after the Second World War?

The role and status of women in 1945

Figure 9.1: Posters showing the role of women in the 1940s (left) and the 1950s (right).

ACTIVITY

Look at the two images in Figure 9.1. The poster on the left dates from 1942, during the Second World War; the advertisement on the right dates from 1950. In pairs, discuss their purpose, value and limitations. Do you think the designs would have achieved their purpose? What do the pictures suggest about how the perception of women changed after the war ended?

The two posters in Figure 9.1 illustrate the huge changes women experienced during the Second World War and the decade that followed it. The legendary 'Rosie the Riveter' poster, produced in 1942 for the Westinghouse Company's War Production Coordinating Committee, has become symbolic of the contribution of women to the war effort. Over 7 million women took on roles in US factories as a result of men being called up. The second image was used to launch the Kenwood food mixer in 1950. Barely five years after the end of the war, a woman's role (as far as advertisers saw it) was back to being the dutiful housewife. Historian Howard Zinn summed up the situation like this:

SOURCE 9.1

It seems that women have best been able to make their first escape from the prison of wifeliness, motherhood, femininity, housework, beautification, isolation, when their services have been desperately needed – whether in industry, or in war, or in social movements.

Zinn, H. 2003. **The Twentieth Century: A People's History.** *New York, USA. Perennial. p. 256.*

Women's war work was vital in both the world wars, and their role in social movements was no less important. Susan B. Anthony and Elizabeth Cady Stanton had endorsed the US Women's Christian Temperance Union (a pressure group founded in 1874 that campaigned for the abolition of the sale of alcohol on the grounds that it damaged physical and psychological health).

The temperance movement was particularly associated with women as they were often left to pick up the pieces of families affected by an alcoholic husband or father, and the work of the Union eventually led to prohibition in 1919. It was the commitment and willingness to do the less glamorous work of social movements, such as delivering newsletters and putting on catering, that made women indispensable to their success, and this was to be the case when the civil rights movement first stirred in the decade after the Second World War.

The relative dormancy of feminism in the US after 1920 was not the case through the rest of the Americas, where other countries moved to catch up, in terms of suffrage at least. Women were given the vote in Chile in 1931, Brazil in 1932, Bolivia in 1938 and Argentina in 1947

1947. However, the Great Depression that rippled out of Wall Street from 1929 until the mid 1930s also showed how economic conditions could affect women's positions – as jobs became scarce throughout the Americas, men were even less inclined to tolerate women 'stealing' their work.

This resentment goes some way to explaining the shift from Rosie the Riveter to the Kenwood housewife. As millions of men returned home from the war, the government felt obliged to reward them by guaranteeing jobs, often at the expense of women. In addition, the annual birth rate increased by nearly 7% between 1945 and 1949. This 'baby boom' resulted in a generation of young people who entered their late teens in the mid to late 1960s and felt that change was in the air. By 1965, four out of ten Americans were under the age of 20, a statistic inextricably linked to the growth of youth protest (see Chapter 8).

The second wave of feminism

The 'baby boom' clearly kept many women busy after the Second World War, but it would be wrong to suggest that it was the only reason that a large-scale women's rights movement did not appear in the late 1940s and early 1950s. The start of the second wave of feminism came about because of three changes in the role they played.

More women at work

The first factor was the increase in female workers, which had continued after the war. These jobs were not in the factories but rather in the burgeoning tertiary, or service, sector. In 1940, women made up 19% of the workforce; by 1950 this figure was 28.8% and by 1960 women took almost half of the jobs available in the US. However, this superficially positive trend had underlying problems, as women suffered much discrimination in the workplace.

In 1960, Eleanor Roosevelt persuaded Kennedy to set up the Presidential Commission on the Status of Women. The commission reported in 1963 that despite women making up almost half the workforce, 95% of company managers were men and 88% of technical workers were men, while only 4% of lawyers and a mere 7% of doctors were women. Worse still, women earned around 50–60% of the wages of men, even when they were doing the same work. The commission concluded that work for women was, almost without exception, poorly paid, part-time and with no responsibility.

Legally, women also suffered, and in some sectors it was common for working women to be dismissed when they married or even reached a certain age. The airline industry was particularly culpable, leading to court cases and even congressional hearings. Congresswoman Martha Griffiths questioned National Airlines about its policy of firing air stewardesses when they married or reached the age of 32: 'You are asking that a stewardess be young, attractive and single. What are you running, an airline or a whorehouse?'

'The problem that had no name'

The second factor evolved out of the 'baby boom'. A decade and a half after the end of the war, many of the women who had married and had children in the baby boom had become disillusioned. In 1963, **Betty Friedan** described the problem in her hugely influential book *The Feminine Mystique*. The title referred to her belief in an ingrained set of ideas that dictated that women's happiness could only come from their roles as wives and mothers.

[handwritten annotation: → kick started 2nd wave]

Friedan said that married women must be helped to continue in paid employment, if they were not to get bored, frustrated and become de-skilled. Friedan's research suggested that there was a generation of college-educated women who felt more like slaves. Banners at some of the marches she organised took up this theme, with slogans like 'End Human Sacrifice, Don't get Married'.

Betty Friedan (1921–2006):

Friedan's 1963 book *The Feminine Mystique* is often credited with kick-starting the second wave of American feminism. In 1966, Friedan founded the National Organization for Women (NOW), which aimed to bring women 'into the mainstream of American society in fully equal partnership with men'. Friedan organised the nationwide Women's Strike for Equality on 26 August 1970, which broadened the feminist movement with actions in 90 cities. The march on Fifth Avenue in New York, led by Friedan, attracted over 50 000 people. In 1971, Friedan joined other leading feminists to establish the National Women's Political Caucus (NWPC). She was also a strong supporter of the proposed Equal Rights Amendment to the US Constitution, and she founded the National Association for the Repeal of Abortion Laws.

Figure 9.2: The feminist activist Betty Friedan (right) on a march, 1971.

SOURCE 9.2

As the American woman made beds, shopped for groceries, matched slipcover material, ate peanut butter sandwiches with her children, chauffeured cub scouts and brownies, lay beside her husband at night, she was afraid to ask even of herself the question 'is this all?'

Friedan, B. 1963. **The Feminine Mystique (2001 edition).** *New York, USA. W.W. Norton. p. 57.*

ACTIVITY

What can you infer about the lives of American women from Source 9.2?

But Friedan was keen to point out the failings of the system rather than just demonising men. For her, the problem went deeper than rights to equal pay and education. Whereas the other social movements in the US focused on tangible problems – civil rights for black people, anti-Vietnam protests for the young, and legal recognition for Native Americans – Friedan expressed women's sense of dissatisfaction with their traditional roles as 'the problem that had no name'.

SOURCE 9.3

Men weren't really the enemy – they were fellow victims suffering from an outmoded masculine mystique that made them feel unnecessarily inadequate when there were no bears to kill.

Friedan, B. 1963. The Feminine Mystique (2001 edition). *New York, USA. W.W. Norton. p. 521.*

QUESTION

What does Betty Friedan mean in Source 9.3 when she says that men felt inadequate 'when there were no bears to kill'?

Friedan's book had an impact beyond the US. In Mexico, Anilu Elias, the journalist, professor and feminist activist, described her feelings after reading the book: 'I put it away because it felt like keeping a bomb in the house. I knew that after reading it the only thing I could or should do is to get a divorce.'

The debate about the influence of *The Feminine Mystique* echoes the discussions about the importance of Martin Luther King to the civil rights movement. The historian Stephanie Coontz argues:

SOURCE 9.4

Feminine Mistique

The Women's Movement certainly would have taken off without Friedan's book, but acknowledging this only makes what the book did achieve all the more powerful and moving. [It] electrified a layer of women 'in between,' women who might otherwise have been lost entirely, to themselves and to the women's movement.

Coontz, S. 2011. A Strange Stirring: the Feminine Mystique and American Women at the Dawn of the 1960s. *New York, USA. Basic. p. 161.*

Theory of Knowledge

History, literature and revolution:

Can a book really begin a revolution? Thomas Paine's *The Rights of Man* is often credited with inspiring the American Revolution, and Karl Marx's *Das Kapital* could be seen as the inspiration for the communist revolution in Russia in 1917. Should *The Feminine Mystique* be seen in the same light? How could we prove this? In addition, has the digital revolution made the wider role of the book redundant? If so, what, if anything, has replaced it?

The experience of the civil rights movement

The third factor affecting women's rights was the influence of the other rights movements. Women had been the unsung heroes of the black civil rights movement. Leading figures such as Ella Baker (see section 5.1) of the SCLC, Fannie Lou Hamer of the Mississippi Freedom Democratic Party, Autherine Lucy and Rosa Parks (see section 4.2) made huge contributions along with the countless thousands who marched, delivered leaflets, boycotted, sat, rode and were arrested as part of the cause.

Historically, however, these women tended to be ignored in favour of Martin Luther King, Malcolm X or Huey Newton. Powerful male figureheads took much of the credit and publicity while the organising and lower-profile work fell to the women.

By the time the civil rights movement began to fracture after the
1965 Voting Rights Act had been passed, many female civil rights
campaigners were disillusioned with the misogyny of Black Power. They
were experienced campaigners, emboldened by the successes they had
achieved, and angry about their treatment as women. The skills and
experience these women were to bring to second-wave feminism was
vital to its successes.

→ animated them to support women's right

SOURCE 9.5

Mary King and Casey Hayden argued in 'Sex and Caste: A Kind of
Oppression', that women were expected only to clean up, make coffee,
and serve men while being denied an equal voice in the decision making.
In so many instances, they suggested, women in the SNCC were treated
by men just like blacks in America were treated by whites. With an
attempt at ironic humour, Stokeley Carmichael infamously commented,
'The position of women in the movement should be prone.'; but the
conflicts suggested in the King-Hayden memo eventually resulted in
white women leaving the movement and becoming the leaders of a new
women's liberation struggle.

Chafe, W. H. 2009. **Rise and Fall of the American Century: The
United States from 1890–2009.** *New York, USA. Oxford University
Press. p. 207.*

QUESTION

With reference to its origin, purpose and content, analyse the
value and limitations of Source 9.5 for a historian studying the
treatment of women in the civil rights movement.

These three factors led to the development of the women's movement
in the US. Like the black civil rights movement, the movement was not
represented by a single organisation, but, instead of four or five groups,
competing, there were thousands of more positive ones, incorporating
housewives, students, former civil rights campaigners and even book
groups and Tupperware parties. The groups had different agendas
but similar aims, namely raising the status of women, ending legal

discrimination against women, and highlighting the social structures that kept women in a subservient position.

9.3 What were the goals of the reformers in the women's movement?

Legislation

While Betty Friedan was inspiring a generation, Congress was reacting to the findings of the Presidential Commission on the Status of Women. In June 1963, Kennedy signed into law the Equal Pay Act as part of his New Frontier programme. One important omission in the report was any mention of the Equal Rights Amendment (ERA) (see section 9.5) which had first been introduced to Congress in 1923.

This was to be expected given the presence on the commission of key figures such as Robert Kennedy and Abraham Ribicoff, the secretary for health, education, and welfare, who were part of an administration that was not fully committed to supporting the ERA. The Kennedy government was keen to avoid discussion of the ERA, owing to its close ties to organised labour.

After President Kennedy's death many of the legislative efforts of the Kennedy executive were then taken on by the Johnson administration, as part of the Great Society programme and the Civil Rights Act of 1964. While this act is best remembered as a vital step in black civil rights, the efforts of Congresswoman Martha Griffiths ensured the act also outlawed discrimination against all women by cleverly arguing that without the Title VII amendment she proposed, the act would protect the rights of black women but not white women.

Organisations and campaigns

With the buzz around *The Feminine Mystique* yet to explode, some writers despaired of the movement despite these legislative advances. The sociologist Alice Rossi wrote: 'There is no overt anti-feminism in our society in 1964, not because sex equality has been achieved, but because there is practically no feminist spark left among American women.'

But the spark Betty Friedan had lit was about to burn much brighter. By the early 1970s, the National Organization for Women (NOW) had over 40 000 members. NOW learned lessons about the dangers of division from the fracturing of the black civil rights movement, and it cooperated with a wide range of other women's groups, such as the National Women's Political Caucus, the Women's Campaign Fund, the North American Indian Women's Association and the National Black Feminist Organization. NOW also picked up valuable lessons from the civil rights movement in terms of how best to gain media attention.

Marches and demonstrations in the streets of major American cities echoed the actions of the SNCC and SCLC earlier in the decade, and the women also challenged discrimination in the courts. In a series of cases between 1966 and 1971, NOW secured $30 million in back pay owed to women by companies who had ignored the Equal Pay Act of 1963. In 1972, the Supreme Court ruled that the US Constitution did give men and women equal rights.

There were also defeats, however. A NOW campaign for the Comprehensive Child Care Act (which would have provided a national day care system that would make it easier for single mothers to work), made it through both houses of Congress, but was vetoed by President Nixon, who dubbed it the 'Sovietization of American children'.

Women's liberation

But as the 1960s drew to a close, NOW was increasingly becoming the conservative part of the women's movement. Friedan herself still believed in traditional family values and marriage, and NOW mostly used conventional methods – such as political pressure and court cases – to achieve its objectives. At the other end of the spectrum, younger, more radical feminists began to employ different methods to achieve more radical aims. These feminists became known as the Women's Liberation Movement (commonly known as Women's Lib).

In 1968, using tactics designed to gain maximum media attention, a group called Radical Women picketed the Miss America pageant in Atlantic City, New Jersey. Claiming that the contest objectified women, they crowned a sheep as 'Miss America' and threw items that they saw as instruments of female oppression, such as dishcloths, make-up, bras and copies of *Playboy*, into a 'Freedom Trash Can'. Jacqui Ceballos, a NOW member who was at the protest, described the plan: 'We learnt very early on that the press liked crazy things. So we used the press.'

Despite the complete absence of any flames, an article in the magazine *Ms.* by Lindsy Van Gelder created one of the most enduring images of the women's movement. The article, which sought to draw parallels with the symbolic burning of draft cards by young men opposed to the Vietnam War, was headlined 'Bra Burners and Miss America'. The phrase 'bra-burning' subsequently became synonymous with the women's movement.

DISCUSSION POINT

The association between feminism and bra-burning has been seen by some as detrimental to the women's movement. Why do you think this might be? Why might some people have wanted a negative interpretation of the 'Freedom Trash Can' protest to become widespread?

Figure 9.3: A women's rights activist 'burns' her bra by dropping it in the 'Freedom Trash Can' at the Miss America Pageant, 1968.

Extremism

Demonstrations such as that at the Miss America pageant raised the profile of the feminist movement, and were widely reported in the USA and overseas (notably in the USSR). However, some feminists felt that this did not help the cause because the protests were not taken seriously. On the fringes of the movement more extreme forms of protest had also begun to emerge. On 3 June 1968, Valerie Solanas, a radical feminist writer, had attempted to murder the artist Andy Warhol. Solanas had self-published a pamphlet called the SCUM Manifesto. SCUM was interpreted to stand for the 'Society for Cutting up Men' and the manifesto, which encouraged male gendercide and the creation of an all-female society, was seized on by the press as an example of radicalism gone too far, though there is much evidence to suggest Solanas had other motivations for her manifesto and for shooting Warhol.

A more stable form of extremism came in the guise of WITCH, the Women's International Terrorist Conspiracy from Hell, who protested against corporations that infringed women's rights globally. Some of the most radical members of Women's Lib were lesbians who regarded men as increasingly redundant. Although the first successful birth of a 'test-tube' baby was a decade away, one popular saying went 'A woman needs a man like a fish needs a bicycle'.

Figure 9.4: Protest banners condemn what demonstrators saw as men's sexist expectations.

'The personal is political'

But away from the attention-grabbing extremism and the glare of the media spotlight, hard-working feminists ran consciousness-raising groups where women, often inspired by the writing of Friedan, **Erica Jong** or **Germaine Greer**, could talk about their lives in depth and debate how they might best challenge discrimination.

A popular phrase at the time was 'the personal is political', which derived from a 1970 essay of the same name by feminist writer Carol Hanisch. The phrase meant that many of the personal problems women experienced in their lives were not of their own making but rather the result of systematic oppression. Of course, the phrase could be interpreted in a more positive way as well, that everything you did in your personal life could affect the way people treated all women. For example, it was an act of protest against male supremacy to choose not to wear a bra or make-up.

> ### Erica Jong (b. 1942):
>
> American novelist and poet, Erica Jong is a key writer of the feminist period. Her book *Fear of Flying* was published in 1973. The frank sexual nature of *Fear of Flying* made Jong an instant celebrity. The book tries to reconcile the different aspects of women's sexuality with the roles imposed upon them by society, and it remains popular today.

> ### Germaine Greer (b. 1939):
>
> Greer is another significant feminist writer and academic. Her first book, *The Female Eunuch*, was in print in the US by 1971. It polarised opinion by arguing that women do not realise how much men hate them, and how much they are taught to hate themselves. Originally from Australia, Greer was appointed in 1979 as director for the Center for the Study of Women's Literature at the University of Tulsa. She continues to write and contribute to political debate, mainly in the UK.

'De-sexing the English language'

In a 1972 edition of *Ms.*, an article entitled 'De-Sexing the English Language' suggested that the English language itself was inherently sexist. The article's authors, Casey Miller and Kate Swift, argued that words such as 'mankind', which were designed to represent all humanity, implicitly gave preference to men. In addition, the language of many professions seemed to have built-in prejudice: a chairman was common but people never referred to a chairwoman; men were always referred to as Mr but women were forced to reveal their marital status when they gave their names in an official capacity as either Mrs or Miss, a distinction which defined them by their relationship to men. The inherent biases in the English language have gone on to be a significant part of the feminist agenda, and raise interesting questions about the nature of language itself.

9.4 In what ways, and to what extent, did the role and status of women change as a result of the women's movement?

Reproductive rights

Perhaps the most important factor in changing the role and status of women was the technological and social changes that enabled them to take control of their own fertility. By deciding when to conceive, women could plan their careers more consciously and aspire to positions of influence and power in ways that previous generations could not.

The pill

The first birth control pill, Enovid, was approved by the Food and Drug Administration for use in June 1960, but it required two key legal battles for it to become available. In 1965, in *Griswold versus Connecticut*, the Supreme Court made the pill available to married women nationwide on the grounds that to prohibit it violated the 'right to marital privacy'. In the 1972 case *Eisenstadt versus Baird*, the Court struck down a Massachusetts law prohibiting the distribution of contraceptives to unmarried people, ruling that it violated the Equal Protection Clause of the Constitution. This case effectively made the pill available to all.

The historian Elaine Tyler May claims the arrival of the pill was the culmination of the work of Margaret Sanger, the founder of the American Birth Control League in the 1920s and the first legal, doctor-run birth-control clinic. May argues that Sanger 'knew that women could not achieve full equality unless they had control over their reproductive lives'.

Control over reproduction meant a number of things. First, it reduced the chances of women dying during pregnancy; second, it meant that they could avoid having more children than they could afford; third, it meant that their careers could be planned more carefully; and finally – and this was the angle the media favoured – it allowed them to take a more liberated approach to their sex lives.

Griswold versus Connecticut, 1965

In the early 1960s, a young woman from Connecticut challenged the anti-contraception laws. Griswold's lawyers were smart; they approached the case using the constitutionally sacrosanct 'right to privacy' in much the same way as the NAACP had used the Equal Protection Clause of the 14th Amendment to remove segregation in education. They argued that the state legislating to interfere in the sexual relationship of married couples was an infringement of the privacy of ordinary Americans. In 1965, the case reached the Supreme Court, where judges under Earl Warren ruled 7 to 2 in favour of Griswold.

Abortion

Controlling pregnancy was one part of controlling fertility; the ability to safely abort was a far more ethically complex area. The debate hinged on when human life was deemed to begin – at conception, at the point of foetal viability or elsewhere. The legalisation of abortion was an issue that feminists had never been united on. Susan B. Anthony and Elizabeth Cady Stanton had both opposed the practice in the first wave of the feminist movement, whereas Betty Friedan supported a woman's right to choose.

The legal situation was complex and in flux even before the development of the feminist movement. Criminalisation had occurred gradually up to 1900, when most states banned the practice, but illegal abortions still took place. These were often unsafe, but sometimes highly organised by underground movements. For example, the Jane Collective performed 12000 abortions in the Chicago area from 1969 to 1973, for

$25 a time. In the early 1960s, abortion was illegal even if pregnancy and birth would threaten the life of the woman involved.

Feminists demanded the 'right to choose' and this 'right' would become a key issue that still provokes exceptionally strong feelings. Their argument, that a woman should not be forced to bear a child if she does not want to, challenged women's perceived role as mothers and their status as subject to male authority.

Roe versus Wade, 1970–73

The success of the Griswold case emboldened feminists and lawyers to attack the issue of abortion, and the pivotal case was that of *Roe versus Wade*, 1970 to 1973. Jane Roe was the legal-use name given to Norma McCorvey to protect her identity. McCorvey had led a difficult life. She was raised in a reform school, she was beaten by her husband, and her three children had been taken away from her because she could not care for them.

Sarah Weddington, a feminist lawyer, met McCorvey when she was pregnant again, and saw this as an ideal test case to get the courts to allow abortion. Unlike the respectable figures the NAACP used for their test cases, such as Rosa Parks and Linda Brown, Weddington realised that McCorvey's troubled background and maternal incompetence would make a convincing argument for the eventual unhappiness of her unborn child.

Weddington's 1973 victory in the case established a legal precedent that led to abortion becoming freely available. *Roe versus Wade* also reshaped American politics, dividing voters and politicians into two clear lobbies – pro-choice and pro-life. In addition, *Roe versus Wade* had a profound effect on America's social landscape: the controversy over a chapter in the best-selling book *Freakonomics*, by Steven Levitt and Stephen Dubner, which claims that the *Roe versus Wade* case was responsible for significant drops in crime in the 1990s, is just one example.

Figure 9.5: The 1976 'March for Life' – demonstrators lobby for a constitutional amendment to ban abortion.

SOURCE 9.6

In the aftermath [of the *Roe versus Wade* decision] abortions averaged 1.5 million per year, or four terminated pregnancies for every ten babies born. To conservatives, and especially many Roman Catholics who had been taught that abortion was murder, these figures suggested that the entire moral structure of the nation had been turned upside down, with no-one defending society's interest in stable family life or strict sexual standards.

Chafe, W. H. 2009. **Rise and Fall of the American Century: The United States from 1890–2009.** *New York, USA. Oxford University Press. p. 231.*

Significance: To what extent can a comparison between *Roe versus Wade* and *Brown versus Board* be made as the most significant Supreme Court cases in the struggle for women's rights and African American rights?

Consequence: Using the sources and your own knowledge, evaluate the consequences of the technological and legal changes on the lives of women in America.

9.5 How successful were the women's campaigns of the 1960s in achieving their original goals?

The 1970s brought a series of legal and social successes for the second-wave feminists. The publication of groundbreaking children's books such as *William Wants a Doll*, which challenged childhood stereotyping, suggested that attitudes were changing. Also, politically, with differing levels of enthusiasm from national to state level, women's rights were being enshrined in law.

In the decade following 1968, a huge amount of legislation aimed at addressing women's rights was delivered:

- in 1968, President Johnson signed an Executive Order extending full Affirmative Action rights to women
- in 1970, the Title X law created publicly funded family planning
- in 1974, the Women's Educational Equity Act was passed

- in 1978, the Pregnancy Discrimination Act extended women's rights during pregnancy
- in 1978, marital rape was criminalised and the legalisation of no-fault divorce allowed many to escape from loveless or abusive marriages.

Roe versus Wade was just the tip of the iceberg. It completed the 'reproductive freedom', a phrase coined by the journalist **Gloria Steinem**, which had been begun by the advent of the pill. Despite this, it is the changing of social attitudes towards women that is often considered the greatest success of the women's movement.

Gloria Steinem (b. 1934):

Steinem was a prominent journalist, feminist and activist who co-founded *Ms.* magazine and whose 1969 article 'After Black Power, Women's Liberation' seemed to bridge the gap between the two movements. In 1970, Steinem provided a passionate Senate testimony in favour of the ERA. In 1971, along with other feminist leaders, she founded the National Women's Political Caucus. She continues to be a vocal advocate for women's rights to this day.

However, Howard Zinn argues that it is important not to see *Roe versus Wade* as an isolated triumph:

SOURCE 9.7

The right of a woman to an abortion did not depend on the Supreme Court decision in **Roe versus Wade.** It was won before that decision, all over the country, by grassroots agitation that forced states to recognise the right.

Extract from 'Don't Despair about the Supreme Court', **The Progressive,** *Howard Zinn. From www.progressive.org.*

Opposition

SOURCE 9.8

And now, our guest speaker – Phyllis Schlafly, Harvard grad, TV Star and radio commentator, whose distinguished career has taken her all over the country during the past three years fighting for the need for women to stay put in the home where they belong!

The caption to a 1975 cartoon by Paul Szep in the **Boston Globe.**

The strides made by the feminist movement in the late 1960s and early 1970s had seemed to be virtually unopposed. The media, the courts and the government all seemed to be inclined to agree with the need to rebalance the ways in which the two genders were treated. Feminists were certainly never dragged off buses or attacked with fire hoses. However, the ending of the Vietnam War and the stagnation and relative calm of the Cold War led to a gap for a new enemy for an increasingly confident right wing in the US, and the gap was filled by the more extreme branches of feminism.

Of course, men attacking the feminist movement could be easily dismissed by the feminists themselves. What the right required was a strong, intelligent and media-savvy woman to take the feminists on, and they found her in **Phyllis Schlafly** and her STOP ERA campaign.

Phyllis Schlafly (b. 1924):

A conservative, Roman Catholic lawyer and activist, Schlafly was a staunch opponent of many aspects of the feminist movement. Noted for her traditional views, a sample quote is: 'A man's first significant purchase is a diamond for his bride, and the largest financial investment of his life is a home for her to live in.' Schlafly opposed the ERA and claimed *Roe versus Wade* was 'the worst decision in the history of the US Supreme Court'. She was never the head of a movement or a key political figure, but her opposition reflected the opinions of a 'silent majority' in the US that was co-opted by the right wing in the 1980s.

The Equal Rights Amendment (ERA)

The Equal Rights Amendment (ERA) was a proposal to change the US Constitution with an amendment that outlawed sex discrimination. It had a long history. Almost every leading feminist since 1923 had had some involvement with it, but it had never been voted on in either house, despite being introduced in every session from 1923 to 1970. Leading figures such as Eleanor Roosevelt and groups such as the League of Women Voters opposed it, arguing that it would take away aspects of the special protection women enjoyed. With the reforms inspired by the civil rights movement, the 1960s Congress was in favour of the ERA and opinion polls suggested 63% of the population agreed.

Phyllis Schlafly's tactics were clever. By arguing that feminists were devaluing women's role in society by making it equal with men's, she successfully appealed to traditional values and ensured mothers across the land felt valued rather than denigrated as a result. And by arguing that feminists denied the rights of the unborn child through their support for abortion, she helped to create the volatile pro-life/pro-choice debate by bringing the complicating factor of religion into the argument.

Schlafly later published a popular book, *The Power of the Positive Woman*, which had shades of the later self-help boom. In the book, Schlafly compared the complaints of feminists to the 'positive' woman's approach: '[The positive woman] understands that men and women are different and that those differences provide the key to her success as a person and fulfilment as a woman.'

While Schlafly was touring the country trying to sabotage the ERA, female representatives were doing their best to push it through Congress, while feminist organisations sought to put pressure on the legislature. In 1969, Representative Shirley Chisholm, the first black woman elected to Congress, gave her famous 'Equal Rights for Women' speech but still the ERA was not introduced. In February 1970, NOW picketed the Senate to demand a hearing on the ERA; in August, millions of women took part in the Women's Strike for Equality, which demanded full social, economic and political equality. Betty Friedan, who organised the strike, linked it to the fight for the ERA.

However, the ERA became bogged down in Congress, partly as a result of Schlafly's campaigning and it was finally defeated – by three votes – in 1982. Schlafly was helped by the fact that by 1980 the political pendulum was swinging away from radicalism. The anti-abortion movement was growing stronger and economic problems for poor women were getting worse, not better – making feminism seem less relevant to their lives. Even mainstream feminists were prepared to accept that women had their own values and that equal rights might be a false objective.

By 1980, second-wave feminism in the US had achieved many of its goals by getting a better deal for women in the workplace, at home and in education. More importantly, it had shocked men out of their complacency and inspired women across the Americas. Changes to cultural norms, relationships and even language made life for women considerably easier and more enjoyable than their grandmothers would have dreamed possible.

The role of government

The greatest success of the women's movement, and its chief target, was to change minds and gain women the respect they deserved. Altering the law was part of this, but never the primary objective, unlike in the early civil rights movement. Nevertheless, as we have seen, legislation did play a significant role in both advancing and sometimes holding up the demands of feminists.

ACTIVITY

Read back through this chapter, noting down the key federal government acts and Supreme Court decisions. Then construct a table with acts and decisions down the side and columns for whether they were promoted by national government, resisted by national government, promoted by the states or resisted by the states. Fill the table in with as much detail as you can, and use it to attempt the following: 'Compare and contrast how the various branches of government in the US dealt with the women's movement after 1960.'

The resurgence in conservative politics

From the early 1970s there was a distinct shift in American politics towards the right, helped by the policies of Nixon and Ford but influenced by many other factors. Disenchantment with Johnson after Vietnam, and the loss of vast numbers of votes in the South from the Democrats following the civil rights legislation of Kennedy and Johnson, were pivotal – symbolised by the defection of Dixiecrat Senator Strom Thurmond to the Republicans in 1964.

The election of Ronald Reagan in late 1980 completed the resurgence of the Republican Party, which now seemed to stand for many of the values that Schlafly promoted. The Republicans opposed feminism, welfare benefits, affirmative action policies, sexual permissiveness, abortion and drug use – all of which, in their view, were responsible for undermining family and religious values. Instead, the party believed in an end to big government, a return to the work ethic and a focus on national security and defeating the Soviets.

The 'silent majority' invoked by Nixon in his November 1969 speech (see source 8.5) were largely in support of Republican policies that aimed for lower taxes and a moral revival brought about by family values and an increasingly fundamentalist form of Christianity. The rejection of Jimmy Carter's presidency was clear when Reagan won over 50% of the blue-collar vote. For the first time since 1954, the Republicans gained control of the Senate by defeating 11 liberal Democrats targeted by the 'moral majority'. The Republicans also gained 33 seats in the House of Representatives, which, combined with the votes of conservative Southern Democrats, gave them a working majority on many key issues.

Case study: Canada

Feminism in Canada was slower in coming and more restrained than in the US. Canadian women had contributed extensively to the war effort, with the rewards of the vote in 1919 and the election of Agnes Macphail as the first woman in parliament in 1921.

Despite these successes, Canadian feminism largely slumbered for the next 40 years. However, the rise of feminist movements in the US prompted the Canadian government to create the Royal Commission on the Status of Women, which reported in 1970 that only 3.9% of managers were women, two-thirds of people on welfare were women and, although eight out of ten provinces did have equal-pay laws, women were still paid less than men for doing the same work.

The commission's report created an agenda for feminism in Canada for the next two decades. It produced 167 recommendations, dealing with equality of employment, training programmes, increased representation for women in the Senate, 18 weeks of maternity leave, access to birth control, and greater equality in pension rights. However, the Canadian government was slow to take on board these recommendations and, in protest, the National Action Committee (NAC) was formed in 1972.

The NAC provided a more centralised voice for women than NOW did in the US, helped by funding from government grants and a great deal of media attention. The NAC's efforts helped to press Prime Minister Pierre Trudeau into passing the Canadian Human Rights Act in 1977, which guaranteed no discrimination based on sex, race, religion or sexuality. It also stated that there must be 'equal pay for work of equal value'. However, in Canada, as in the US, by 1985 there was still disparity – with female employees earning only 72% of the wages of their male counterparts.

In 1982, Bertha Wilson was the first woman appointed to the Supreme Court of Canada. This showed the progress women had made in the workplace, and Wilson's position would be crucial in achieving the abortion rights that Americans had gained in *Roe versus Wade*. The contraceptive pill was legalised in 1969, and the *R. versus Morgentaler* case in 1988 finally led to the decriminalisation of abortion in Canada.

Canadian feminism paralleled its southern counterpart in many ways. Laws that were liberalised in the US were sooner or later liberalised in

Canada, but the process was much easier due to the campaigning of the American feminists.

Case study: Argentina

The patriarchal influence of the Catholic Church and the long-term presence of military dictatorship prevented large-scale feminist movements in Argentina in the latter half of the 20th century. Before the Second World War, Argentinian feminists were divided between the philanthropic, who devoted their time to active improvements in the working lives of the poor, and the educated élite, whose claims for social equality never achieved mass support.

In this environment, the role of Eva Perón (Evita) was crucial. Born into a poor, working-class family, she pursued a career on stage before marrying Colonel Juan Perón in 1946, the same year he was elected president. Evita threw herself into the business of government, speaking out for labour rights, running the Ministries of Labour and Health, agitating for women's suffrage (which was achieved in 1947) and founding the nation's first large-scale female political party – the Female Peronist Party.

Evita turned down the opportunity to become vice-president because of her declining health and opposition from the military and upper classes, but her status among the working classes was so great that she was given the title 'Spiritual Leader of the Nation' in 1952 by the Argentine parliament, shortly before her death. Evita's potent legacy was as an inspiration for women's rights in a culture traditionally associated with 'machismo', and she did more for feminism in Latin America than any woman before her.

It was the spirit of Eva Perón that was invoked by Las Madres de Plaza de Mayo (the Mothers of Plaza de Mayo). In 1977, 14 women gathered in the large square in Buenos Aires, in spite of a ban on public gatherings ordered by the military government. The women demanded information about their missing children, who had 'disappeared' as part of the government's 'Dirty War' against all forms of opposition.

'Las Madres' were initially ignored by the government, but this error allowed the group to grow in size and fame. Once the junta realised the severity of its miscalculation, the women had sufficient support to ensure that the political cost of suppressing them would have been too great, particularly in the light of international media interest.

9

Although their agenda was never women's rights, Las Madres de Plaza de Mayo was the only political group that dared challenge the military government, and its role in helping point the country back to democracy was vital.

Case study: Guatemala

See the case study in Chapter 2 for the work of Rigoberta Menchú, a female leader in the macho culture of Central America. The fact that she has stood for political office also points to her having an impact in terms of changing the nature of what is expected of women in Guatemala.

Case study: Mexico

As in the US, Mexico in the 1920s saw a series of developments that could have led to a successful feminist movement if not for the advent of the Second World War. Political parties began to include women's issues in their manifestos, often focusing on social and economic concerns such as prostitution and the legalisation of abortion in case of rape, which occurred in 1931. This was achieved despite the lack of full female suffrage until 1953.

Following the war, and particularly the granting of suffrage, the feminist movement was inspired by events in the US. In 1968 a group of female students participating in the 'Mexico 68' protests began a fledgling feminist movement. Women were vital to the movement as a whole, exploiting the macho culture of the police to bypass barricades. Despite the suppression of the protests by government forces before they had achieved their political goals, the status of women was changed by their participation both in terms of the female student radicals and the working-class mothers who challenged the government over the deaths of their children in the Tlatelolco massacre when police killed between 30 and 300 students and civilians as part of the protests.

The action of these 'Mother's Movements' spread from Mexico City into other urban centres and beyond into rural Mexico, and demands for justice began to incorporate further demands for food, sanitation and work. The Mother's Movements were also vocal in their questions about the disappearances of protesters.

As the media revolution that had begun in the US spread south the anger at government corruption found a voice in Alaíde Foppa's 1972 radio show *Foro de la Mujer* (Women's Forum) which discussed inequalities within Mexican society and broke the taboo against discussing violence against women. Foppa went on to co-found with Margarita García Flores the feminist magazine *Fem* in 1975.

Fem intellectualised the debate over women's concerns and the movement looked back to the work of the artist Frida Kahlo, who had died in 1954, and found inspiration in her willingness to depict and celebrate the female form in her work. In July 1975, the UN World Conference on Women was held in Mexico City giving further impetus to the movement and leading Mexico's six major women's organisations to merge to form the Coalicion de Mujeres Feministas (Coalition of Feminist Women) in 1976.

The Coalition had fractured by the early 1980s as progress slowed over contraception and abortion with an intransigent government unwilling to risk the anger of the Catholic church. The movement was brought back to its working-class roots as an economic crisis led prices to rise forcing more women into the work place. Companies began hiring women because they were cheaper and initially feminist activity declined, but as male unemployment rose and conditions for women in work declined women's groups began to mobilise. The catalyst came with the devastating 1985 earthquake in Mexico City that killed 5000 people and left 700 000 homeless.

Women's groups were vital in addressing the immediate needs of families and providing aid on the ground and the bonds formed, respect earned and the strength derived from their success inspired loose groups of women to coalesce and traditionally male groups to take on female representation. Several textile workers' unions created female advisory boards aimed at educating, training and politically organising garment workers. Feminists serving on advisory boards within organisations focused on addressing sexual harassment and demanding provision for childcare and health care along with training.

By 1989, feminist groups were confident enough to begin working with indigenous women in rural states like Chiapas, Morelos and Sonora. The Center for Research and Action for Women and the Women's Group of San Cristóbal de las Casas initiated programmes for indigenous women in Chiapas that addressed sexual and domestic violence.

In the same year, the progress that had been made was evident in condemnation of a police raid on a private abortion clinic in Tlaxcoaque. A notice condemning the raid published in the national press by members of the Women's Studies Department at the Metropolitan University of Mexico City showed 283 signatories, including members of the ruling party, lined up to condemn the actions of the police. The organiser, Marta Lamas, founded the magazine *Debate Feminista* (Feminist Debate) in the following year. *Debate* went on to be a key voice in the protests of the 1990s and 2000s which eventually led to the decriminalisation of abortion in 2007 in Mexico City. A campaign to extend this provision nationwide is ongoing.

ACTIVITY

Although it is easy to generalise about the progress women have made, particularly in the US where basic human rights were already well established, examiners appreciate concrete evidence of progress to support analysis. Split the class into groups, with each group taking a country to research. In particular, look at the following:

- the number of women in political office (national or local government)
- voting rights and statistics on women voting
- the number of women in full-time/part-time employment, and how this has changed since 1945
- the gap between average wages for women and those for men
- attitudes towards abortion and contraception.

Summary

As with other areas of minority rights, the US led the growth of feminism and adoption of feminist policy demands in the Americas. While the Canadian experience paralleled that in the US, in other countries the issue of women's rights was inextricably linked with other groups such as native rights and youth protest.

The common thread was a growing belief among the younger generation that women were entitled to equal treatment and opportunity, but there was a proportionately slower acceptance of the need to legislate among politicians and an even more tardy willingness to accept women as equals among the older generation of both genders. By the end of the century much progress had been made across the continents but equality was undoubtedly still a distant dream for many.

Paper 3 exam practice

Question

To what extent do you agree that the Supreme Court was the most important factor in promoting women's rights in the 1960s and 1970s.
[15 marks]

Skill

Using your own knowledge analytically, and combining it with awareness of historical debate

Examiner's tips

Always remember that historical knowledge and analysis should be the core of your answer – aspects of historical debate are desirable extras. However, where it is relevant, the integration of relevant knowledge about historical debates and interpretations, with reference to individual historians, will help push your answer up into the higher bands.

Assuming that you have read the question carefully, drawn up a plan, worked out your line of argument and approach, and written your introductory paragraph, you should be able to avoid both irrelevant material and simple narrative. Your task now is to follow your plan by writing a series of linked paragraphs that contain relevant analysis, precise supporting own knowledge and, where relevant, brief references to historical debate interpretations.

For this question, you will need to:

* give brief explanations of the key cases where the Supreme Court decisions were important to women's rights, in particular *Roe versus Wade*
* outline an argument that the Supreme Court decisions were not vital in terms of promoting women's rights
* consider the other reasons that might be argued to have been more important than the Supreme Court.

Such a topic, which has been the subject of some historical debate, will also give you the chance to refer to different historians' views.

Common mistakes

Some students, aware of a historical debate (and knowing that marks can be gained by showing this), simply write things like: 'Historian x says… and historian y says…' However, they make no attempt to evaluate the different views (for example, has one historian had access to more or better information than another, perhaps because they were writing at a later date?); nor is this information integrated into the answer by being pinned to the question. Another weak use of historical debate is to write things like: 'Historian x is biased because she is American.' Such basic comments will not be given credit – what is needed is explicit understanding of historians' views, and/or the application of knowledge to evaluate strengths and weaknesses of these views.

Sample paragraphs containing analysis and historical debate

Although the Supreme Court made pivotal decisions, not least Roe versus Wade in 1973, it can be argued that this was merely confirming rights that had been attained elsewhere. Three states, including Alaska and Oregon, provided abortion on request, and 14 others in either the event of rape, incest or medical complications. Howard Zinn argued that 'grassroots agitation forced states to recognise the right' to abortion, and although this supports his central thesis about the importance of the actions of ordinary people in history, the evidence of state law preceding Supreme Court law agrees.

EXAMINER'S COMMENT

This is quite a good example of how to use historians' views. The main focus of the answer is properly concerned with using precise own knowledge to address the demands of the question. The candidate has also provided some brief but relevant knowledge of historical debate, smoothly integrated into the answer. However, there is no attempt to evaluate the views of the historians.

Activity

Using the information in this chapter, and any other sources available to you, copy this Summary Chart of the aims, activities and achievements of feminist movements in the Americas post-1945. As well as developments in the US, Canada and Argentina, which are covered in this chapter, try to make notes on at least two other countries – such as Chile, Brazil, Mexico or Guatemala:

Country	Aims	Actions	Successes	Failures
USA				
Canada				
Argentina				

Then write a couple of paragraphs to explain why some of these feminist movements were more successful than the others.

Remember to refer to the simplified Paper 3 mark scheme given in Chapter 11.

Paper 3 practice questions

1   Examine the social and cultural impact of the women's movement in one country in the Americas.

2   Compare and contrast the role of the media in the women's movement in at least two countries in the Americas in the second half of the 20th century.

3 Examine the contribution of women to political change in one country of the region in the post-war period.

4 Compare and contrast the progress of women in two countries in the region in the period after the Second World War.

5 Evaluate how far the role and status of women changed in one country of the region during the post-war period.

Hispanic American movements in the United States

Introduction

The teaching of US history normally focuses on the founding of the original 13 colonies under the British, their emergence as an independent nation in 1776 and the subsequent development of the United States from east to west as a European achievement. This traditional story has been questioned in the last three decades as Native Americans, Hispanic Americans and African Americans have sought to have their own roles and positions within US history affirmed. By 1992 Hispanic Americans numbered over 22.4 million legal citizens of the US and, as such, made up the second largest minority in the nation after African Americans. In addition, their presence in the south-west of the country from the 16th century onwards means that Mexican Americans at least can lay claim to being the second oldest demographic group in American society.

not homogenous groups c̶d̶t̶ diff. countries associate with their own ↳ splits .

The term Hispanic American describes Spanish-speaking people living in the US. The dominant group were and are Mexican Americans, many of whom can trace their citizenship back to the Treaty of Guadalupe-Hidalgo of 1848 that ended the Mexican-American War of 1846–48. The Treaty ceded to the US a third of Mexican territory, an area approximately the size of Western Europe and including nearly all of present-day California, Utah, Nevada, Arizona and New Mexico. However, the Treaty also promised to protect the rights of Mexican Americans in the newly won territories.

due to valuable labour supply + reduce friction of border

→ properties cultural traditions language

In common with the Treaties signed between the federal government and the Native American tribes (see Chapter 2), most of the provisions for Hispanic Americans were not honoured by the United States. Huge areas of land were taken from the new Mexican American citizens both by dubious legal practices and by violent theft. The immediate effect was the impoverishment of the Mexican Americans in relation to their white countrymen. This economic inferiority was then compounded by a perceived social inferiority stemming from the fact that the Mexican Americans were not only Spanish speaking but also Roman Catholic, setting the tone for social, political and economic grievances that persist to the present day.

TIMELINE

1953 'Operation Wetback' from 1953 to 1958, leads to the deporting of over 3.8 million Latin Americans

1954 *Hernandez versus Texas* is the first Hispanic rights case heard in the Supreme Court after the Second World War; it establishes a precedent against discrimination based on ethnic distinctions

1962 200 000 of Cuba's wealthiest citizens flee to the US following Fidel Castro's revolution

1965 César Chávez and Dolores Huerta found the United Farm Workers association, in Delano, California

1968 The Mexican American Legal Defense and Education Fund becomes the first legal fund to focus on the civil rights of Mexican Americans

1969 Puerto Rican youths in Chicago form the Young Lords Organization, inspired by King and X

1974 The Southwest Voter Registration Education Project founded by William C. Velasquez

1975 Congress votes to expand the 1965 Voting Rights Act to require language assistance at polling stations

1986 Congress passes the Immigration Reform and Control Act (IRCA), providing legalisation for some undocumented workers

1989 Miami's Ileana Ros-Lehtinen, a Cuban American, becomes the first Hispanic woman elected to the House of Representatives

KEY QUESTIONS

- What was the position of Hispanic Americans before the Second World War?
- Why did Hispanic Americans begin to protest for their civil rights after the Second World War?
- Why was César Chávez so important to the campaign for Hispanic American rights?
- What role did the Chicano movement play in Hispanic rights protests?
- What were the circumstances of non-Mexican Hispanic groups?

10.1 What was the position of Hispanic Americans before the Second World War?

This period following the Treaty of Guadalupe-Hidalgo to 1895 was characterised by Anglo-American assimilation of the new territories in the south-west. Wealthy Mexican American landowners managed to hold on to some measure of political power and often benefitted from their lighter skin tone in comparison with African Americans. The first Hispanic American elected to Congress from the south-west was Romualdo Pacheco who served first as Governor of California and then in the House of Representatives from 1877. Poorer, often darker-skinned Hispanic people however found themselves working largely as itinerant labourers and sharing these roles with the Chinese immigrants who came to the US following the California Gold rush of the late 1840s and subsequently found employment building railroads and working in agriculture.

Although Hispanic Americans suffered less overt discrimination than African Americans in the South and Chinese Americans whom the media dubbed the 'yellow peril' their position was not helped by the growing numbers crossing the Mexican border in search of work. The cheap labour they provided angered white workers and their cultural, religious and language differences exacerbated tensions that were felt most keenly during times of recession when there was competition for scarce jobs. In addition, a new influx of Hispanics came to the South East from Puerto Rico and Cuba following the US victory in the 1898 Spanish-American war, which meant for the first time there was a substantial Hispanic presence in most of the major cities.

labour shortages attracted them

Many Hispanic workers did not come to the US with the intention of staying. Instead they left the relative poverty of Mexico, Cuba and Puerto Rico to do seasonal agricultural work. Their geographic proximity also meant they were easier to repatriate in times of ethnic tension, an action undertaken by the government frequently in the period leading to 1900.

- *treated as inferior*
- *fed govt. ignored the issue*

The turn of the century did bring an increased consciousness among Hispanic Americans of the rights that had been neglected since the Treaty of Guadalupe-Hidalgo. Like the Native and Chinese Americans Hispanic immigrants arrived from countries that lacked established traditions of civil rights but by 1903 in California over a thousand Mexican and Japanese farm workers organised the first farm-worker union, the Japanese-Mexican Labor Association (JMLA), which went on to win a strike against the Western Agricultural Contracting Company at Oxnard, California that same year. Elsewhere in the country, the American rights campaigner Lucy Gonzales Parsons, who claimed Native, Mexican and black heritage, was part of the group that founded the Industrial Workers of the World (IWW) in Chicago in 1905. Disparagingly nicknamed 'the Wobblies', the IWW's goal was to promote worker unity in the revolutionary struggle to overthrow employers as a class. This idea was influenced by the theories of Karl Marx which were growing in popularity in Europe and would become the basis for Russian communism after 1917. The IWW motto 'an injury to one is an injury to all' reflected an idealistic solidarity that advocated improved rights for all workers, regardless of ethnicity.

Figure 10.1: Members of the Industrial Workers of the World (IWW), known as the Wobblies, gather during a rally in Union Square, New York City, April 1914.

These early ventures into rights advocation were boosted when the 1910 Mexican Revolution increased the flow of workers in search of both physical and economic security. Numbers of Mexicans coming into the US increased to 20000 per year during the 1910s and then

1st large organisation 1911

50 000 per year in the 1920s. With greater numbers came greater consciousness, and in 1911 El Primer Congreso Mexicanista met in Laredo, Texas. The Congreso was the first large-scale organisation focused on Hispanic rights and considered issues of schooling, discrimination in work, treatment of Mexicans at the border and the growing problem of lynching of Mexicans by whites. The brainchild of journalist Nicasio Adar, the Congreso also rejected assimilation and supported language retention as a way of maintaining Mexican culture.

Outside Texas and California, the treatment of Mexican Americans was less harsh. In 1912 New Mexico's new constitution was drawn up as an officially bilingual state and prohibited segregation for children of 'Spanish descent'. The historian Julia Young attributes this better treatment to a perception that Mexicans had qualities that made them 'better' immigrants than other non-whites, including their supposed docility, physical strength and stoicism in the face of harsh working conditions. Young argues that, most importantly, 'they were perceived as temporary migrants, who were far more likely to return to Mexico than to settle permanently in the United States'.

US entry into the First World War also served to increase Mexican immigration as factories involved in war-related production required workers to replace American conscripts. As a result, Mexicans from the south-west begin moving north in large numbers for the first time, paralleling the 'Great Migration' of African Americans out of the rural South. The war years also saw the 1917 Jones Act which granted citizenship to all Puerto Ricans.

Hispanic Americans in the First World War

The First World War had seen a removal of many Mexican immigrants. The 1917 Zimmerman telegram, a secret communication from the German government to the Mexican president suggesting a potential military alliance against the US between the two countries, had been intercepted and published outraging public opinion. Congress quickly acted to pass the Selective Service Act which required all men between the ages of 21 to 30 to register for duty as the electorate finally became willing to countenance entering the war in Europe. While some immigrants feared the discrimination they might face in the US military and returned to Mexico others signed up determined to prove themselves as loyal Americans.

In total over 200 000 Hispanic Americans were mobilised in the First World War, with the majority being Mexican Americans; 18 000 Puerto Ricans also showed their gratitude for being made citizens by volunteering for service. Hispanic Americans were integrated throughout the armed forces and one David Barkley (formerly David Barkley Hernandez) of the 89th Infantry Division's 356th Infantry Regiment won the Medal of Honor posthumously for his actions near Pouilly, France on 9 November 1918.

[handwritten margin note: led to belief of needed recognition]

Civil rights before the Second World War

Mexican American veterans expected the country to recognise their contribution but, as historian Cynthia Orozco argues, while the efforts of Mexican American soldiers demanded respect a flood of new Mexican immigrants undermined their status. Movements such as San Antonio's 1921 Orden Hijos de América (Order of the Sons of America) organised Latino workers to raise awareness of civil rights issues and fight for fair wages, education and housing were joined by the Confederación de Uniones Obreras Mexicanas (Federation of Mexican Workers Union-CUOM) in Los Angeles in 1927. In 1929 a group of organisations merged to form the League of United Latin American Citizens (LULAC), which remains the largest and longest-lasting Latino civil rights group in the country. However, the vast majority of Mexican Americans remained as labourers living in ghetto areas known as *barrios* (slums) in cities such as Los Angeles and San Francisco and their numbers were swollen by a growth in immigration from Mexico encouraged by economic opportunity and a desire to escape from political persecution.

[handwritten margin note: pressure group. middle class focus on improving lives of them there. assimulate]

Nevertheless, the 1920s was a relatively benign period for Hispanic Americans. The 1921 Immigration Act restricted the entry of southern and eastern Europeans into the US, but successful lobbying of Congress by the large-scale agricultural businesses of the south-west successfully prevented any curbs on the immigration of Mexicans. Politically the situation seemed to be improving as well when in 1928 Octaviano Larrazolo of New Mexico became the first Latino US Senator and was followed in the New Mexico seat by Dennis Chávez in 1935. LULAC also began to have some successes and, in both organisational structure and method paralleled the NAACP, although the group was at pains to stress that their campaign was not over race but over cultural prejudice.

[handwritten margin note: 40s–60s achieved deseg brutality jury selern voter registrn]

LULAC were keenly aware that to ally with the NAACP would be to undermine their argument and potentially equate Hispanic rights with African American rights, which at the time were considerably inferior.

Salvatierra versus Del Rio School District, 1930

LULAC's first key case in the era was *Salvatierra versus Del Rio School District* which took place in Del Rio, Texas, in 1930. Jesus Salvatierra and other parents sued the Del Rio school board on the grounds that Mexican American students were being deprived of the resources that were given to white students. The district judge ruled in favour of Salvatierra, but the state's higher courts were to overturn the decision. The following year, in a case known as the Lemon Grove incident, a group of parents in the Lemon Grove suburb of San Diego successfully sued their local school district when the principal of the local elementary school prevented Mexican American children from enrolling in his white school and instead directed them to a new school built specifically for the Mexican American community. Historian Robert Alvarez Jr points out the significance of this case, declaring: 'This was the first situation when a group of immigrants had gotten together, challenged a school board and won.'

The Depression and Hispanic Americans

However, the political and legal success occurred in a climate of economic deprivation brought about by the 1929 Wall Street Crash and resulting Great Depression. In these circumstances the pressure on local politicians to repatriate immigrant workers became too great to resist and between 1929 and 1936 a forced return to Mexico of people of Mexican descent took place which ignored fundamental constitutional principles and resulted in the repatriation of between 500 000 and 2 million people, 60% of whom were American citizens.

Recovery from the Great Depression was slow with Roosevelt's New Deal concentrated in the eastern and central areas of the country and focused primarily on generating jobs for white workers. Indeed, the cutting of production on farms as a result of the Agricultural Adjustment Agency (AAA) actually affected Hispanic agricultural workers badly.

QUESTION
What does Source 10.1 suggest about the effect of the Great
Depression on Hispanic Americans on the East Coast?

SOURCE 10.1

The economic crisis of the Great Depression was devastating to Latino
workers. Union strength among Cuban tobacco workers in Florida
declined as cigar factories introduced automatic cigar making machines
with women operators and as Havana regained its primacy as the
center of cigar manufacturing. Cuban cigar workers began to leave Ybor
City for Havana, New York, and elsewhere to find work. Those workers
who remained precipitated a general strike in 1931 organised by the
Tobacco Workers Industrial Union and the workers once more were
brutally suppressed. In New York City, despite high representation in the
textile and the garment trades, one of three Puerto Rican workers could
not find work because of prejudice and competition for menial jobs.
Consequently, many Puerto Ricans returned to Puerto Rico.

Extract from an essay entitled 'Latino Workers' by Zaragosa Vargas,
Kenan Eminent Professor in the Department of History, University of
North Carolina, Chapel Hill.

The pressure on employment did produce advances in labour
organisation however. In 1931 a failed strike by Cuban immigrants
working in a cigar factory in Ybor City Florida caught national
attention and inspired a 1933 strike at El Monte, California. Here, in the
largest agricultural strike at that point in US history, Mexican strawberry
pickers demanded a wage rise from nine cents an hour to 20 cents,
which they achieved. In this environment of increased political
confidence El Congreso del Pueblo de Habla Española (the Congress
of Spanish-Speaking Peoples) held its first conference in Los Angeles in
1938. Founded by Luisa Moreno and led by Josefina Fierro de Bright,
the Congreso sought to bring together Hispanic workers from different
ethnic backgrounds and link Cubans and Spaniards from Florida, Puerto
Ricans from New York, Mexicans and Mexican Americans from
the south-west.

Where other civil rights groups such as LULAC favoured an assimilation with American norms, the Congress of Spanish Speaking Peoples promoted a wider agenda of Hispanic unity that incorporated immigrants and Central and South American countries. It supported a wide range of campaigns against racial oppression, including support for improving medical care, improvements to education, the building of federal housing and fairer wages and encouraged members to join unions, register to vote and to take active roles in electing candidates who fought for racial equality.

The Second World War and Hispanic Americans

While the war was being fought in the Pacific and in Europe, it was not an entirely different story at home. With 3 million Hispanic Americans in the country by 1939, tension was inevitable in areas of deprivation, and the Los Angeles barrios were the worst example.

The Los Angeles media had begun to use the derogatory term 'Chicanos' to refer to younger Hispanic Americans who seemed to be a visible example of laziness and indolence at a time of war. Some of this was down to the style they favoured: zoot suits were a long flamboyant jacket with baggy trousers, sometimes accessorised with a pork pie hat, a long watch chain, and shoes with thick soles, and the music they listened to, a new genre of 'Chicano music' popularised by Lalo Guerrero.

Riots and civil unrest

In the summer of 1942 the Sleepy Lagoon murder case had made national news when teenage members of the 38th Street Gang were accused of murdering a man named José Díaz in an abandoned quarry pit. The nine defendants were convicted at trial and sentenced to long prison terms. The historian Eduardo Obregón Pagán summarised the situation arguing that 'Many Angelenos saw the death of José Díaz as a tragedy that resulted from a larger pattern of lawlessness and rebellion among Mexican American youths, discerned through their self-conscious fashioning of difference, and increasingly called for stronger measures to crack down on juvenile delinquency.'

Into this febrile atmosphere, thousands of predominantly white US Navy sailors were added and they began to clash with the Hispanic street gangs in larger and larger numbers, often stripping the captured gang members and burning their suits. For this the military received praise from the local press, but were condemned nationally as the riots triggered similar attacks that year against Hispanics in Chicago, San Diego, Oakland, Philadelphia and New York City. Meanwhile in Detroit, while the LA riots died down, the white youths began to attack African Americans, leading to the worst race riot in the city's history. For the first time, the erroneous stereotypes of African American youths had bled across into the Hispanic youth culture, tainting Hispanics by association.

Figure 10.2: Two Hispanic youths having being stripped of their zoot suits during the riots of 1943.

Employment

Where the rioting highlighted the prejudices against young Hispanics, the majority of Hispanic Americans had at least benefitted from a limited number of the measures Roosevelt had taken since the New Deal began. The Farm Security Administration had established camps for migrant farm workers in California, and the CCC and WPA hired unemployed Mexican Americans on relief jobs. Further federal intervention came in the form of the 1941 Fair Employment Practices Committee, which handled cases of employment discrimination; Hispanic workers filed more than a third of all complaints the FEPC received from the south-west.

→ developed to Equal Employment Opportunities Commission
  ⤷ Equal Employment Act 1972
    • affirmative action

303

10

The Bracero Program

*[handwritten: opposed by LULAC
coz poor + uneducated
→ undermine their status]*

In addition, the 1942 Bracero Program (*bracero* means day-labourer) agreed between Roosevelt and the Mexican president Manuel Ávila Camacho allowed Mexican citizens to work temporarily in the United States. *[handwritten: to deal with shortages during the war.]* Inevitably the impetus for the Bracero deal came from farming companies keen to tap the Mexican labour market as demand soared during the war. One key advantage of the Bracero Program was its legality. The United States government kept records of the immigrant workers. After the programme ended many undocumented workers kept pouring into the United States, creating the massive problem of illegal aliens. In total over 4.5 million Mexican immigrants crossed the border under the programme, although conditions in the temporary accommodation in which they were housed were tough, with one worker commenting: 'In this camp, we have no names. We are called only by numbers.' The scheme led to a ballooning in the significance of the Mexican American labour force that César Chávez was to call on in the 1960s.

Hispanic Americans at war

The outbreak of the Second World War repeated the opportunity for Hispanic American soldiers to distinguish themselves and with a more sustained campaign than in 1917–18 they were able to do this in greater numbers. Around 500 000 Hispanic Americans served in the US military during the Second World War, with most being Mexican Americans. Hispanics won 20% of the awards for bravery given to soldiers from Los Angeles despite only constituting 10% of the population.

Aside from the notable successes of soldiers from LA, General Douglas MacArthur was on record as calling the Arizona National Guard's 158th Infantry Regiment (which consisted of large numbers of Mexican and Native Americans) 'one of the greatest fighting combat teams ever deployed for battle' following their service in the South West Pacific theater.

The 141st Infantry Regiment, part of the Texas National Guard's 36th Infantry Division, was another unit with a large Hispanic contingent and suffered almost 7000 battle casualties, in the gaining of three Medals of Honor, 31 Distinguished Service Crosses, almost 500 Silver Stars and almost 1700 Bronze Stars. Although 350 000 Puerto Ricans registered for military service in the Second World War, only 65 000 actually fought and most served in segregated units.

10.2 Why did Hispanic Americans begin to protest for their civil rights after the Second World War?

By September of 1945 the war was over and it seemed that the US was set for peace and prosperity, for Hispanic Americans however, like other ethnic groups, the end of the war seemed to have changed little. Jobs in the war industries were lost and there remained disparities between their access to the 'American Dream' and that of their white counterparts. In contrast to the pre-war period however, some Hispanic Americans began to agitate for their share of the dream and the rights that were a precursor to it.

Education

At the end of the war, Hispanic veterans returned with a new feeling of unity and, paralleling the experience of black soldiers, Hispanic veterans were also more conscious of what they had been fighting for in terms of equal rights in the country they defended. Many also benefitted from the 1944 GI Bill through which they could gain a university education and buy a first home. ⟶ active govt.

The issue of education immediately came to the fore with the 1947 case *Mendez versus Westminster* in which the Supreme Court of California agreed that segregation of all kinds violates children's constitutional rights. Though little remembered now, the Mendez case had important consequences for the later campaigns of the African American movement with Thurgood Marshall and Robert L. Carter attending the deliberations and Governor of California Earl Warren paying close attention to the outcome. Unlike the Linda Brown case (see 4.2, *Brown versus Board of Education of Topeka*, 1954), there was no Hispanic rights organisation that took a lead on the Mendez case.

Jewish American civil rights lawyer David Marcus took the case on and the parents of one of the students affected provided much of the initial funding but, like the 1930 Jesus Salvatierra case, *Mendez versus Westminster* became a precedent not just legally but in the minds of an increasingly rights–conscious Hispanic population, leading to a gradual integration of Californian schools.

LULAC
achievement

Immigration

The Bracero Program and the number of jobs available in factories serving war contracts meant that Mexican immigration during the war had largely been adult males, but after 1945 whole families began to arrive. These families arrived at the same time that the US began to experience a more problematic economic climate with five recessions between 1945 and 1960 and government spending switching from the production of war commodities to other areas. In the barrios where the Mexican families ended up they shared the curses of poverty with Native Americans and blacks, higher unemployment rates, lower life expectancy and increased prevalence of curable disease. Meanwhile the derogatory term 'Chicano' had gained more currency in the press and among a population made increasingly aware of the issue of race by the black civil rights movement, which had been visibly growing nationwide since 1950.

Theory of Knowledge

History, language and bias:

As with the words 'nigger', 'gay' and 'queer', the term 'Chicano' began as a derogatory term and is still seen in that way by many conservative whites, some older members of the Hispanic American community and, interestingly, in Mexico itself as a term describing a poor Mexican American. However, attempts to reclaim the word as part of the Chicano movement of the 1960s and 1970s were successful and many Mexican Americans, particularly the young, began to see the term as a badge of pride. To what extent is it possible for a group to deliberately re-engineer the definition of a term. Are there examples that do not have racial connotations?

Other derogatory words used to describe Hispanic Americans include 'spic', and the compound word 'wetback' also began to be used in the 1950s. The latter term became synonymous with government efforts to deport Hispanic Americans from 1953 to 1958. 'Operation Wetback' was begun by the Eisenhower administration (the term deriving from the fact that Mexican migrants coming into the US would often have to swim or wade across the Rio Grande) as a response to problems with the bracero programme and pressure from the Mexican government.

[Handwritten margin notes: over 1 mill deported incl. citizens. → to stop overflowing → message that it's not an open border]

As Mexico's own agri-business grew, producers found they could not get labourers to pick the crops as so many were in the US both illegally and legally through the Bracero Program. US farmers had continued to hire illegal Mexican workers, which had also served to keep wages down and leave returning soldiers with little opportunities for work across the south-west. President Truman had previously commissioned a report on the breakdown of the programme, which hyperbolically concluded: 'The magnitude of the situation has reached entirely new levels in the past seven years. In its newly achieved proportions, it is virtually an invasion.'

President Eisenhower appointed General Joseph Swing to head up Operation Wetback which began in May 1954 and saw 750 immigration and border patrol officers focusing on quick processing and deportation of illegal immigrants in cities as far afield as Los Angeles, San Francisco and Chicago. The main targets however were border towns in Texas and California. In 1954 over a million apprehensions were made but the numbers involved fell rapidly in the second year to under a quarter of a million.

This second wave of deportations followed on from those of the 1930s prior to the Bracero Program. They were initially supported by Mexican American groups such as LULAC, which, according to historian David Gutierrez, highlights the fact that some Mexican Americans resented the braceros for depressing the wages of those who had to earn their whole year's income just during the harvest season. However, Gutierrez believes, 'Not even the most politically conservative Mexican American organizations could ignore the fact that immigration dragnets not only were affecting putative illegal aliens but also were devastating Mexican American families, disrupting businesses in Mexican neighborhoods, and fanning interethnic animosities throughout the border region.'

Alfonso Aguilar, who headed the Citizenship and Immigration service under George W. Bush, goes further, arguing that Operation Wetback was a tragedy: 'Human rights were violated. People were removed to distant locations without food and water. There were many deaths, unnecessary deaths. Sometimes even US citizens of Hispanic origin, of Mexican origin were removed. It was a travesty. It was terrible. Immigrants were humiliated. So to say it's a success story is ridiculous.'

One of the initial problems with the deportation was that many illegal immigrants soon returned to the US: in 1960, for example, 20% of those deported had already been removed once. Consequently, a decision was taken to deport those detained much deeper into Mexico, sometimes far from family or even the prospect of work. Some were even left in the desert, with 88 reported to have died in 44-degree heat in July 1955.

LULAC also began to receive reports of beatings and imprisonment before deportation and in the ten years of the programme over 11 000 formal complaints were received from documented bracero alone. A congressional investigation later compared the conditions on ships to those experienced on an 'eighteenth-century slave ship'.

Operation Wetback was deemed to be a success by the government but some historians have argued that it only served to show that the federal authorities were willing to take action (rather than ensuring that any actions were consistent). However, the programme did serve to illustrate the precarious nature of civil rights for Mexican Americans who could be deported summarily deep into Mexico for failing to produce their papers sufficiently quickly. Worse still, Operation Wetback provided a template for exclusion that was invoked by Donald Trump in the 2016 presidential race.

Hispanic Americans and the law

While Operation Wetback and the Bracero Program showed the two sides of the issue of Mexican American employment, the 1954 *Hernandez versus Texas* case set a precedent that widened the issue of discrimination beyond just race. In 1950 Pete Hernández, a migrant cotton picker, had been accused of murdering tenant farmer Joe Espinosa in Edna, Texas, a small town in Jackson County, where no person of Mexican origin had served on a jury for at least 25 years.

Hernández's lawyer Gus García fought the case as a challenge to the systematic exclusion of Mexican Americans from jury service across Texas. Hernández was found guilty both locally and at the Texas Court of Criminal Appeals, so Garcia took the case to the Supreme Court where he was supported by James de Anda and Chris Alderete of the American G. Forum and Carlos Cadena and John Herrera of LULAC. García argued that the 14th Amendment guaranteed protection not only on the basis of race but also on the basis of class, and consequently the absence of Mexican American jurors was a form of discrimination. The state conceded that no person with a Spanish surname had served on a jury for 25 years, but claimed that this was a coincidence.

Two weeks before the Brown decision Chief Justice Earl Warren delivered the unanimous opinion of the court in favour of Hernández accepting the concept of distinction by class. The court held that Hernández had 'the right to be indicted and tried by juries from which all members of his class are not systematically excluded'.

The Hernández decision was a significant success for the legal strategy of the Mexican American civil-rights activists. Although not as simple as the Brown case, nor as media-friendly the case helped to undermine the separate but equal doctrine and paved the way for Brown as well as incrementally increasing the rights of Hispanic Americans, the so called 'other white'. The Hernández case set a valuable precedent until it was replaced in 1971 by *Cisneros versus Corpus Christi*, which saw Hispanics finally identified as a distinct minority group.

MEXICAN AMERICAN AWAKENING

before 60s kicked interest presidential election 1960 → greater militancy

10.3 Why was César important to the can Hispanic American ri

Organised Hispanic workers were a threat to the powerful agricultural interests of the south-west and prior to the arrival of **César Chávez** they had largely been sidelined. However, Chávez was tireless in his organising and encouragement and used the models of the black civil rights movement as both inspiration and template. Soon, his organisation, the United Farm Workers of America (UFW), was holding strikes and organising boycotts and other protests such as hunger strikes. In the San Joaquin valley area Chávez developed credit, insurance and shopping facilities following the example of the Nation of Islam. In a letter to Coretta Scott King in 1968 Chávez said, 'We owe so much to Martin.'

César Chávez (1927–93):

Chávez is the name synonymous with the Hispanic civil rights movement. Born in Yuma, Arizona, his family was cheated out of a land claim by a local white settler and the injustice stuck with him into his teenage years. The family eventually settled in San Jose, California where they lived in a barrio nicknamed Sal Si Puedes ('Get Out If You Can'). After settling down with his own family – going on to have eight children – Chávez took various labouring jobs but began to be interested in ideas of social justice and the writings of St Francis of Assisi and Gandhi, as well as biographies of labour leaders Eugene Debs and John L. Lewis. Working with the community organiser Fred Ross, Chávez first met Dolores Huerta and the two of them founded their own organisation in 1962 initially called the National Farm Workers Association but later to become the United Farm Workers (UFW), the key civil rights group for Mexican Americans.

Figure 10.3: United Farm Workers leader César Chávez, with pictures of Robert Kennedy and Mahatma Gandhi in the background.

In 1968, too, Chávez himself went on a hunger strike in support of non-violent methods, demonstrating his own willingness to put his life on the line to gain recognition for the rights of Hispanic workers. This water only, 25-day fast was repeated by Chávez in 1972 for 24 days, and again in 1988, this time for 36 days.

Fasting was a new tactic in the post-war civil rights movement but had an extensive precedent in the actions of Gandhi and suffragettes on both sides of the Atlantic. Chávez himself argued that farm workers were worried that they wouldn't win without violence and needed to be shown the power of non-violence. He cited the terrible suffering of farm workers and their children, the denial of farm worker rights, the dangers of pesticides, and the denial of fair and free elections.

By invoking both the religious aspects of fasting and the connection to the environmental issues – popularised by Rachel Carson's 1962 book *Silent Spring* – Chávez was able to gain more media attention than any previous Hispanic leader.

SOURCE 10.2

A fast is first and foremost personal. It is a fast for the purification of my own body, mind, and soul. The fast is also a heartfelt prayer for purification and strengthening for all those who work beside me in the farm worker movement. The fast is also an act of penance for those in positions of moral authority and for all men and women activists who know what is right and just, who know that they could and should do more. The fast is finally a declaration of non-cooperation with supermarkets who promote and sell and profit from California table grapes. During the past few years I have been studying the plague of pesticides on our land and our food. The evil is far greater than even I had thought it to be, it threatens to choke out the life of our people and also the life system that supports us all. This solution to this deadly crisis will not be found in the arrogance of the powerful, but in solidarity with the weak and helpless. I pray to God that this fast will be a preparation for a multitude of simple deeds for justice. Carried out by men and women whose hearts are focused on the suffering of the poor and who yearn, with us, for a better world. Together, all things are possible.

César Chávez talking about his 25-day water-only fast in 1968 which he undertook on behalf of suffering farm workers, quoted on the United Farm Workers' website, www.ufw.org.

ACTIVITY

What are the advantages and disadvantages of the type of protest described in Source 10.2? Why was it not used as prolifically by the African American and other civil rights movements?

However, Chávez was not the only activist involved and, like Martin Luther King, was sometimes accused of hijacking others' work. The Delano grape strike, which began in 1965 was a labour strike by the Agricultural Workers Organizing Committee and the United Farm Workers, against grape growers in California. The strike began on 8 September 1965, and lasted more than five years. It had come about when the Agricultural Workers Organizing Committee, whose members were mostly Filipino, and led by Philip Vera Cruz and Pete Velasco, walked off the grape farms in Delano, demanding wages equal to the federal minimum wage.

Figure 10.4: 'Marchers as Far as the Eye Can See', the first Grape Strike by the National Farm Workers Association (NFWA) and AWOC. The joyous march of campesinos (peasant farm workers) led by Cesar Chavez (fourth from right), the leader of the United Farm Workers' Union in Delano, California, 3 January 1966.

A week later the Mexican-American National Farmworkers Association, led by César Chávez, joined the strike and then, in March 1966, led a 340-mile protest march from Delano to the state capital of Sacramento. Eventually the two groups merged, forming the United Farm Workers of America in August 1966. The strike eventually spread to over 2000 workers and led to a consumer boycott of grapes from non-unionised farms. The strike ended with a significant victory for the United Farm Workers in 1967 when both the major companies involved accepted the UFW as representatives of the workers.

By 1970 the UFW had forced grape growers in California to accept union contracts and had effectively organised most of that industry. As a result, the organisation's membership had swollen to over 50 000. Chávez was not a hierarchical leader and made a point of training UFW workers and then to send many of them into the cities where they were to use the boycott and picket as their weapon but although both Chávez and **Dolores Huerta** were committed to the rights of Hispanic Americans both were against immigration and opposed the Bracero Program.

While this may seem counter-intuitive, their opposition was rooted in the belief that braceros undermined the resident workers for whose rights they were campaigning. In addition, immigrant workers were far less likely to protest against infringement of their rights for fear of losing the valuable seasonal work. In 1973, the UFW was one of the first labour unions to oppose proposed sanctions against employers who hired illegal migrants.

Such was the confusion caused by this stance that in 1969, on a UFW march to the border of Mexico in protest at growers' use of illegal aliens as strikebreakers, Chávez was accused of being anti-immigrant. In 1973, the UFW set up a 'wet line' along the US-Mexico border to prevent Mexican immigrants from entering the United States, and this confrontational stance led to physical attacks on migrant workers by UFW pickets.

> **Dolores Huerta (b. 1930):**
>
> Dolores Huerta was the co-founder of the National Farmworkers Association, alongside César Chávez, which later became the United Farm Workers (UFW). Huerta began fighting for the rights of farmworkers in 1955 and has been arrested 22 times for non-violent protests. She was speaking on the same platform as Robert Kennedy on the night that he was shot and she has been named among the 100 most important women of the 20th century alongside Rosa Parks, Betty Friedan, Eleanor Roosevelt, Gloria Steinem, Rachel Carson and Margaret Sanger. As a role model to many Hispanics, Huerta has been immortalised in corridos (ballads) and murals.

Though Chávez and Huerta clearly favoured grassroots actions and employing economic pressure against companies rather than against the state or federal government they did also push for legislation when it seemed the most viable way of making progress. In 1974, encouraged by the election of the pro-union Democrat Jerry Brown as governor of California, Chávez decided to try to focus on legal victories.

Chávez put pressure on Brown through a 110-mile march from San Francisco to the Gallo Winery in Modesto in February of 1975. The media coverage of the event forced Brown into action and in June 1975 he signed the California Agricultural Labor Relations Act (ALRA), which established collective bargaining for farmworkers. The act also set up the California Agricultural Labor Relations Board (ALRB) to oversee the process. Chávez continued to protest through to his death in 1993, and while his actions were increasingly on the margins of the rights movement his success in mobilising and organising Hispanic workers has seen his birthday, 31 March, made into a state holiday in California, Colorado, and Texas.

Chávez's success came from his ability to inspire and mobilise the residents of what was often referred to as the 'third country', the region of the south-west United States where characteristics of both Mexico and the US blended across the borders. With the increased protection of rights for workers and the numbers, both legal and illegal that had arrived since the war, the use of the Spanish language became predominant in the area and there was growing recognition of Hispanic culture.

In 1967 the epic poem 'Yo Soy Joaquin' (I Am Joaquin) was published by Rodolfo 'Corky' Gonzales, a Mexican American boxer, poet and political activist, and it became a rallying call for the Chicano movement and Hispanic culture in general by documenting the struggles of Mexican Americans in achieving economic and political rights. The following year President Johnson designated one week in mid-September to be National Hispanic Heritage Week.

KEY CONCEPTS QUESTION

Significance: How significant was the role of César Chávez in the civil rights movements in the Americas in the period after 1945?

KEY CONCEPTS ACTIVITY

Significance: The California state senator Art Torres, who is both Hispanic and gay, spoke about Chávez after his death in 1993 saying: 'He was our Gandhi… our Martin Luther King.' Are comparisons like this helpful to a historian? Or do they trivialise the role of one figure by conflating them with another? Draw up a table of similarities and differences between King and Chávez and use your own criteria to judge whether Torres was making a serious or superficial comparison.

ACTIVITY

How far can a poem such as that in Source 10.3, following, provide us with knowledge about the experience of Mexican Americans? Is it comparable with other works of literature that had a political impact?

SOURCE 10.3

My hands calloused from the hoe. I have made the
Anglo rich,

Yet

Equality is but a word–

The Treaty of Hidalgo has been broken

And is but another treacherous promise.

My land is lost

And stolen,

My culture has been raped.

I lengthen the line at the welfare door

And fill the jails with crime.

These then are the rewards

This society has

For sons of chiefs

And kings

And bloody revolutionists,

Who gave a foreign people

All their skills and ingenuity

To pave the way with brains and blood

For those hordes of gold-starved strangers

Rodolfo 'Corky' Gonzales, 'Yo Soy Joaquin' (I Am Joaquin), 1967.

Representation

Despite certain civil improvements, Hispanic Americans still
experienced the same types of *de facto* segregation as their black
counterparts in most areas. Access to local facilities such as schools,
restaurants and parks was still *de facto* segregated and Hispanics were
also under-represented politically in the 1960s. In towns like El Paso,
Texas and San Diego, California gerrymandering of electoral boundaries
ensured Hispanic candidates failed to win elections despite majority
Hispanic populations. In 1968 a million 'Chicanos' lived in Los Angeles
but none sat on the city council. Nationally the picture was no better
with over five million Hispanic Americans registered as voters but none

serving in a state government role. This was most notably outrageous in California where there were over 2 million out of a total population of 20 million. However, the one bright spot was the election of Henry Gonzales to the House of Representatives in 1961 for the state of Texas. As with African American representation, the subsequent progress of Hispanic legislators and judges was slow but steady and helped by grassroots voter registration campaigns of education.

In 1974, Willie Velásquez established the Southwest Voter Registration and Education Project, motto *Su voto es su voz* (Your vote is your voice). SWVREP succeeded in registering more than 2 million Hispanic voters in the following two decades and historian Julie Pycior believes that it 'succeeded in extending Johnson's Voting Rights Act to Mexican Americans and in eliminating most other barriers to minority voting'.

Figure 10.5: Willie Velasquez, left, head of the Southwest Voter Registration and Education Project, taking local residents' details.

Even in the fledgling days of SWVREP things were changing, though. In 1975, Raul Castro became the first Mexican American to be elected governor of Arizona and the Carter administration saw the appointment both of more Hispanics and African Americans to be federal judges than any president before him. Despite the increased conservatism of the Reagan years, progress continued. In 1981 Henry Cisneros was the first Mexican American to become the mayor of a major city when he was elected in San Antonio, while in 1985 Xavier Suarez became the first

Cuban American mayor of Miami. As local politics embraced Hispanic politicians so national government followed when in 1988 Ronald Reagan appointed Dr Lauro Cavazos as Secretary of Education, the first Hispanic member of a president's cabinet, and the following year President Bush appointed Puerto Rican Antonia Novello as Surgeon General of the United States. In the same year Miami's Ileana Ros-Lehtinen, another Cuban American, became the first Hispanic woman elected to the US House of Representatives.

While still under-represented at all levels of government, Hispanic Americans had made significant political progress in the years following Chávez's breakthrough. The issue of representation became less of an outrage to be fought and more of an incremental progression. This progress was slow, however, and the appointment in only 2009 of Sonia Sotomayor as the first Hispanic Supreme Court judge, 42 years after Thurgood Marshall became the first African American on the top bench, illustrates how Hispanic rights have lagged behind those of African Americans.

Perhaps the most overtly political efforts in the period were those of the La Raza Unida Party which also began in the south-west in January 1970 at a meeting of 300 Mexican Americans in Crystal City, Texas. The meeting, chaired by José Ángel Gutiérrez and Mario Compean, who had been involved in the Mexican American Youth Organization (MAYO) in 1967 decided that La Raza Unida would focus on improving the economic, social and political aspects of the 'Chicano' community in Texas.

less successful due to dispersed population in California

Following success in municipal elections in Texas the party expanded into neighbouring states, notably Colorado, where it allied with Rodolfo 'Corky' Gonzales and the Crusade For Justice. In California the party also grew rapidly with 20 different chapters by 1972. RUP politicians were naive in power and the party's reputation was damaged as a result of overspending, but it remained active throughout the 1970s running candidates for governor of Texas in 1972 and 1974 and for the US Senate in Colorado. The RUP's candidate, Secundion Salazar, received only 1.4% of the vote and this led to a refocusing of the party on grassroots activism linking the needs of not only Hispanic people but those of Native Americans in the south-west as well. By 1978 the party's candidate for governor of Texas only gained 15 000 votes and this result effectively saw its death as a political force.

Although its achievements were limited on a national scale, the RUP had demonstrated that the Hispanic vote could be mobilised as well as bringing attention to Hispanic concerns, particularly over the issue of education, notably the development of multilingual and multicultural curriculums, equal funding for all school districts, that local school boards should proportionately reflect their communities and that early childhood education should be free. Perhaps more importantly the party had shown that Hispanics could hold the balance of power in the dominant two party system of state governance and that meant that their needs could no longer be ignored.

SOURCE 10.4

The expansion of participation throughout society was reflected in the markedly higher levels of self-consciousness on the part of blacks, Indians, Chicanos, white ethnic groups, students, and women – all of whom became mobilised and organised in new ways to achieve what they considered to be their appropriate share of the action and of the rewards. The results of their efforts were testimony to the ability of the American political system to respond to the pressures of newly active groups, to assimilate those groups into the political system, and to incorporate members of those groups into the political leadership structure. Blacks and women made impressive gains in their representation in state legislatures and Congress, and in 1974 the voters elected one woman and two Chicano governors.

Extract from **The Crisis of Democracy: On the Governability of Democracies**, *a 1975 report co-written by the political scientist Samuel P. Huntington.*

ACTIVITY

To what extent was Samuel Huntington right to be positive about the political representation of Hispanic Americans in 1975?

Education

In much the same way as political representation, the issue of Hispanic education showed incremental improvement largely through the actions of multiple organisations working with different demographics. In 1961 Dr Antonia Pantoja founded ASPIRA ('aspire' in Spanish) to address the high drop-out rate and low educational attainment of Puerto Rican youth in New York. Pantoja, who is described by historian Virginia Sánchez-Korrol as 'one of the foremost figures in community activism from the 1950s to the present' built ASPIRA into a nationwide organisation and expanded its scope to incorporate all elements of the Hispanic community.

Parent groups were also key to progress. In 1963 in East Los Angeles, local parents formed the Mexican American Education Committee, which called for a recognition of Mexican culture and bilingual teaching, echoing the actions of Miami's Coral Way Elementary School, which in 1963 offered the first bilingual education programme in public schools in the country.

The issue of bilingual teaching was brought to nationwide attention by California State Assistant Superintendent Eugene Gonzalez whose 1966 research found that 86% of Californian districts lacked programmes for students with limited English proficiency and 80% had inadequate financial resources to serve migrant children. In 1968, after a three-year lobbying effort by NEA under Braulio Alonso, Congress passed the Bilingual Education Act, which compelled all school districts with significant numbers of Spanish-speaking students to provide special programmes for those students' education. This was followed by further success as the minutiae of access was fought for.

In the 1974 *Lau versus Nichols* case, the Supreme Court ruled that students' participation in education could not be denied because of their inability to speak or understand English. The lawsuit was begun on behalf of a Chinese student but the decision brought increased rights of Spanish-speaking immigrants in the same year that Congress also passed the Equal Education Opportunity Act.

Figure 10.6: Miss Socorro Dejesus teaches her fourth-grade public school class about American history, in Spanish, in one of the many bilingual school lessons underway throughout the nation. 23 February 1971.

Universities

In Universities things were also changing as Hispanic history and culture courses were introduced and, in 1974 the future Supreme Court Judge Sonia Sotomayor filed a formal letter of complaint about the lack of Latino staff on Princeton's faculty.

Sotomayor's actions were part of wider calls for change that came from students themselves, particularly those galvanised by the Chicano movement. In 1968 high school students in East Los Angeles presented a list of demands to the Los Angeles Unified School District Board of Education. When the Board failed to act, the students, and a high school teacher called Sal Castro, began a strike which led thousands of students from five schools to walk out. A violent police response followed.

Sal Castro was not the only teacher for whom protest about education morphed into protest over wider issues. In 1967 Braulio Alonso became the first Hispanic President of the National Education Association. Among his first actions was the to merge the NEA with the American Teachers Association (ATA), the organisation that represented black teachers in segregated schools.

In so doing Alonso linked the issue of Hispanic education with the more media spotlighted problems affecting black educational standards and successfully tied Hispanic rights to the growing federal efforts to deal with black education.

It was from the educational community that the largest Latino civil rights organisation derived. The National Council of La Raza's origins were in the pioneering work of Herman Gallegos, a community organiser, and professors Julian Samora and Ernesto Galarza whose Southwest Council of La Raza (SWCLR) formed in Phoenix, Arizona in 1968 grew to become a national group by 1973. Through grant funding from the Ford Foundation, the National Council of Churches and the United Auto Workers the organisation was able to grow and move from the south-west to Washington, DC, expanding its focus and representation to encompass 41 states and become the largest Latino civil rights organisation in the US.

ACTIVITY

Research the work of the National Council of La Raza in the time since its move to Washington, DC. What has been its greatest success? Which of the African American civil rights groups would you compare it to?

10.4 What role did the Chicano movement play in Hispanic rights protests?

Police and power

While treatment of Hispanic Americans by the police forces in the major cities and south-west was less institutionally racist than that experienced by black Americans, the high levels of crime in the barrios and the pejorative terminology attached to Hispanic Americans embedded and legitimised the prejudice they experienced in their daily lives. The absence of Hispanic people on juries or in the police force meant that rights were still not protected in the 1960s and 70s. Hispanic officers in the FBI and local or state police were also limited with only six out of over a thousand FBI officers in the south-west being of Hispanic descent into the late 1960s.

The Chicano movement of the 1960s and 1970s is a more nebulous idea than the African American civil rights movement. It certainly incorporates the work of Chávez, the increased cultural awareness among Hispanic Americans and the campaign for bilingual education and higher standards. However, in popular culture the Chicano movement is most commonly associated with the protests of young Hispanics and their clashes with the police, particularly in Los Angeles and most notably in the events that led to the death of the journalist Ruben Salazar.

In 1968, the LA Police Department arrested 13 Chicano leaders, including the teacher Sal Castro after the school walkouts. The 13 were indicted on charges of conspiracy and Castro was banned from teaching. After years of heavy-handed policing in the barrios the actions of the LAPD brought tension to a head, but following pickets of police headquarters and a sit-in in the boardroom of the LA School District for the teacher that lasted seven days the Board agreed to reinstate Castro. Among those arrested with Castro were several 'Brown Berets'.

Inspired by the ideas of Black Power, members of a new group, the Young Chicanos For Community Action, or YCCA, decided to change their name to the 'Brown Berets' in 1967. Their agenda was no less radical than that of the Black Panthers (see section 7.3) and called for the return of all United States territory once held by Mexico to Mexico and an end to police brutality, while also promoting free breakfast programmes and medical services. By September 1968, the Brown Berets had become a national organisation, having opened chapters in California, Arizona, Texas, Colorado, New Mexico and as far afield as Milwaukee, Chicago, Detroit and Oregon. However, the Brown Berets were afflicted by similar problems to the Panthers.

Grace Reyes, a Beret and writer for their magazine *La Causa*, repeatedly complained of sexism within the wider Chicano movement and by 1972, when 26 Brown Berets occupied the Santa Catalina Island off the coast of California and claimed it for Mexico, the group had already been weakened by internal conflicts and police and FBI infiltration as part of the latter's COINTELPRO operations (see 7.3, The Black Panthers).

The high point of Chicano action came in 1969 and 1970 when the Berets joined the first Rainbow Coalition – led by the Black Panther Fred Hampton – and also joined in with the Poor People's Campaign, then organised the first Chicano Moratorium against the Vietnam War in 1970 and a few months later the National Chicano Moratorium, at which 30 000 Hispanic Americans marched in protest against the disproportionately high casualty rate of Hispanics serving in Vietnam.

Figure 10.7: Two young Chicano men ride on the front of a car and raise their fists during a National Chicano Moratorium Committee march in opposition to the war in Vietnam, Los Angeles, California, 28 February 1970.

When the LA County Sheriff's Department tried to end the march, riots broke out, resulting in the deaths of three Chicano activists, including the journalist Rubén Salazar. Salazar was well known for his reporting on civil rights and police brutality, and his death gained national attention.

Although no police officer was successfully prosecuted for Salazar's death, a settlement of $700000 was paid to his family three years later and the exposure and cost ensured that policing of Hispanic protest in the south-west was more even handed in subsequent years, particularly with the increasing experience of the Mexican American Legal Defense and Education Fund (MALDEF), which had been founded in 1967 and grew into a major advocate group for Hispanic civil rights, including equal access to a quality education.

Initially co-funded by the NAACP, LULAC and the Ford Foundation (a philanthropic fund founded by Henry Ford in 1947 that contributes to organisations involved in education, human rights, democracy and creative arts), the group had an increasing profile and worked to train Mexican American lawyers as well as taking on numerous legal aid cases, which gave Hispanic Americans, particularly in the south west where the group was predominantly based, considerably more confidence in their relations with the police.

ACTIVITY

Create a table like the one below. Using the other chapters in the book, summarise the extent to which youth protest affected each of the movements listed.

	Aims	Actions	Results
Women's movement			
Native American rights movement			
Civil rights movement			
Hispanic rights movement			

10.5 What were the circumstances of non-Mexican Hispanic groups?

[handwritten: 80s + 60s Noiked sepentely]

The growing immigration of other Hispanic people

[handwritten: 70s cooperation new Latino identity helped interests]

Although Mexican Americans dominate the make-up of the Hispanic American community in the US, and are concentrated in the south-west of the country and have also been the group that have most notably been denied and fought for their civil rights in the post war period, other groups of Hispanic Americans and the roles they have played are worth noting. The modern migration of Cubans to the United States began in 1959 when Fidel Castro appeared to be on the verge of deposing the US puppet dictator Fulgencio Batista. Unlike the Mexican and Puerto Rican immigrants, those Cubans who fled to the US were not from the poorest parts of society but were members of the prosperous middle class. In the decade following the revolution in Cuba, 256 769 Cuban immigrants were admitted to the United States. In 1966 Congress passed the Cuban American Adjustment Act allowing Cubans who had been living in the US for at least one year to become permanent residents. This was a clear example of the different status both economically and politically of these new Cuban Americans. As 'refugees' from a communist country they had propaganda value and federal sympathy and hence were far less affected by issues of the denial of rights. Their status created an interesting split in the Hispanic community with Cuban Americans far more likely to vote Republican than other Hispanics.

Immigration after 1965

Wider Hispanic numbers were boosted considerably by the 1965 immigration act. From 1968 the act led to a substantial increase in immigrants from Mexico and Puerto Rico and for the first time immigration from the countries of central and southern America. This had the most significant impact on the Dominican Republic and Dominicans soon become the second largest immigrant group from the western hemisphere. They were joined in the 1990s by large numbers of Columbians fleeing from the drug wars that wracked Columbia in the period. However, the presence of both migrants and illegal aliens put considerable financial strain on the public services offered by the states, especially following a Supreme Court ruling in 1982 that states must pay for educating the children of illegal aliens. With states already providing substantial social services and with an increase in drug smuggling across the border into the south-west and into Florida anti-Hispanic feeling grew through the late 1970s and with the arrival of Ronald Reagan and a more robust attitude to law enforcement Congress passed legislation in 1986 that increased fines and other penalties for employers who employed illegal immigrants.

The impact of non-Mexican Hispanic Americans was dissipated by their lack of geographic concentration and the natural divisions of nationhood that they brought with them, Puerto Ricans in New York felt they had little in common with Cubans in Florida either geographically or culturally. Nevertheless, they certainly played a role in terms of sheer numbers alone in bringing the issue of Hispanic rights to the attention of the media and legislators from the local to the national level wherever they settled.

→ 90s white backlash.

By the early 1990s more than 90% of Mexican Americans, and Hispanics as a whole, were living in or near cities, completing the urbanisation that their white compatriots had undergone a century before. Indeed, the Los Angeles–Long Beach area has the second-largest Mexican community in the world after Mexico City itself. With substantial communities in Denver, Kansas City, Chicago, Detroit and New York City as well, Hispanic Americans made up a significant proportion of the modern United States. In addition, there were an estimated 2 million 'illegal aliens' in the US by 1990, of whom 55% were estimated to be Mexican.

Summary

A debate continues as to whether this illegal immigration has been beneficial or detrimental to the country, with opinions divided along both party and economic grounds. While Republicans on the right of their party advocate the building of a wall on the Mexican border, leading Democrats call for a pathway to citizenship for illegal immigrants. Meanwhile, many farmers and factory owners, traditional Republicans, approve of 'illegals' working in low-paying jobs that Americans do not want anyway and thus keeping wages and costs low.

It would be easy to see the Hispanic rights issue as an agglomeration of both the problems and actions of the other groups in this book. Hispanics today are a younger, less affluent and less educated group than the rest of the population but are better off than both African and Native Americans. However, more than 23.4% lived below the poverty level in the early 1990s. As with African Americans and Native Americans, the earning of rights on the political, judicial and educational fields does not necessarily seem to have translated to the economic equality that activists such as César Chávez and Corky Gonzales would have hoped for.

DISCUSSION POINT

Vladimir Lenin, the leader of the communist revolution in Russia in 1917, talked about the importance of the 'vanguard' in a movement. The vanguard are the most class-conscious and politically advanced sections of the working class who provide the leadership that stimulates change.

Having studied some of the different civil rights movements to emerge after 1945 would you agree with the idea that African Americans were the vanguard of the rights movements? If so, does that give them greater historical significance and hence merit their inclusion in school history at the expense of Hispanic rights or Native American rights?

Paper 3 exam practice

Summary activity

Copy the spider diagram below to show:

- the main reasons for the emergence of Hispanic rights protests after 1945
- the main actions taken
- the results of those actions.

Then, using the information from this chapter, and any other sources available to you, complete the diagram. Make sure you include, where relevant, brief comments about different historical debates and interpretations.

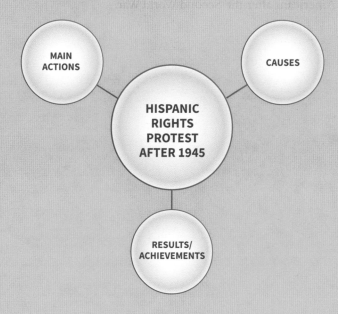

Paper 3 practice questions

1 Examine the reasons why, and the extent to which, a Hispanic rights movement developed in the US between 1960 and 1974.

2 'César Chávez achieved more for Hispanic Americans than any other figure.' To what extent do you agree with this statement?

3 To what extent was the Hispanic rights movement dependent on the techniques of the other civil rights movements?

4 'The main reason why the Hispanic rights movement moved slowly was a lack of media attention.' How far do you agree with this statement?

5 Evaluate the reasons why there was an improvement in civil rights for Hispanic Americans after the Second World War.

Exam practice

11

Introduction

You have now completed your study of the origins, nature, challenges and achievements of civil rights and social movements in the Americas after 1945. You have also had the chance to examine the various historical debates and differing historical interpretations that surround some of these developments.

In the earlier chapters, you have encountered examples of Paper 3-type essay questions, with examiner's tips. You have also had some basic practice in answering such questions. In this chapter, these tips and skills will be developed in more depth. Longer examples of possible student answers are provided. These are accompanied by examiner's comments that should increase your understanding of what examiners are looking for when they mark your essays. Following each question and answer, you will find tasks to give you further practice in the skills needed to gain the higher marks in this exam.

IB History Paper 3 exam questions and skills

Those of you following Route 2, HL Option 2 – History of the Americas – will have studied in depth three of the 18 sections available for this HL Option. *Civil Rights and Social Movements in the Americas post-1945* is one of those sections. For Paper 3, two questions are set from each of the 18 sections, giving 36 questions in total; and you have to answer three of these.

Each question has a specific mark scheme. However, the 'generic' mark scheme in the *IB History Guide* gives you a good general idea of what examiners are looking for in order to be able to put answers into the higher bands. In particular, you will need to acquire precise historical knowledge so that you can address issues such as continuity and change, significance, causation, perspectives and consequence.

This knowledge will be required in order to explain historical developments in a clear, coherent, well-supported and relevant way. You will also need to understand relevant historical debates and interpretations, and be able to refer to these and critically evaluate them.

Essay planning

Make sure you read each question carefully, noting all the important key or 'command' words. You might find it useful to highlight them on your question paper. You can then produce a rough plan (for example, a spider diagram) of each of the three essays you intend to attempt, before you start to write your answers. That way, you will soon know whether you have enough own knowledge to answer them adequately.

Next, refer back to the wording of each question. This will help you see whether or not you are responding to all its various demands and aspects. In addition, if you run short of time towards the end of your exam, you will at least be able to write some brief condensed sentences to show the key issues or points and arguments you would have presented. It is thus far better to do the planning at the start of the exam; that is, before you panic, should you suddenly realise you don't have time to finish your last essay.

Relevance to the question

Remember, too, to keep your answers relevant and focused on the question, it can be a good idea to use the language of the question in your answer, for example if the question is asking about the impact or success of something you should be using the words 'impact' and 'success' in your answer repeatedly. The dates offered in the question are vital, don't go outside the dates mentioned, it can be a good idea to jot down a quick chronology of all the events that you can remember in the period so you can see how they relate to the question as you plan.

In a similar way, don't write answers on subjects not identified in the question. Also, don't just describe the events or developments. Sometimes students just focus on one key word, date or individual, and then write down everything they know about it. Instead, select your own knowledge carefully, and pin the relevant information to the key features raised by the question. Finally, if the question asks for 'causes or reasons' and 'results', 'continuity and change', 'successes and failures' or 'nature and development', make sure you deal with all the parts of the question. Otherwise, you will limit yourself to below half marks at best.

Examiner's tips

For Paper 3 answers, examiners are looking for well-structured arguments that:

- are consistently relevant and linked to the question
- offer clear and precise evaluation and analysis
- are supported by the use of accurate, precise and relevant own knowledge
- offer a balanced judgement
- refer to different historical debates and interpretations or to relevant historians and, where relevant, offer some critical evaluation of these.

Simplified mark scheme

Band		Marks
1	**Consistently clear understanding of and focus** on the question, with **all main aspects addressed**. Answer is **fully analytical, balanced** and **well-structured/ organised**. Own knowledge is **detailed, accurate and relevant**, with events placed **in their historical context**. There is **developed critical analysis**, and **sound understanding of historical concepts**. Examples used are **relevant**, and used effectively **to support analysis/evaluation**. The answer also integrates **evaluation of different historical debates/perspectives**. All/almost all of the main points are **substantiated**, and the answer reaches a **clear/reasoned/consistent judgement/ conclusion**.	13–15
2	**Clear understanding of the question**, and most of its **main aspects are addressed**. Answer is mostly **well-structured and developed**, though, with **some repetition/ lack of clarity** in places. Supporting **own knowledge mostly relevant/accurate**, and events are placed **in their historical context**. The answer is **mainly analytical**, with relevant examples **used to support critical analysis/evaluation**. There is **some understanding/evaluation of historical concepts and debates/perspectives**. Most of the main points **are substantiated**, and the answer offers a **consistent conclusion**.	10–12
3	**Demands of the question are understood** – but some aspects **not fully developed/ addressed. Mostly relevant/accurate supporting own knowledge**, and events generally placed **in their historical context. Some attempts at analysis/evaluation but these are limited/not sustained/ inconsistent**.	7–9

Band		Marks
4	**Some understanding** of the question. **Some relevant own knowledge,** with some factors identified – but with **limited explanation. Some attempts at analysis,** but answer **lacks clarity/coherence, and is mainly description/narrative.**	4–6
5	**Limited understanding of/focus on** the question. **Short/generalised** answer, with very **little accurate/relevant own knowledge.** Some **unsupported assertions,** with **no real analysis.**	0–3

Student answers

The following extracts from student answers have brief examiner's comments in the margins, and a longer overall comment at the end. Those parts of student answers that are particularly strong and well-focused (such as demonstrations of precise and relevant own knowledge, or examination of historical interpretations) will be highlighted in red. Errors/confusions/irrelevance/loss of focus will be highlighted in blue. In this way, students should find it easier to see why marks were awarded or withheld.

Question 1

Compare and contrast the contribution of the federal government under Eisenhower and Johnson in the achievement of African American civil rights. **[15 marks]**

Skills

- Factual knowledge and understanding
- Structured, analytical and balanced argument
- Awareness/understanding/evaluation of historical interpretations
- Clear and balanced judgement

Examiner's tips

Look carefully at the wording of this question, which asks you to compare and contrast how the Eisenhower and Johnson administrations helped in the achievement of African American civil rights. This means you would need to show both how they are similar and how they are different. It is perfectly all right for you to draw parallels between the two presidents – as long as you support your arguments with relevant and precise own knowledge. All aspects of the question will need to be addressed in order to achieve high marks. Remember: the question refers to the federal government under Eisenhower and Johnson, not just the presidents themselves – this means the Supreme Court should feature in your answer as well.

To begin to answer a question such as this, draw up a rough plan with headings for 'comparisons' and 'contrasts'. Then make notes on where aspects of their policies were similar under 'comparisons' and where and how they were different under 'contrasts'. Remember: don't just describe what their policies were. You need to focus on similarities and differences.

At the most sophisticated level you can also engage with the question. This question makes an assertion, that African American civil rights were achieved. Consider whether there is any evidence to challenge this, specifically here you might look at how political rights were achieved but economic rights were not, as evidenced by the actions and rhetoric of groups like the Black Panthers.

Student answer

Eisenhower himself was a reluctant exponent of civil rights, famously declaring that it was 'difficult through law and through force to change a man's heart'. His introduction of two Civil Rights Acts in 1957 and 1960 were a positive step, but both acts were watered down in congressional committees by Dixiecrats such as James Eastland and achieved little. Eisenhower's legislative contribution can therefore be seen as symbolic rather than effective. His acts were the first civil rights legislation passed by Congress since Reconstruction, but the fact that the Voting Rights Act had to be introduced in 1965 demonstrates clearly how little the 1957 Civil Rights Act did to help African Americans gain the right to vote.

Eisenhower's reticence when it came to intervening on behalf of the movement can be seen in his negotiations with Orval Faubus over the Little Rock crisis in 1957. Despite the fact that his Civil Rights Bill was passing through Congress at the time, the president refused to force Faubus to integrate Little Rock High until the situation had escalated wildly out of hand.

EXAMINER'S COMMENT

This is a clear and well-focused paragraph, showing accurate knowledge of the topic, and a good understanding of Eisenhower's attitude to civil rights. It shows precise knowledge in terms of the overlap between the 1957 Civil Rights Act and the Little Rock crisis.

The federal government during the Eisenhower administration did, however, make a profound difference to the achievement of African American civil rights through the actions of the Supreme Court. Earl Warren's leadership of the court during the Brown case, and in particular his conviction that a unanimous verdict must be delivered, was vital in providing the movement with a legal victory that destroyed Jim Crow and the Plessy versus Ferguson precedent.

Historians differ about the importance of the Eisenhower administration to the achievement of African American civil rights with some, such as Robert Cook, describing it as a period of 'relative federal inactivity' whereas others, such as Harvard Sitkoff, see the Brown decision as the start of the effective civil rights movement. Eisenhower's reluctance to commit the federal government to supporting the movement is all the more embarrassing in the light of the efforts of the Kennedy and Johnson administrations, who risked fracturing their own parties for the sake of civil rights and the fact that what Mary Dudziak called 'the Cold War imperative' made the need to achieve equality for all US citizens part of the wider propaganda war with the USSR.

EXAMINER'S COMMENT

Although this historiography is accurate and exhaustive, it has been placed in a separate paragraph after the Eisenhower material has been discussed. It will earn some credit with the examiner, but the student has missed an opportunity to weave the historiography in with the factual content.

In contrast to Eisenhower, LBJ was a committed and proactive exponent of African American civil rights. When his body lay in state in Washington after his death, around 60% of those who came to pay their respects were black. Johnson's alleged comment after signing the 1964 Civil Rights Act – 'we have lost the South for a generation' – reflects the political sacrifice he was willing to make for the sake of the civil rights movement.

EXAMINER'S COMMENT

This paragraph shows how the student is approaching the question with a clear but not sophisticated structure. In approaching the question as negatives and positives of Eisenhower followed by positives and negatives of Johnson, the material is covered well but opportunities are missed to make direct comparisons. If the structure had been political/legal/social/economic, the student would have had far more opportunity to compare the two. For example, the Supreme Court under Eisenhower was highly influential but was not as significant under Johnson, because of the latter's more proactive approach to civil rights and the fact that the key battle of **Brown versus Board** had already been won. This is a good example where a chronology of key events would have helped the student. If he/she had noticed that there were violent attacks on protesters under both Eisenhower and Johnson from their chronology they could easily have seen a way to produce an effective paragraph comparing the response of the two.

In terms of legislation, it was the Johnson government that truly brought an end to segregation. The pivotal pieces of legislation were the Civil Rights Act of 1964 and the Voting Rights Act of 1965, together with the 24th Amendment of 1964. These enforced the civil and political rights that had been provided de facto but denied de jure since the Civil War amendments of 1865–70. However, it should be noted that it was Johnson, as Senate Democrat leader in 1957, who had helped James Eastland to water down Eisenhower's 1957 Act. After dealing with political rights, LBJ turned his attention to the economic segregation that particularly affected blacks in the North. His 'Great Society' programme built on JFK's 'New Frontier' and provided a host of legislation dealing with elementary and secondary education, higher education, social security and healthcare in 1965 alone.

EXAMINER'S COMMENT

Again, there is accurate own knowledge in this paragraph – but this is not what the question requires. Despite an opening sentence which suggests the correct focus might be applied, the candidate then goes on to talk exclusively about Johnson-era legislation instead of making comparisons. There is recognition of Johnson's role in the passing of the 1957 Civil Rights Act but no comparison of the two acts, which would be directly focused on the question, remember the question specifically asks the student to 'compare and contrast'.

[There then follow several more paragraphs giving detailed and accurate accounts of Johnson's Great Society programme.]

Johnson was also hampered by an uncooperative Congress featuring Dixiecrats determined to make a last stand against civil rights. Here there is a direct parallel with Eisenhower, whose 1957 and 1960 Civil Rights Acts were both badly damaged by Dixiecrat opposition. The 1964 Bill brought a 54-day filibuster and in 1966 Congress rejected a Civil Rights Bill that was designed to prevent housing discrimination. However, Johnson differs from Eisenhower in that he skilfully managed to keep most of his Bills together, whereas the 1957 was badly diluted by Eastland.

Johnson also eventually achieved the 1968 Fair Housing Act, skilfully invoking public sympathy after the assassination of King in the same way he had after Kennedy's death. It is interesting to note, however, that a section of the 1968 act that criminalised interstate travel to incite a riot was used to prosecute the Black Panther H. Rap Brown. Johnson's experience of Southern politics enabled him to force through ambitious legislation that would have been beyond Eisenhower, but the obduracy of his southern partners and the white backlash that followed the riots of 1964–68 hampered his efforts to manipulate Congress just as it had with Eisenhower. Johnson even commissioned the Kerner Report to look into the causes of the riots, despite the damage they did to his programme.

EXAMINER'S COMMENT

Here there is some relevant focus on the demands of the question – coupled with good own knowledge which is accurate, and sometimes precise, although the line on H. Rap Brown, though undoubtedly 'interesting to note', does little to aid the argument. However, the inclusion of the line about the Kerner Commission is largely irrelevant and weakens the end of the paragraph. This suggests that Kerner and possibly the end of the course had not been well revised.

In conclusion, it can be seen that Johnson made the greater contribution to the attainment of African American civil rights: his wide-ranging legislative agenda finally achieved desegregation and his social measures made a difference to the lives of the very poorest in society. While it is true that Johnson drew on the precedents established by Eisenhower in the 1957 Civil Rights Act and presidential intervention at Little Rock, it was Johnson's willingness to be proactive, despite the damage it would cause to his party, that deservedly earned the admiration of African Americans. As Thurgood Marshall said of him, 'You didn't wait for the times, you made them.'

EXAMINER'S COMMENT

There is then a brief conclusion, which makes a valid judgement. Unfortunately, this is not really a supported judgement because there has been little discussion of the comparisons and contrasts between the presidents, aside from the paragraph highlighted. In addition, it could be argued that this conclusion is slightly too long given the limited time available in the exam; the quote from Marshall, though showing impressive recall, adds little.

Overall examiner's comments

There is plentiful and accurate own knowledge – but it is not used as well as it could have been. The fundamental problem of this answer is that the structure is not appropriate for the question. By dealing with the two presidents separately, the candidate has lost the opportunity to compare and contrast, and so the bulk of the answer is not really focused on the demands of the question. However, there are some sections which are relevant, so the answer is thus probably just good enough to be awarded a mark at the top of Band 3: 9 marks. What was needed was an answer that focused on comparing and contrasting, and to achieve this a thematic rather than chronological structure was required. The candidate also needed to make more use of their excellent understanding of historical debate instead of relegating it to virtual footnotes to the discussions of the presidents.

Activity

Look again at the simplified mark scheme at the beginning of this chapter, and the student answer to this question. Now draw up a chronology and use it to complete a plan, with a structure focused on comparing the two presidents. Then try to write several paragraphs that will be good enough to get into Band 1, and so obtain the full 15 marks. As well as making sure you address all aspects of the question, try to integrate into your answer some references to and evaluation of relevant historical interpretations.

Question 2

Examine the reasons for, and effects of, the emergence of the women's movement in the Americas in the second half of the 20th century.
[15 marks]

Skills

- Factual knowledge and understanding
- Structured, analytical and balanced argument
- Awareness/understanding/evaluation of historical interpretations

Examiner's tips

Look carefully at the wording of this question, which asks you why the women's movement emerged in the Americas in the second half of the 20th century and what the effects of its emergence were. Questions such as this show how important it is to study all the material in the chapters. If you only focus on the US, you will seriously limit your options in the exam. To answer questions like this in the most effective way, it is best to structure your answer thematically and then try to find examples that fit into each section. For example, you might like to look at economic, political, technological and social reasons. Technological reasons, such as the invention of the pill, might be important in the US but not, for example, in Guatemala. Here, because of the action of brave women such as Rigoberta Menchú, political reasons might be considered to be much more important. However, there were also political reasons why the women's movement emerged in the US, so that paragraph might need to be larger to reflect its superior significance.

Student answer

Although the women's movement emerged for a variety of reasons in the Americas, the fundamental reasons were political, economic and social. The economic impact of the Second World War was particularly important, but other political reasons, such as equal rights and standing up to oppressive male-dominated governments, were the most significant factors. To show this, I will focus on the emergence of the women's movement in the US and its results.

EXAMINER'S COMMENT

This introduction starts in a generally promising way. However, the final sentence in this paragraph is very worrying. This is because such an approach will almost certainly result in a narrative answer and is likely to ignore, despite the talk of oppressive governments, women's movements in other countries. As has been seen in previous answers, a narrative account, without clear focus on all the demands of the question, is unlikely to get beyond Band 4 (maximum 6 marks).

In the USA, the Second World War was a pivotal experience for many women. After the achievement of the vote in 1920, women were largely confined to running the home, owing to the huge amount of time taken up by caring for the large families that were typical of the early part of the 20th century. However, with the drafting of thousands of men into the armed forces, the need for labour led many women to take jobs in factories where they often excelled in their contribution to the production process. Figures such as 'Rosie the Riveter' inspired many, and women enjoyed the responsibility of their new positions. However, when the war ended, jobs were returned to men, creating an underlying level of resentment that was hidden by the enthusiasm that greeted the defeat of the Nazis. Alongside this enthusiasm came a 'baby boom', which kept women busy for much of the next decade and a half.

EXAMINER'S COMMENT

This paragraph contains a lot of very good information – and is clearly the result of solid revision. However, it is mainly background material – there is little detail on how this led to the emergence of a women's movement and its connection to the question is implicit rather than explicit.

The invention of the contraceptive pill in 1960 allowed women to take control of their own fertility for the first time. They could embark on careers with the confidence that they would not have to give them up to look after children. In addition, the pill was liberating sexually and some women took advantage of this, advocating free love and siding with the hippy movement. Two years later, the publication of Betty Friedan's book The Feminine Mystique elucidated for many women the 'problem that had no name' – this was the sense of disappointment with a life of pseudo-slavery to the family. At the same time that these technological and social developments were taking place, the black civil rights movement provided a template for how a minority group could gain political recognition and redress for their grievances. The successes of the civil rights movement inspired women to campaign for their own rights, and the experience of women such as Ella Baker, Rosa Parks and Fannie Lou Hamer showed that women could fight for their own rights and inspired others to do so.

EXAMINER'S COMMENT

Again, there is a lot of accurate own knowledge – this time, some of it is relevant, as it deals with technological and social developments. However, this answer seems to be turning into a descriptive account of what happened during the period. The sentences on the influence of the civil rights movement suggest that the candidate has an understanding of how to answer the question, but this is being lost in the desire to show how many facts he/she knows; mixing technological developments with social ones is a clear sign of a narrative answer.

The influence of the media was also important in the emergence of women's rights movements. Protesters such as Jaqui Ceballos learned valuable lessons from the civil rights movement, such as how the media would give huge coverage to stories that provided powerful images, such as the sit-ins and Freedom Rides. As a result, protests such as the throwing away of symbols of women's oppression, and the crowning of a sheep as Miss America, drew attention and spread the word to other women.

EXAMINER'S COMMENT

Again, there is accurate own knowledge here, some of which addresses the question. However, the problem here is that this information is from 1968, after the women's movement could be said to have emerged. The student has not focused sufficiently on the question, and their unwillingness to abandon facts they have made an effort to learn hampers their ability to answer it.

[There then follow several paragraphs on legislation, especially *Roe versus Wade* and the efforts to ratify the Equal Rights Amendment, both of which are after the 'emergence' of the movement in the US. The paragraphs fail to address these as 'results'. There is still no discussion of the women's movement in other countries in the Americas.]

Women gained a great deal from the emergence of the women's rights movements in the US – increased sexual equality through the pill and Roe versus Wade, and legislation that attempted to address the pay gap. There was also increased representation, as women such as Shirley Chisholm were elected to Congress. Writers such as Betty Friedan, Erica Jong and Germaine Greer had opened up the possibility of women changing the way they were perceived, and made it impossible for male oppression to be so widespread in the future. However, pay was still not equal, women were still under-represented, and there remained an expectation that women would continue to do most of the home-making.

EXAMINER'S COMMENT

This is a good conclusion – brief and to the point. However, it does not reflect the line of argument adopted in the essay and it fails to give any consideration to any other country in the region.

Overall examiner's comments

Though there is precise and accurate own knowledge, the essay is basically a story of women's advances in the US, and lacks a focus on results or consideration of other countries in the region. If the candidate had dealt with these other countries in the same way, then the answer would have been awarded Band 4 – maximum 6 marks – even though it hasn't really addressed the demands of the question.

However, because it only deals with the US, this answer can only be awarded a low mark in Band 4 – which would be 4 marks at most. To reach Band 3 and higher, the answer would need some explicit and well-structured treatment of other countries and the results of the emergence of the women's movement.

Activity

Look again at the simplified mark scheme at the beginning of this chapter and the student answer to this question. Now draw up a plan, with a structure focused on the demands of the question. Then write your own answer to the question, making sure you consistently make comparisons and contrasts. Attempt to make your answer good enough to get into Band 1, and so obtain the full 15 marks.

Question 3

'The youth protest movement in the USA in the 1960s and 1970s failed to achieve any of its goals.' To what extent do you agree with this statement? **[15 marks]**

Skills

- Factual knowledge and understanding
- Structured, analytical and balanced argument
- Awareness/understanding/evaluation of historical interpretations

Examiner's tips

Look carefully at the wording of this statement. The focus is purely on the USA, so there is no need to consider other countries. However, there is a subtlety to the question. You must consider what the goals of the youth protest movement were, and whether these were achieved, but you must also consider whether these were achieved because of youth protests or because of other factors. It is also worth remembering that the civil rights movement can be seen as part of youth protest movements through the actions of the SNCC and Black Panthers among others, as can aspects of the Native American protest movement (through the National Indian Youth Council (NIYC)) and the women's rights movement. There are also some relevant historical debates, which could be made part of the answer.

Student answer

Youth protest movements in the 1960s and 1970s rarely had clearly defined goals unless they were part of a wider movement. Young people involved in the protests against segregation – for example, in the sit-ins and Freedom Rides – could be said to have achieved their goals, but the vague protests against 'the man' that characterised the counter-culture can be seen merely as a form of privileged teenage rebellion stretching into college years. Moreover, it is important to appreciate that where the goals of specific movements, such as withdrawal from Vietnam, were achieved, this was not necessarily purely because of the youth protest but other factors should also be considered.

EXAMINER'S COMMENT
This is a clear and well-focused introduction, showing a good appreciation of all the demands of the question, and indicating an analytical approach is likely to be followed. This is a good start.

In many ways, it is difficult to justify the use of the term 'youth protest movement' when looking at the USA in the 1960s and 1970s. Young people were in fact involved in many protests. For instance, during the period from 1960 to 1965 young people provided the 'shock troops' for the civil rights movement, showing huge bravery in endangering their safety at Greensboro sit-ins and marches in places such as Selma and Washington.

Outside the major movements, young people's protests were often badly organised and not clearly defined. A series of movements in the 1960s and 1970s seemed to change with the frequency of the Billboard Chart, and incorporated environmental issues, university teaching, the actions of the CIA and FBI, and other issues that never coalesced into a coherent political movement.

Youth protest in the 1960s and 1970s can be seen to have contributed to the success of the civil rights movement. Images of Freedom Riders being beaten in Montgomery and Birmingham, and marchers having snakes thrown at them in Selma, outraged the nation and kept up the pressure on Kennedy and Johnson to legislate to enforce black civil rights. However, after the passing of the 1964 Civil Rights Act and the 1965 Voting Rights Act, the increasing radicalisation of the civil rights movement – through the rhetoric of angry young blacks such as Stokeley Carmichael and Huey Newton – did much to undermine the protest movement. The subsequent four summers of rioting from 1964 to 1968 made it difficult for Johnson to argue for the expansion of his Great Society programme when it seemed that black youths were rapidly turning cities such as Detroit into war zones.

The greatest success of the youth protest movement can be said to be over the issue of the Vietnam War. Here, sustained protest – which often turned violent, such as the shootings at Kent State University in 1970 or the self-immolation of Norman Morrison outside the Pentagon in 1965 – kept up a highly visible and consistently outraged protest movement with a clearly defined goal. Marches and protest rallies in major cities and at major universities escalated as the war went on, and chants like 'Hey Hey, LBJ, how many kids did you kill today' were a key factor in Johnson not seeking re-election and in Nixon's policy of 'Vietnamisation' as a prelude to withdrawal of troops.

However, even here other factors were possibly more important than youth protest. The cost of the Vietnam War was putting huge strains on the economy in the US, and led to unpopular tax rises in 1970. This and the opposition of powerful politicians such as William Fulbright could easily be argued to have been more important in ending US involvement in Vietnam, especially as much of the youth protest could be dismissed by critics as the actions of self-interested young men trying to avoid the draft.

EXAMINER'S COMMENT

A very relevant paragraph, focused on how Vietnam can be argued to be the greatest success, but that even this wasn't purely down to youth protest. The approach is still mainly analytical, and focused on the demands of the question.

[There then follow several paragraphs – with detailed supporting own knowledge – analysing other areas of youth protest, such as the actions of the Yippies and other members of the counter-culture. However, there is no mention or evaluation of different historians' views.]

In conclusion, youth protest was important in some of the successes of protest movements in the period, especially in the civil rights movement and the Vietnam War. However, this success could also be attributed to other economic and political factors and, in the case of Black Power, youth protest actually undermined the wider goals of the movement.

However, when it lacked a coherent cause, youth protest – of the 'tune in, turn on, drop out' kind favoured by the counter-culture – was never more than a disparate collection of vaguely disgruntled middle-class teenagers, and any hope of the emergence of a powerful, left-leaning protest movement willing to engage with issues such as the environment, social deprivation and the provision of education had been lost by the time of Reagan's election in 1980.

EXAMINER'S COMMENT

The conclusion is well focused, and ends an increasingly analytical argument.

Overall examiner's comments

This is a good, well-focused and analytical answer, with some precise and accurate own knowledge to support the points made. The answer is thus certainly good enough to be awarded a mark in Band 3 – and possibly at the lower end of Band 2. To reach the top of Band 2, and to get into Band 1, the candidate needed to provide some reference to historians' views and historical interpretations, and some critical evaluation of these interpretations.

Activity

Look again at the simplified mark scheme and the student answer. Now write your own answer, and attempt to make it good enough to get into Band 1 and so obtain the full 15 marks. In particular, make sure you are aware of the main historical debates about this topic – and incorporate some critical evaluation of them in your answer.

Further reading

Dierenfield, Bruce. 2008. *The Civil Rights Movement*. Edinburgh, UK. Pearson Education.

Fairclough, Adam. 2002. *Better Day Coming: Blacks and Equality, 1890–2000*. London, UK. Penguin.

Gair, Christopher. 2007. *The American Counterculture*. Edinburgh, UK. Edinburgh University Press.

Jackson, Troy. 2008. *Becoming King: Martin Luther King Jr. and the Making of a National Leader*. Lexington, USA. University Press of Kentucky.

Marable, Manning. 2011. *Malcolm X: A Life of Reinvention*. London, UK. Allen Lane.

Oates, Stephen. 1998. *Let the Trumpet Sound: A Life of Martin Luther King*. Edinburgh, UK. Payback Press.

O'Neill, William L. 1969. *Coming Apart: An Informal History of America in the 1960s*. New York, USA. Ivan R. Dee Inc.

Orozco, Cynthia E. 2010. *No Mexicans, Women, or Dogs Allowed: The Rise of the Mexican American Civil Rights Movement*. Houston, USA. University of Texas Press.

Pawel, Miriam. 2015. *The Crusades of Cesar Chavez: A Biography*. New York, USA. Bloomsbury Press.

Reich, Charles. 1970. *The Greening of America*. New York, USA. Random House.

Rosales, F. Arturo and Rosales, Francisco A. 1997. *Chicano! The History of the Mexican American Civil Rights Movement*. Houston, USA. Arte Público Press.

Sanders, Vivienne. 2006. *Race Relations in the USA, 1863–1980*. London, UK. Hodder Education.

Sitkoff, Harvard. 1993. *The Struggle for Black Equality*. Toronto, Canada. Harper Collins.

Tuck, Stephen. 2010. *We Ain't What We Ought To Be: The Black Freedom Struggle from Emancipation to Obama*. London, UK. The Belknap Press of Harvard University Press.

Bibliography

Baldwin, James. 1963. *The Fire Next Time*. New York, USA. The Dial Press.

Carson, Clayborne. 1981. *In Struggle: SNCC and the Black Awakening of the 1960s*. Boston, USA. Harvard University Press.

Chafe, William H. 2009. *Rise and Fall of the American Century: The United States from 1890–2009*. New York, USA. Oxford University Press.

Cook, Robert. 1998. *Sweet Land of Liberty?: The African-American Struggle for Civil Rights in Twentieth Century*. Harlow, UK. Pearson Education.

Coontz, Stephanie. 2011. *A Strange Stirring: the Feminine Mystique and American Women at the Dawn of the 1960s*. New York, USA. Basic.

Dierenfield, Bruce. 2008. *The Civil Rights Movement*. Edinburgh, UK. Pearson Education.

Fairclough, Adam. 2002. *Better Day Coming: Blacks and Equality, 1890–2000*. London, UK. Penguin.

Franklin, J. H. and Moss, Alfred. 1994. *From Slavery to Freedom: A History of African-Americans*. New York, USA. McGraw-Hill.

Friedan, Betty. 1963. *The Feminine Mystique*. New York, USA. W.W. Norton.

González, Rodolfo. 1967. *Yo Soy Joaquin*. La Causa Publications.

Goodman, Paul. 1960. *Growing Up Absurd*. New York, USA. Random House.

Goodman, Paul. 2010. *New Reformation: Notes of Neolithic Conservative*. New York, USA. PM Press.

Hertsgaard, M. 2002. *The Eagle's Shadow: Why America fascinates and infuriates the world*. New York, USA. Farrar, Straus & Giroux.

Huntington, Samuel. 1975. *The Crisis of Democracy: On the Governability of Democracies*. New York, USA. New York University Press.

Jackson, Troy. 2008. *Becoming King: Martin Luther King Jr. and the Making of a National Leader*. Lexington, USA. University Press of Kentucky.

Lawson, Steven and Payne, Charles. 1998. *Debating the Civil Rights Movement, 1945–1968.* Lanham, USA. Rowman and Littlefield.

Marable, Manning. 1991. *Race, Reform and Rebellion: The Second Reconstruction in Black America, 1945–1990.* Jackson, USA. University Press of Mississippi.

Marable, Manning. 2011. *Malcolm X: A Life of Reinvention.* London, UK. Allen Lane.

Nagel, J. 1997. *American Indian Ethnic Renewal: Red Power and the Resurgence of Identity and Culture.* Oxford, UK. Oxford University Press.

Norrell, Robert. 2005. *The House I Live in: Race in the American Century.* Oxford, UK. Oxford University Press.

Oates, Stephen. 1998. *Let the Trumpet Sound: A Life of Martin Luther King.* Edinburgh, UK. Payback Press.

Olson, James S. and Wilson, Raymond. 1986. *Native Americans in the Twentieth Century.* Chicago, USA. University of Illinois Press.

Polenberg, Richard. 1980. *One Nation Divisible: Class, Race and Ethnicity in the United States since 1938.* London, UK. Penguin.

Reich, Charles. 1970. *The Greening of America.* New York, USA. Random House.

Roszak, Theodore. 1969. *The Making of a Counter Culture: Reflections on the Technocratic Society and its Youthful Opposition.* Los Angeles, USA. University of California.

Sanders, Vivienne. 2006. *Race Relations in the USA, 1863–1980.* London, UK. Hodder Education.

Schlafly, Phyllis. 1978. *The Power of the Positive Woman.* New York, USA. Jove/HBJ Books.

Sitkoff, Harvard. 1993. *The Struggle for Black Equality.* Toronto, Canada. Harper Collins.

Trotter, J. W. 2001. *The African-American Experience, Volume 1 Through Reconstruction.* Boston, USA. Houghton Mifflin.

Tuck, Stephen. 2010. *We Ain't What We Ought To Be: The Black Freedom Struggle from Emancipation to Obama.* London, UK. The Belknap Press of Harvard University Press.

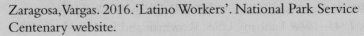

Zaragosa, Vargas. 2016. 'Latino Workers'. National Park Service Centenary website.

Witt, Shirley and Steiner, Stan (eds). 1972. *The Way: An Anthology of American Indian Literature*. 1972. New York, USA. Alfred A. Knopf.

Zinn, Howard. 1980. *A People's History of the United States*. New York, USA. Harper & Row.